Native of Eskdale
ANOTHER COUNTRY

Native of Eskdale
ANOTHER COUNTRY

Margaret Armstrong Elliot

HAYLOFT PUBLISHING LTD.
CUMBRIA

First published by Hayloft 2016

Hayloft Publishing Ltd, South Stainmore,
Kirkby Stephen, Cumbria, CA17 4DJ

tel: 07971 352473
email: books@hayloft.eu
web: www.hayloft.eu

ISBN 978-1-910237-19 -9

ISBN regisgtered but no longer applicable & will have to unregister

A CIP catalogue record for this book is available
from the British Library

Papers used by Hayloft are natural, recyclable products made from
wood grown in sustainable forests. The manufacturing processes   conform to the environmental regulations of the country of origin.

Designed, printed and bound in the EU

Frontispiece: Granda Leece leading his horse,
Margaret Armstrong Elliot, SFCA, CSPWC

For Ava and Ruby, DeeDee and Catherine

Acknowledgements

I have been heavily dependent on the family trees created by my cousin Sara Holliday and my neice Jane Holmes and her husband John. The trees were a helpful resource in the effort of keeping the family generations straight. Both Sara and Jane read selected chapters and provided some specific family references for the narrative.

I am grateful to my friend Norma Pitfield for initial encouragement and for the push to write. My siblings, Richard H. Armstrong and Helen Woodall, kindly read the first draft and answered a lot of my questions. I used some family information from my cousin Marjorie Mallinson. Thank you for all of that, it was essential for me.

I am indebted to my friend Noreen Fairweather for her kind encouragement; she carefully read and annotated the first entire draft and gave constructive advice. Maddaline Enns gave me valuable insight into writing style. Cecilia Mavrow kindly reviewed the entire text and gave me much appreciated editorial assistance, moral support and professional advice. My daughter Catherine bore with the writing and gave generously of her time on the text from an insider's viewpoint. I am also indebted to Catherine for computer assistance, as well as to my sons-in-law Craig Bourget and Kevin Armstrong.

Finally, I am appreciative of Hayloft Publishing for their interest in Eskdale and the Lake District, and for their committment to rural matters. I much appreciated Dawn Robertson's friendly style and for keeping me in the picture.

Contents

The past is never dead. It's not even past.
William Faulkner.

Preface

l found myself confiding to Norma Pitfield, a friend of over sixty years, and familiar with Eskdale over that time span, that I was thinking that it might be a good idea if I put down a few things about growing up in Eskdale: what it was like, the children might like to know about it. Norma got the point immediately; she observed that in some respects I had never really left.

I had the idea of simply describing what Eskdale was like in my early life, seeing as my readers my grandaughters, Ava and Ruby (and I thought to fill in a few gaps for my daughters DeeDee and Catherine), expecting that there might be things in it that would interest them. The ultimate imperative to me was that if I did not write it all down it would be lost, and Eskdale seemed far too good for that: it is an interesting subject, has promising material, and finally it is important – somebody had to record how it was for a native.

I felt completely free to indulge in detail, to an extent that might be tedious for a contemporary, since anything that I could say would be news to the grandchildren, living as they do in the New World of today. How it was, on an ancient farm with its inn, in a relatively isolated place in the Old Country, at a time for us when horses and carts, and candlesticks, were just being replaced by cars and electricity. In Eskdale we were a bit of an anachronism in that at the beginning of the World War Two we were to some extent living in a past, a bit behind the rest of England. And for us there was the added component of being so curious and attractive to the country at large that we were to be made into a National Park.

Putting it all down has been a positive experience, firstly on a personal life-story level: trying making some sense of it all. I was surprised to find that it turned out to be much more than that. I, myself, disappeared into history: my boundaries expanded. I am conscious now that I was there in Eskdale for a short time, hardly even a footnote. My limited project of describing life in Eskdale, from about 1931 through to the late 1950s, grew into something more of a project, became a bigger subject than me and my interractions, and doubtless got me into areas for which I have little qualification.

I heard somewhere that one discovers the nature of one's real subject in the course of the writing of it – and so it was for me, in much the same way that one does not know exactly how a painting will turn out. I did start out by doing a few watercolours in my preparation for writing as that comes more naturally to me, and gets more easily to the 'totality' of the place: how it looked, how it felt, how it came to be. I think that my ultimate subject is 'land use', a term that comes near to my meaning: how one regards and treats land, how one feels about it, how it affects life. We had a different view from that I see in much of modern thinking.

Geographically Eskdale is in the county of Cumbria, which is in the north west corner of England, on the Scottish border. While England is generally flat, central Cumbria is mountainous, and that explains the historical isolation. Scafell is the highest point in the centre and the valleys radiate out from it, many of them have lakes, which gives the name of the Lake District. Upper Eskdale is in the central area, close up against Scafell. Eskdale and the other valleys have a unique landscape: many farms have managed to remain little changed since the medieval period, and the constant grazing has given a character to the fells (mountains). Everything about it is of compelling interest to the family since it was our home.

All things Bright and Beautiful

We grew up singing this hymn. It was said to have been inspired by a line of the poet Samuel Taylor Coleridge, 'He prayeth best who loveth best all things both great and small.' And Coleridge loved Eskdale.

In order to tell you how it was in upper Eskdale, in the 1930s, and to give a flavour of the time, I will start back in 1936, just after I turned five. I will drop into that time and place, by describing the route from our farm, Paddockwray, to the school. The village school was a mile or so away, down the valley, and run by my Aunt Gladys, Father's oldest sister. I walked there alone at five, as was customary.

My problem in writing this narrative is that I cannot go even a few feet along the way without some memory intruding from my later elementary years, or from my life as an adult, looking over my shoulder. So we will all have to cope with that variety, these three voices. The five year old would have understood perfectly this added complication, since I was already a babysitter for two younger brothers, Alastair and Hughie. And if there was one thing upon which the adults in upper Eskdale were crystal clear, it was that the job and first responsibility of an older child, of any age, was to look after any younger ones present. I was to keep them from harm, and to generally explain the world. (Immediately we get intruding observations from the adult.)

Coleridge recorded his thoughts about Eskdale in his notebook as he walked down the valley in 1802, more than a century before my walk to school: '… but never sure was lovelier Human Dwellings than those nestled in the Trees at the foot of the Fells, and in among the intervening Hills.' Paddockwray must have been one of those dwellings. And he was right, the farms 'sat well' in the landscape. Importantly, in the intervening years, between Coleridge's walk and me starting school, and I would join the road that he took, I would imagine that it would be hard to find anything at all much changed.

We had been noticed by an important poet. This would have been meaningful to the psyche of the nation, and to the 'educated', but not, at

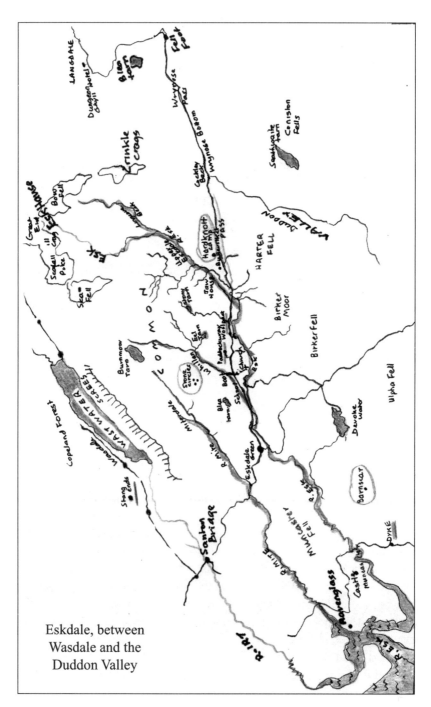

Eskdale, between
Wasdale and the
Duddon Valley

the time, mean much to the natives of the area, in their relative isolation. Not many of the natives would be reading the poets then. But in the end, the idea that there was something attractive here would change everything. I can see that, for us, Coleridge's writing on his walk down Eskdale was less of a poetic observation and more of a 'warning shot across the bow'.

The valley had an ancient, ageless, pastoral and uncluttered look. It was a harmonious and beautiful landscape: the old farm buildings with the drystone walls around their little fields, were constructed of the same weathered granite seen in outcrops on the fells all around, and at the head of the valley, and in the erratic rocks still lying in the fields. When first quarried the stone is pink with iron, but as it weathers, various lichens grow all over the surface, giving a mostly gray and white mottled look, with an occasional bit of sulphurous yellow, or sometimes an outright black. The valley floor was a fresh and luscious green.

One might ask why the farmsteads were nested at the foot of the fells? While there was an occasional farm in the middle of the dale, they were usually set into the fell side, away from possible flooding and also, one assumes, to avoid the valuable, slightly deeper, soil in the middle. The farms were convenient to the basic building material from the quarries in the fell sides. Nowhere was the soil very deep. In the quarries it could be seen to be a very thin layer over the reddish rock. Like Paddockwray, the farmsteads were mostly on the north side of the valley and so got the most sun. Less often there was a farmhouse built into the south side and it must have had a good reason to be there: presumably ownership of the fields around it, and the south side was in a different ancient manorial jurisdiction. That side got very little direct sunlight, being blocked as it was by the steep Harter Fell range. We were living in a deep valley, that had been scoured out by an ice-age glacier long, long ago.

Meanwhile back to the five year old – the day inevitably started with the essential oatmeal porridge cooked over an open fire in the dark north facing kitchen that looked out intimately into the fellside. Porridge was most likely followed by an egg. We certainly had plenty of eggs, our hens were all around in the yard, and they would come almost up to the kitchen door. As children we learned to avoid those sharp beaks and the cold reptilian eyes. The hens were a cheeky lot. They thought the yard to be theirs, and understandably, since the hen house was only a few yards away in a section of the huge granite barn. They retired to it at dusk, and arranged themselves along the tree trunk perches slotted into the stone walls.

At this time, and place, parents did not normally walk their children to school. A mother might turn up at school on a child's first day, for extra support, but that would be all. There were only a few farms in the upper valley and so we knew most people well. Escorting a child daily would have entailed walking there and back twice a day, a serious loss of time and daylight; and we must have been thought to be safe enough. Cars were little known at this time, when I started school there were probably only two resident cars further up to the head of the valley from Paddock-wray. The one at the Woolpack Inn that Father drove on inn business, and one at Wha House where Father's sister Sallie and and her family farmed. At this time a stranger in a passing car was still an event.

Since we wandered around the paths and fields a lot even a five year old had a good idea of the surrounding geography; I most certainly knew the way to school. The lane from Paddockwray to the main road was long and gravel, grassed on both sides and in the middle – what in Ireland they call a 'green road.' It was hemmed in by granite walls that were just wide enough for a horse and cart. To begin with, the lane was shaded by sycamore and hazel. The leaves of the first sycamore at the yard gate had the raised black spots of a fungus, handy for learning to count, since they went from one to forty or so, and we did occasionally line them up in numeric order.

The lane passed the stone hulls on the left, for calves and the like. And, on the right, was the dipping tub and the quarry into the fell. Finally, situated high on the bank and so well placed for sunshine was the large vegetable and soft fruit garden with the much desired berries and currants. The lane wandered around the Big Meadow and turned sharply left at the drinking trough, where a high placed spout delivered a constant stream of cold, pure water from the fell. Immediately ahead was the stile over a wall onto a path leading up the fell to the Howes Farm. (A stile is a narrow slit built into the top half of the wall which allows a person to squeeze through sideways, but is too narrow for sheep.) It was at this stile, on a remarkably thick and dark night, that Tyson Cowman, our farm man heard inexplicable moans. The owner was Auntie Gladys, who was found in a heap amongst the tall grass with a broken ankle, apparently having missed a step down.

Our lane continued on to a small bridge over a stream that meandered through the middle of the meadows. The stock got their water from the fresh streams in the fields. Although small, this stream had a name, Eel Beck – but we saw no eels in our time. In the spring its banks were dotted with our iconic primroses – of a devastating pale yellow tint, with the tiniest hint of pale green. Their delicate, notched, petals spoke to the humidity that was our lot. Also in spring there were the white lambs that tottered around, unsure of their long legs, their little black faces alert to you, their mothers all attention, stamping a hoof if you got too close.

It was here, at the little bridge, a few years later, that Auntie Gladys came another cropper. She was driving her new Austin and for some reason abandoned it skewed sideways and hanging over the water. She then walked on to Paddockwray and imperiously demanded of a farm man, fortuitously present, that he deal with the situation. He might not yet have learned to drive himself. It was to become one of our classic 'Auntie Gladys car stories', and there were to be many.

The Big Meadow on the left was, a few years later and early on in the war, to be drained by Italian soldiers from a nearby prisoner-of-war camp. They sang memorably as they dug ditches to the main stream, and laid the drain tile. Glad to be well away from it all, one imagines. Singing like that in the open was something new; it brought us a bit of southern warmth. Our farm men sang only at milking time – and then really only for the cows. One of these singers made me a ring out of a threepenny bit; he had been a jeweller in civilian life.

The soldiers arrived for work in an open lorry, driven by a young boy with a difficult teenage skin. This boy, who looked scarcely old enough to hold a licence, was teased mercilessly during their picnic lunches. All the while, we children wandered among them and enjoyed the excitement, it was a change from our usual country quiet. It was not exactly high security as anyone wanting to escape could just have walked away. There was nothing like a guard, and not even a telephone at the house. Some did wander off, but mostly to look for rabbits, which were plentiful at the time.

After the Big Meadow the lane passed a rocky field on the left, really just a bit of rough pasture. On the right was a rare arable field. It was narrow and with earth deep enough for a plough. As children we had followed behind the ploughing team. There could be one horse or two yoked to the plough with a complicated harness system enabling the metal ploughshare to point sharply forward. The ploughman hung onto the handles of the plough, guiding the ploughshare and keeping it upright; at the same time talking to the horses. And it was a tough job; men had to be men. The plough had to be held steady as it went, so that the furrows curled nicely over in a straight line, parallel with the last one. Not infrequently the metal cutting edge struck a significant cobble, that was a shock to both the horse and the ploughman and an interruption to be sorted out. Gulls wheeled about, diving greedily down on what was uncovered.

At the gate, where our lane met the main road, there was a smallish and struggling larch tree, not doing too well. A teasing farm man tried to tell us that this tree fruited sugar cubes – a story on a par with reindeer on the roof. I have to say that we were serious as children, a fact confirmed by the sombre faces in the school photograph. We were not at all entertained by misinformation, we had a struggle to find it in any way amusing, we were almost to the point of being censorious about it. Doubtless that was the largest part of our charm as subjects.

Over the other side of the main road was our other hen house. These hens had acres over which they could potentially range. They were entirely free, but in practice they stayed close to their house. Someone had to walk to them in the morning to let them out, and again to feed them in the afternoon and collect the eggs, then again to shut them in at night. We listened to many stories about foxes and the damage they wrought in the night. Gory details about what had been needlessly killed, what had been taken, about the tell-tale feathers and remains lying about. The pity of it all. Once I had the good luck to meet a fox on my way, and in broad daylight. It trotted by me, sporting a healthy red coat and brush, and with a confident air quite at odds with its poor reputation.

It was a westward turn onto the main road down Eskdale, the direction also taken by Coleridge. It was not much different in width than the lane, but smoothed over with tar macadam. It had the same enclosing drystone walls and these could frighten unfamiliar drivers, so much so that they tended to drive dead centre, as far away as possible from the narrow hedges and the granite. Father joked that he too wanted just a little bit – in the middle. Two cars could just pass if they slowed down and took it inches at a time, and it was always possible that one might have to back up to a more hopeful looking passing place at a field gate. A bigger problem could arise with a lorry. Still in 1936 the chances were slim that I would meet anyone at all on the road, and if I did it would almost certainly be someone who would address me by name.

Paddockwray with Aberdeen Angus cattle.

There were no noticeable airplanes about at this time either. In fact we listened to conversations about conversations that the family had held in the past, about the implausibility, and the difficulties, of such a weight staying up in the air. Unfortunately we were, very shortly, to become familiar with planes: they came with the Second World War. Since there were as yet no tractors in upper Eskdale, and we did not yet have mains electricity as far up the valley as Paddockwray, there was not much machine noise. Plastic was similarly hardly known to us, so there were no bits of it about, and very little paper either. In short it would have been difficult to find any pollution at all: no unwelcome detritus or discordant racket, and only country smells.

We were accustomed to this pervasive quiet. The usual background sounds on this walk would have been an occasional sheep blare, and the two nearest and sizable waterfalls of Birker Force and Stanley Ghyll, coming down from the Harter Fell range. The falls were noticeably more insistent after rain. One might meet rain itself, or the prevailing strong wind from the west, driving up the valley. My own footfalls would likely be the loudest thing on my way down the road. And there was always the murmur of water somewhere, the ground was usually damp, the grass soft

17

and cool. To quote Coleridge again, and this time completely out of context … 'there was water, water everywhere' (even up on the fell), but this water was all fit to drink, and we were free to do so. For this reason dry ground is still exotic to me, even dust; even the very idea of 'drinking' water still provokes thought.

The seemingly endless and unfolding landscape was a patchwork of small fields enclosed by their walls, completely pastoral and much changed from the wild. It had been worked over for countless generations, for a thousand years at least, according to the sparse records that remain, but was attractive as remarked on by the poet, and still productive.

Going to school one had the time, and the expectation, to acquire a knowledge of the wild and the domesticated life encountered along the way. Hedgerows were good for the wild. There were no immediate threats to safety. Children were not continually warned, as yet, to 'stop, look and listen' with some apprehension, before proceeding. In this tranquil near silence, a car or a motor-bike echoed down the valley. As children we had all the time in the world to concentrate on the surrounding countryside. One could take in the whole thing, focus at a distance, register a mile or two away on the valley floor, check on the tops of the fells, survey the sky, track the clouds. We had space – both physical and mental.

The main road passed a ruin called the Old Shop – short for workshop – which was a place where miners stored tools and stayed while working. In our time most of its old granite walls still stood, but they were overgrown with sycamores, some rising from out of the middle of the house and growing right through vestiges of the slate roof. Later on, after the war, wandering men might camp here while passing through the valley. They were said to be 'unable to settle' on account of their war experiences. They were a shock to us, in our rural self-sufficiency, but they were fed by the locals, albeit with some apprehension.

The road meandered around corners and then up to Cross How, then a sharp, dangerous, left turn, and a long, narrow, steep drop down hill. Tiny bilberries grew on the hedges, good for a snack on the way to school. In the middle of this hill, at the age of five, was the start of my first remembered humiliation. I was on my way back from school when a farmer with his horse and cart stopped. He told me that he was calling in at Paddockwray for tea, and would I like a ride? I answered that I was sorry but I could not, since I did not know him, so he had to go on without me. When I got home a bit later, there he was having tea with Father, and the laughter over my refusal comes back. No laughter from my mother I am quite sure; she had very likely been the one to programme me against this potential danger, either she or Auntie Gladys, and possibly both. The farmer was from Ghyll Bank, just up behind Paddockwray, part way up the fell to Burnmoor, and he became a family friend.

At the bottom of Cross How there was another bridge over Eel Beck, the stream now certainly big enough to be called a beck. It was here one morning that a horse and cart came through the gate from Hollings Farm, carrying a coffin on a bed of straw. The two Benson brothers had farmed there – one had died and was being transported to church by his brother. The bereaved brother was lying on his back by the side of the coffin, his hat pulled down over his eyes in his grief. What seemed most extraordinary was that the horse appeared to be doing the navigating.

Finally there was the really important Cross Roads at Brook House – civilization to us. The way to school was straight ahead, the road up to Boot village was to the right, the road to the church was to the left. The church road was gravel, another green road, and wound around two farms before ending at St Catherine's, with the Esk river flowing musically past. The road up to the village was short, and the village tiny.

There was a single row of stone whitewashed cottages on one side, flanked by farmsteads at each end, Fold End and Bridge End, and with the inn and a post office. At the end of this intimate space there was an old packhorse bridge to the water mill on the Whillan Beck, and two cottages. The beck here was swift moving and stained with a clear sienna bog colour; it rushed down from Ghyll Bank, and beyond that from Burnmoor. The mill was still working then, grinding local oats (called corn by us), but it was very close to going out of business after hundreds of years of important life. In my mind I can see the wooden wheel turning, the cross sections scooping up the water as it flowed past. As children we wandered up and down these roads and knew all the residents.

The school was straight ahead past Brook House and past the terminus of a small gauge railway that was a left over from a period of iron ore mining in the valley. The school was right on the roadside. It consisted of one long single room with two porches and a cloakroom, earth toilets outside in two separate gravel yards. There were no swings or other playground equipment. The official name was Eskdale High School, but that title always had to be followed up with a clarification. The High did not mean it was a secondary school, the High referred to upper Eskdale, and distinguished it from Eskdale Low School, the elementary school in the village of Eskdale Green, two miles further down the valley. (Spelling out Eskdale so formally sounds strained since we heard it in the local dialect in which it came over as Eshdle.)

Our teacher, my Aunt Gladys, had taught many in the valley, the consequence being that no one readily questioned her authority on anything. The locals were still her children, and living up to her expectations. And, since she played the piano for the local dances held in the school, they were always coming back for a refresher. There was an enduring respect. So when she got her car, and it was one of the earlier ones in the valley, they were surprised to discover that she was an indifferent driver. This revelation caused wild entertainment and the locals were breathless about their close calls and narrow escapes.

My first challenge at school was the roll call at the start of the day. I had a struggle learning to say 'Present Miss Armstrong' instead of the compromise that first came naturally, 'Present Auntie Gladys'. I had another relative at school for a short while, my cousin John Bulman. His family were at Wha House before they went to the Old Dungeon Ghyll Hotel in Langdale. Then there was his car story, gone over and dissected for us by the relatives. He had been in the car with Auntie Gladys when she had driven straight into one of our stone walls and done significant damage to the car. John's complete delight was the dominant factor in the story; the valley's dire expectations appeared to him to have been met. He had danced around the car singing – with real hope. 'Oh Auntie Gladys... you've absolutely buggered it!' John's curly hair and his long curled eyelashes, his somewhat Tony Lumpkinesque outlook, had the same kind of energy integral to the story.

The school had about eighteen children, of ages five to school leaving. I am not sure when school-leaving was then, possibly as late as fourteen. There cannot have been more than two or so in each Standard (year), so the teaching had to be pretty much aimed at all Standards simultaneously. Fortunately Auntie Gladys had Montessori training so we were set to instruct each other. Only a year later, Mother was astonished to hear from her six year old that she was '... teaching the little ones!'

Parents calling in at the school assured us that the noise was incredible, they never failed to remark on it. Since our teacher was serious about the Montessori method we felt a great deal of personal liberty. We were allowed to walk around and speak to anyone pretty much any time we felt so inclined, indeed a significant number of us had become teachers ourselves. One imagines older generations to have been more disciplined and confined to their desks in a Victorian fashion, hence their amazement when they visited us. In addition children quite commonly wore wooden (alder) clogs, with steel caulkers on the bottom, and they made their own din on the bare wooden floor. Granda Leece would later put leather strips on ours, in place of the steel, to ameliorate the problem. We may have been the only quiet ones.

At the age of five we started out with slates and chalk. When we got the hang of that we graduated to pencils and paper, and then finally on to pens with removable nibs, ink wells being sunk into the desks. There were plenty of blue stained fingers. There was no library as such, in fact very few books at all. Craft materials and supplies were stacked in one of the porches. There was the piano for Auntie Gladys, since all female teachers of the era were required to play the piano. In addition to teaching children of all ages at the same time, two of our number had Down's syndrome, but they were well integrated and notably attached to Auntie Gladys. They spent a bit of their time at her desk, helping her out wherever they could, like distributing or collecting whatever was required.

Some children walked as much as three miles to school, like those off a Birker Moor farm, on the fell to the south. They were said to milk the cows in the morning, then change into their school clothes before leaving for the day. Indeed most of the children lived on farms and certainly helped with the milking, but after school, after their walk home, and after their tea-time. After milking we then helped attend to the stock and feed what was required: that is hay for the cows, milk and gruel for the calves, slops for the pigs, and make the dog food, scatter grain and grit for the hens. General assistance all around was the norm.

Auntie Gladys was a 'born' teacher with serious ambitions for us all. On the lighter side she was much given to drama and throwing chalk about when she wanted us to know that she was displeased at some perceived lack of earnestness, some apparent lack of total commitment towards learning. I recall a chalk eraser sailing through the air; she had no sense of humour at all about education. She would even correct me for laughing. She taught all the required subjects but found time for additional things like knitting and sewing. The girls knitted woollen vests to wear, plain, ribbed or moss stitch, and we sewed blue calico knickers. We had a vegetable garden at the bottom of the boys' playground, so that was part of the curriculum too. I don't remember planting so that possibly that was mainly for the boys.

She had us singing the old songs, certainly a lot of sea shanties. 'Hearts of Oak' for instance '…steady boys, steady' and Scottish songs like 'Over the sea to Skye'. We became familiar with the old ballads spoken, or sung. 'I fear ye are poisoned Lord Randal, my son,' and in response Randal's white lie, 'I am weary with hunting and fain would lie doon.' And what had he eaten? 'Eels Mother – make my bed soon.' We spent a lot of energy on English and Country dances: 'Nuts in May', 'Ring of Roses', 'The Grand Old Duke of York', 'London Bridge is falling down' and 'Oranges and Lemons'. We had Highland dancing and Scottish reels, and Sword Dancing in the quarters between wooden swords dramatically crossed on the floor. Dancing was for both boys and girls and we loved it.

It was there that I discovered that drawing was a skill, a skill with which apparently, and most curiously, not everyone was born. I recall the hush of a crowd around my desk one day. I was carefully demonstrating the drawing of the legs of prehistoric animals, sabre-toothed tigers certainly. And this was to an informed group: these were children who knew how animal legs should look and work. They were serious and attentive.

Apart from the two playgrounds we had an entire field, the School Field, on the opposite side of the road. There was a conveniently placed stile for us to hop over into it. The field had a flat part adjacent to the vicarage and its field, and that was used for drill, or organized games like rounders, the rest was a rough and rocky tree clad rise over which we ranged in our playtime. A little bit of it was cut out as a World War One Memorial listing those past students (scholars was the local word) who had not come home. At Whitsuntide we had Maypole dancing, and what a problem it was to get the ribbons into the right pattern, we had to concentrate on the top of the pole while skipping around and there appeared to be a fair number of mistakes. Even then, I think that we knew that Maypole dancing was some kind of historic re-enactment. Whitsun was historically a time of relaxation in the farming year, being about seven weeks after Easter and so after spring activities like planting and lambing, and so had been a time for dancing.

The school playing field was deep, and at the back, and over the top of the rise, it went down steeply to the river Esk at Trofuss Bridge (the name possibly a corruption Trough Force). Trofuss had a very deep slow moving pool with high smooth rocks on the far side, and it was overhung with trees. The pool was so deep that it was here we eventually learned to dive. On the school side it was a dangerous looking wooded fall-off, but we managed to get down it to the river somehow. The boys were always checking for salmon if it was that time of year. It is true, very occasionally a rash salmon might be out in the middle, and so not to be missed in the clear water, water so clear you could see every fin and spot. More likely the fish were at the banks, sensibly out of direct sight. If one laid flat on the rocks, and leaned out and perilously over, one might see their brown backs with their fins slowly moving as they idled in formation. They hugged the sides of the rocks, camouflaged by the shade. 'Tickling' was the boys preferred method of fishing, and it wasn't at all easy to get close enough for that, but they were forever fancying their luck.

Naturally it was possible to get lost in the field when immersed in activity, possible indeed to forget to go back into the schoolroom after a playtime. This did happen now and then, and once Auntie Gladys registered our casual approach she sought to demonstrate the importance of time keeping. She did this by lining up the entire school to be caned on the hand. The reason was given – failure to return from a playtime at the correct time. That smack on the hand was certainly dramatic, a bit of a surprise, the first time I had personally met such a thing, but it fitted in with her serious approach to learning. We got the point. Auntie Gladys had a hand bell that she wielded outside when playtime was over, but it was sometimes not in our immediate interest to listen for a distant tinkle. Perhaps we were doing somersaults in the branches of a sycamore at the back of the field. Tree climbing could be a major all-consuming activity.

You will notice that there was ample opportunity for getting hurt in our lives. Fortunately for all, we were country children and not victims abroad. We were always to be aware of where we were, what we were doing and who we were supposed to be looking after. It's true we had a lot of independence, were often alone, mostly unsupervised. Imagine today a whole rocky field for a school playground, sloping down at the back and out of sight, dropping off to a deep part of a river! Then, if a country child should come a cropper crying was not automatically the first response, it was rather viewed as a learning experience: considered more of a lapse in common sense.

Older children, both boys and girls, took their supervisory responsibilities seriously. I remember instances of their instruction and explanation, and am still grateful for it. There was a bit of 'us and them' about, that is

Paddockwray Lane.

of children versus adults: we worked out a lot between ourselves. We didn't particularly go off into age groups but boys and girls might play separately, co-operating sometimes, should a game require it. Fighting was thought of as a very shameful thing, but now and again the boys might descend to a stand-off. Alastair once got into such a fight which was an embarrassment for me, the older one, since I was supposed to be in charge, but was powerless to stop it.

One curious thing we local children noticed about visiting children, those who came for holidays in the valley, was how readily they got cuts and bruises and experienced near drownings. Even how ready they were to howl and appeal to adults. In short, how much they foolishly got themselves noticed and into trouble, making themselves quite unnecessarily the centre of attention.

In spite of all of our usual and customary freedoms Auntie Gladys did, on occasion, shock the natives. She would walk the entire school down to the river near the church, in order to have a paddle about. Hardly swimming – one hopes in retrospect. Our rivers were cold and fast and the rounded beck stones slippery. On one particular school outing we crawled, on bare knees, over the river on two parallel old rusty iron girders. We had to crawl since there were no railings at either side, or even slats across between the girders. Just two narrow aging, peeling girders. We were following the narrow gauge track of a disused railway, leading to a long ago iron ore mine, and specifically looking for kidney ore (haematite). 'They have to learn!' Auntie Gladys would announce to the more fainthearted parents. Learning to cope with physically challenging situations we understood; they were all around.

Since the school was run by the county council there was an education inspector. He arrived with much commotion on a motorbike. He was very large and encased in an old Burberry mac with canvas bags crossed over his chest and had a florid complexion. He chain-smoked and sported yellowed nicotine stained fingers. He was altogether an unprepossessing figure. Auntie Gladys, we readily understood, didn't have much patience with him or for his mission. She harangued him in a somewhat patronizing fashion. I recall helping her in this performance during a drill class in the field, put on for the inspector's benefit, by waiting obviously and expectantly for a command. I overheard her drawing the inspector's attention to my diligence. She was always convinced of the superiority of her children: had complete confidence in all that we were doing. Indeed, at the time she advised me personally not to be too impressed with government inspectors.

I do not know anything about the inspector's reports but our school was, later on, when the eleven-plus exam came with the war, found to have twice the national average number of candidates for the newly vamped grammar school entry. At the time this was said to be remarkable since we were country children, without any of the urban advantages that might have helped in the testing procedure. It would have been a source of wonderment to us to hear that we might be considered in any way deprived, but some must have thought so. It was also judged by the authorities of the time that our Down's syndrome classmates were to remain where they were, instead of go to a special school, since they were reported to be doing well with Auntie Gladys. And right enough, when the time came, they readily found work near home and were good employees.

The school inspection was pretty much our only contact with officialdom. We did get free school milk, delivered daily in small bottles, from a neighbouring farm. A boy from the farm was a classmate. School milk was part of a national program. We were of course, mostly entirely off farms and well nourished, particularly with fresh milk, but it was a drink after all. The programme received a lot of criticism from our parents because sometimes not all of the milk was drunk. And this was a society to which any kind of waste was an unforgivable crime, absolutely no food was thrown away at home. The cost was not simply to be seen as money; they knew intimately about the work and care that went into it, and there was always some animal to feed left-overs. When it was cold in winter we had lunch around an open fire at one end of the schoolroom, there the milk bottles were ranged to warm them up, I think there was sometimes ice in them. One child who had had some surgery for a hare-lip entertained us by taking the milk into her mouth and spectacularly bringing it down her nose! Now there was an example of waste alright, and just as well for us it was that it was not ever witnessed by a parent, or by Auntie Gladys.

Occasionally at Easter we got an official visit from Miss Fair, she too was attired in an old mac with crossed canvas bags, and she had a one-of-a-kind cloche hat. She was a local character and well respected, was in fact a serious antiquarian and photographer. Her father had been a previous vicar and she had stayed on after his stint. She was suitably chosen to distribute 'historic' money to each of the pupils. It seemed that there was an ancient bequest, early enough and important enough to have been printed on a large board and displayed inside on the church wall, dated 1798, where local benefactors of the school had left money for its operation, and extra, so that poor children could pay the school fees of the time. Since by our time school education was completely free for all, the money was divided up between the pupils of the day. We would surrender it at home. We had no shops anyway, so it could not be easily spent.

Our education was not completely secular, our vicar at the time, the Reverend Hall, came to school, now and then, accompanied by his very exotic dog Slavasha, a Russian Wolfhound. All we saw were sheepdogs for herding stock, occasionally the fox hound pack or the fox terriers for hunting. All our dogs had a job: a reason for being. Slavasha was clearly not useful: stood about, was of aristocratic aspect, a fantastic height and had long wavy golden hair. Presumably the vicar came to school to teach us something. I try to remember some words of wisdom but the mind is a blank, the talk was not as memorable as Slavasha. Was the presence of a cleric in the school religious discrimination against anyone? Hardly, we were not religious by nature, but we did enjoy that dog; the vicar and his wife, were rumoured to comb it and save the hair, causing wild speculation on a use for dog hair.

We were homogenous in origin, and Anglican by definition, but did not routinely go to church on Sundays. Nevertheless the church was important to the valley: there were births, deaths and marriages to observe. And there was a spell of singing in the choir when we had the war evacuees, and there were the tombstones of the forebears in the churchyard. Our idea of difference was one classmate with an Irish father, at the time that meant being an obligatory Roman Catholic, but since there was no Catholic church within easy reach she may have got the same negligent religious instruction as the rest of us. We did become familiar with bible stories, so maybe it was for that the vicar came to school.

Another vicar, sometime after the Reverend Hall, once announced that the parishioners were close to being pagan. Now that did raise a few eyebrows, but then there came a spirited riposte that he was close to communist. It all did nothing to swell the congregation. It is true we were quite untroubled by our souls, were not harassed in any religious way, we were left to concentrate on our landscape and to discover how things hung together. While the church was central to the valley, outward religious enthusiasm was in fact quite suspect, there was much more sympathy for the rare case of a mental illness, or a special medical condition.

Still the Liturgical Year was constantly referred to by adults: Shrove Tuesday (for pancakes), Ash Wednesday (for stew), Palm Sunday, Good Friday, Easter Sunday (for rolling onionskin and spring flower stained Pasche eggs), Whitsun, Michaelmas and of course Christmas. One imagines that the Liturgical Year had been more tied to the agricultural year in the past, and it was the grandparents who generally drew attention to its markers, there were occasional references to farm events on that calendar. Father talked about farmhands attending some event in the ecclesiastical year, and wearing straw in their hats to indicate they were for hire. My recollection is that the fair was at Michaelmas, although that seems to be an odd time, since it was in the autumn when the work was winding down.

An interesting phenomenon was that even though people did not regularly attend church they seemed to have assigned pews when they did, and ours was second on the right from the front. Like our cows in the byre we preferred an assigned space. For children there was nothing special at the church, I do not remember any attempt at Sunday School, Mr. Pedder did once try a youth group, but I have no memory of it taking off. Young people were kept busy and were maybe a bit suspicious of anything new.

Auntie Gladys, on the other hand, did seem to be somewhat religious, she was the organist and part of the tiny congregation, which was sometimes only two in winter. In summer the numbers would swell with a sprinkling of visitors. Once or twice I heard her remonstrating with my parents on the absence of her nephews and nieces in church. Sunday was still busy in the inn even though the farm might have no special project for the day after the absolute essentials. We could easily have been dispatched to church. It was apparent that there was not much enthusiasm for it at home, although to us children just the time off would have looked like a holiday.

There were two exceptions to the general lack of regular church going, and those were Harvest Festival and Christmas Midnight Mass. We might go to both. On both these occasions the church was packed, just as it was for weddings and funerals. Since both Harvest Festival and a Winter Mass could be said to have been associated with the pagan, the vicar who sensed the paganism might well have had a point.

There was plenty of unsupervised time in our school life, a minor bit of theatrical corporal punishment, but overall a memorable school and a teacher with vision and drive, never to be forgotten. Her pupils must all have felt that they owed a big debt to her and ran their lives to meet her expectations. It is true that there was plenty of child labour at home on the farm, but we were healthy, well exercised and warmly dressed. That is, apart from the red knees in winter that long pants would have helped – unfortunately for us custom still required girls to wear skirts, and the younger boys to wear short pants. We were learning a lot about subsistence and the costs of producing food, and this in our most formative years. We knew all too intimately where all our food came from, followed its life cycle, and on to the table; it was personal. And Auntie Gladys made reference to farming matters at school. By school leaving age children would be well on the way to being able to run a farm.

Even in the 1930s we must have looked like a backwater to city people since at that time we knew practically nothing of libraries, museums, galleries, theatres, cinemas, even shops and the like. The men did not even have football or cricket teams nearby. Women went out to meetings even less, and for them any sport was a non-starter. All of these things were not many miles away, but transport was limited and the work was all consuming. It goes without saying that the natives were not knowledgeable about any cultural activity with a big C. They may even have suspected it as belonging to another class, to some kind of incomer perhaps, that is the 'professionals' that were around, or the summer holiday makers. It is quite true we hardly knew how to operate around urban places: streetwise we were most emphatically not. Auntie Gladys was however again the exception, a 'one-off', she had an open mind and was interested in absolutely everything, willing to give anything a try. She once hauled us off to see the small travelling Ballet Rambert in Whitehaven, 22 miles away, I don't know how.

As children we must have encountered urban institutions in outings and holidays you say? Well, not much. Outings and holidays were thin on the ground and the only bus service from the village was on market days. On the farms the cows had to be milked twice a day, animals had to be fed and looked after seven days a week, year round. And farms took visitors to supplement their hardly won income, so it was never easy. While today, we might worry about leaving a cat or a dog, or worry about a water leak, our farm families would have to get someone capable of running a farm where there were constant decisions to be made. We were in an even more difficult position with the addition of the Woolpack Inn.

And then, where would we go? We were justifiably apprehensive of towns and the life we saw lived there. London was a world away and spoken of rarely, and with some horror; Edinburgh was closer and thought rather more desirable. Nobody went very far.

When we did get to a major shopping centre on the coast it seemed quite depressed. It was the 1930s after all. We in the country were fairly well insulated from all of that, being pretty well self sufficient. In White-haven we occasionally saw rather grubby looking children, some without shoes, playing in the (to us) drab, bare, cobbled streets. Once Mother gave a sobbing child a piece of fruit. The general appearance of the town, at the time (quite different now – it is described as a 'jewel town') was generally sobering to us. What we were seeing I suppose was the effects of the Industrial Revolution, as well as urbanization, and as yet we did not have anything like that in our experience. Our experience was a world away. We were in an older situation, working the land and with scattered households. We were not accustomed to the sight of anyone with an insecure life, or living in anything but picture perfect surroundings, and as children we were thoughtful at the contrast, almost struck dumb by it.

Did we have any days out at all, apart from the occasional and obligatory shopping trips? Some of us did, now and then, get to the beach and swim, about seven miles away, but it was just a beach with sand, waves, and the dunes, no urban excitements generally speaking. We would have had the swim, a picnic, and inspected the marine and dune life. It was still the natural world. Father very occasionally took us out on a drive around somewhere in the Lake District, by extension it was all ours, and we enjoyed picnics.

In the summertime there were agricultural shows that were important to the locals and children went to those, events that we understood, showing off the stock, and the awards. There was produce in the tents and needlework, also competing for awards. The shows were taken very seriously, and were marvellous days out. The events that got our most admiring attention as children were the equestrian, especially the jumping rounds. One memorable year there was a bare-back rider, who styled himself as a Cossack, and showed off his stunts: he raced around the track, facing backwards, rode standing up, jumping on from behind, risking kicks. Sadly, none of it to be tried at home. A show was our one chance for ice cream, which was high on the agenda, and we expected to get a lot. Close to home we did have a memorable sports day for the Coronation

High Eskdale School, 1937 – the author is on the front row on the right, and cousin John is on the back row standing beside Auntie Gladys.

of George VI, in May 1937, in a Brook House field at the Crossroads, which the whole valley seemed to attend, I won a china coronation cup for winning a three-legged race, or was it the egg-and-spoon, or a sack race? They all blur together in the excitement of the day.

There was one summer event completely dedicated to sports and that was Grasmere Sports Day. It took place in Grasmere of course, and so a fair distance away, but still in the central Lake District. The most memorable events there were the Fell Races, for the men and for the boys. The runners set off from the show field and one could track them going up the fell-side into the distance, the course eventually returning them to the field. Besides the climb up and down, fell racing took judgment because feet had to land correctly with regard to the stones concealed under the bracken and other vegetation.

The other main event there was Cumberland and Westmorland Wrestling, for men and boys again. There was a special costume for that: a white vest and white long johns, with embroidered brief swimming-style-trunks worn over the top. The two opponents faced off, their bodies hinged at the hips and the arms draped over the back of the other, with the hands clasped. Thus joined there was a lot of tentative circling, and a lot of footwork. The rules were simple and the objective was to cause a part of the opponent's body to touch the ground. It looked something like judo, and when something happened it was fast, a contestant was suddenly on the grass and it was all over. As children this too became one of our skills – we practiced the tricks. Since this was the only place in the world you could witness this exact kind of wrestling the champion was, of course, styled 'World Champion'.

Then there was an odd happening called the Egremont Crab Fair. I cannot explain the name. To my knowledge there were no crabs, or crab apples. A main event was the gurning through a horse collar. The prize went to the worst facial expression, the most crabby expression perhaps. That just must have been a survival from medieval times.

Hound-trailing too was popular all over, not just in the valleys. It was a fell race for hounds following a scent, previously laid by a runner dragging a bag. The owners released the hounds at the start of the race in the field, who raced around the scent trail and then were greeted back at the starting point, with whistles and general encouragement from their owners.

At this time and in this place we were in some kind of time capsule in upper Eskdale. We lived at the head of a then isolated valley, blocked by the pass. Ours was a very stable population, not moving far over the centuries, and hardly touched by the industrial revolution. Our old buildings had survived unaltered, presumably, because the ancestors had been too poor to change them, the district too 'marginal' to get attention. To some degree we were a hang-over from medieval times: in a bit of a time warp. Most of England would by this time have been living in a more modern fashion, even in the countryside. And we were the last generation born before the Second World War, and the war was to change everything. We were the first generation that would not automatically stay on the family farm, the first to be offered more than an elementary school education and the possibility of another kind of job.

2

Paddockwray

We were at Paddockwray until I was six. Four of us were born there, literally at home, as was customary then. I am told that I arrived before the doctor so he could not present a bill. I remember Helen being born, vividly. The aunts including Father's sister Sallie were in attendance, while Alastair and I waited on the turn in the stairs observing the comings and goings – the placenta going by for instance. I don't recall the doctor there either.

Paddockwray Farm was, and is, old, very old, the buildings not younger than the sixteenth century. And one assumes that it was a farm well before that time. Just one look at the long house and the barn gives a feeling of their age; and leads to a compulsion to know something of their history, and that of previous lives lived there. Unfortunately there are only a few local records to go on: some information about tenancy and the connection to the Manor, sales or disputes, church records of births, deaths and marriages, and the government censuses.

The name itself, Paddockwray, is Old Norse for 'place of the toads'. Padda was the word for toad, and possibly also used for frogs, and wray means dwelling. Since place names are generally accepted as a good indicator of provenance, then Paddockwray was named by a Norse owner, if not built by one. The Norse were said to have preferred hill country and their names are all around in Eskdale. Paddockwray fields had a reputation for being wet; but while we had frogs and toads they did not appear to be present in any unusual numbers. Still there were a few seaves (rushes) growing in the fields proving it was wet. Good drainage was important in the area on account of the high rainfall, and particularly so at Paddockwray. I would imagine that over the generations there had been a continuous effort to drain the fields.

Existing records show family names that recur over and over. For instance the Eskdale and District Local History Society lists Paddockwray's previous tenants over a period of 135 years:

Dec. 1759 – Edward Hartley
May 1770 – Henry Hartley, the son
April 1779 – Henry Hartley, different family
April 1815 – Elizabeth, the heir, and George Tyson presumably her husband
April 1883 – Jonathan Benson
May 1852 – Jonathan Benson, the son
May 1875 – Joseph Tyson
May 1876 – Towers Tyson
April 1842 – George Tyson, heir at law
April 1849 – George Tyson, heir at law
1894 – Towers and George Tyson.

Remarkably there are only three family names covering what must have been five generations. The amazing thing is that, when we lived there, those family names were still around, they were the names of our neighbours: we had the Bensons on the next farm at Hollings, the Hartleys lived on a farm on the way to the church, and we had a farm man at Woolpack named Hartley. My maternal grandmother, Granny Leece, was born Hannah Tyson. While I do not know how related Granny was to Paddockwray Tysons, it is not unlikely that she could have been, in some distant way. She was born in 1876 about three to four hours walk away in Nether Wasdale. To get there the climb was over the fells behind Paddockwray, by

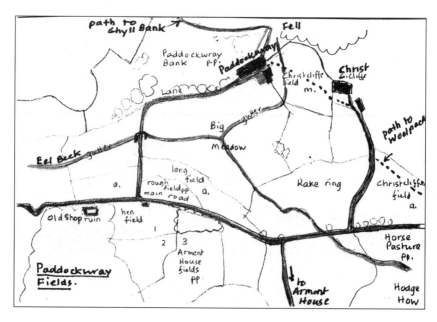

Ghyll Bank, over Burnmoor and down into Wasdale Head, half way around the lake to the west and you are at Rainors, her first home. Not such a great distance in this fell walking culture.

This looks like a very stable population, with a long history in the area. Local people were an intermarried mixture of Celt, Norse, Anglo-Saxon, and Norman. People had come in waves into central Cumbria. According to Angus Winchester, in his informative book *The Harvest of the Hills*, a reason for the stability of names in central Cumbria over the centuries was the medieval institution of tenant-right: the Lord of the Manor gave the tenant farmer the tenancy of his farm for life. That right could be re-newed with a son, or possibly two sons, but further fragmentation of a farm was not encouraged. One deterrent to fragmentation was that the rent was fixed, and not divisible. Winchester also tells us that the agree-ment of tenancy could also carry an obligation of the farmer to serve, if so required, in defence of the Border from Scottish incursions.

While the exact date of the Paddockwray buildings is not known, in the Percy survey of 1578 there is a record of a Nicholson tenant (and yes, there were Nicholsons still around in our time – three miles away in the next village). This survey lists the holdings of Henry Percy, Earl of Northumberland, in the Forest of Copeland: that is in Eskdale, Wasdale and Miterdale. Paddockwray also appears as one of the Earl's holdings.

The Percy survey refers to a basic annual rent at Paddockwray of three shillings, and for that the tenant had the house, barn, garth, arable land and adjacent meadow, and the job of maintaining the flock that went with the holding. The survey lists Wood How and Moss (a parcel of wood ground) as part of the property, but that was a name that I never heard in conversation. It might possibly have been behind the orchard and rising up to the Barrows, or even in the fields on the other side of the road. The survey mentions an old 'improvement', maybe a cottage, above the ten-ement that carried an additional rent of 6d. (pence), possibly draining the land, or walling fields. There were broken down walls in the Rake (the small enclosure behind the house leading to the path up the fell) but they were sheep folds. Perhaps the improvement was an addition to the long-house.

The 'moulture' and the 'walker' were listed at two pennies. So, in 1578 the total yearly rent for Paddockwray was three shillings and eight pence. 'Moulture' means corn (oat) milling, 'walker' means the fulling of wool and the charges at the mills for these services for the farm were set, just like the rent. It sounds as if there was an obligation to use the mill, not to be able to make a private arrangement. By our time at Paddockwray fulling was a thing of the past, and we were freehold.

In the fulling process short staple wool was scoured with Fuller's earth and then matted, for a felt like quality. Short wool staples were made into fine woollens. Long staples were treated differently and became worsted; Granny Leece talked a lot about worsted, she considered it a very fine item. Presumably this treatment of wool was done either at the Boot Mill, or the mill up behind Paddockwray at Ghyll Bank. In the past working with the wool provided a lot of extra employment for women. There are tantalizing references to linsey workers in history; and Granny herself used the word linsey. I have a memory that she also talked about linsey-woolsey which was material with a linen warp and a wool weft. Working with wool, in that sense, was all history to us; we sold our wool in bales, it was still valuable, but not as a secondary local industry. We bought it back as knitting wool and cloth. And we had a local tailor called Youdal at Eskdale Green; he sat cross-legged on a raised platform and when I saw him working he was sewing by hand.

Apart from the buildings and the small fields in the valley Paddock-wray had the ancient medieval grazing rights for the flock attached to it. The rights were to an area up the fell behind the farmstead, and some distance away, towards Black Apron. This was a dedicated section of the un-fenced area called Eskdale Common. Angus Winchester has done wonderful work here, uncovering and mapping each farm's allocated part of the grazing within the Common. The Eskdale Common was, and still is, a large area, about 15,000 acres in all, and it was common grazing for the farms of three valleys, Eskdale, Miterdale and Wasdale Head. Pad-dockwray's flock of sheep were heafed to their area of Common – a type of homing instinct taught by ewes to their lambs. The documents known as the Eskdale 24 Book, of 1587, lumps Paddockwray Farm in with the neighbouring farms of the Howes and Ghyll Bank when considering these sheep pasture rights on the Common.

Over the centuries, and in general, the geography was thought of as having three levels, as far as farming practice was concerned: at the top the high fell, then an intermediate level, and finally the valley floor. The high fells were for sheep, and the Eskdale Common went up to Scafell, and according to Angus Winchester it included part of Scafell. Scafell is the central mountain in Cumbria, and the highest in England, between

Eskdale and Wasdale and we were close to it. The Lord of the Manor, at one time, had a hunting preserve on Scafell, adjacent to the Common.

The intermediate fell level was the Burnmoor expanse, and there were rights that gave farms their grazing there for 'geld goods', both cattle and horses, and at certain times of the year. There were rules about using the Common, fines for breaches of them, and a committee of local farmers to oversee it all. At valley level were the fields and the 'intakes' (pronounced intacks by us) on the lowest bit of the fell behind the farm for cattle. Paddockwray had its three levels in the Eskdale fashion, that is the high fell bit, then the Burnmoor level, and below that the intack and the valley fields (known as the in-bye). It was the lower fell that had the deciduous trees left from the once extensive tree cover. In our day we used the allotted sheep fell grazing, but not so much that allowed for grazing cattle and horses. Our previous generation had used Burnmoor for horses at certain times. We did not much use the intacks for cattle pasture, our cows were kept in the fields.

The Eskdale 24 Book, of 1587, has information about the 'drift' (path on the fell) on which Paddockwray sheep had to be driven up to the grazing on the fell. Again Paddockwray is linked with the Howes and Gillbanke. To give a flavour of the time:

> ...and for the Drifts of Edward Tyson, John Nicholson, Richard Tyson and Edward Nicholson and every one of these, to drive their Sheep in their own order to Cookrigge, and in his own Order every one of them till they come on the west side of the Greathow, and to drive them forth to the Broadtongue as farr as the h(blank) upon their own Ground and then let them go.

Let them go... I like the phrase. With the help of the dogs one drove the flock up the fell on the assigned drift road, then when you got to the right marker ... you let the sheep go. Presumably you called off the dogs and halted; one supposes the sheep knew the signs, and dispersed to start cropping. Those place names on the fell used in the Eskdale 24 Book can be identified today.

The rules of 1587 also describe the allowed drift road for cattle up to the allowed pasture, and here Paddockwray is lumped with the farms of Hollings and the Howes. To quote again: '... every one of them shall drive forth at the Stongs, and so to any Place to the Stoney Gate.' Some of these marker names I recognize and some I do not, my brothers were more likely to know them, since it was their job to 'go to the fell' – that was not considered a job for girls at the time. We still abided by the rules for the flock, and knew them if we wanted to put cattle or horses on the fell. In the past it seems that there were more cattle and horses needing pasture. Indeed there were more people to feed: families were much larger and life may have been a lot tougher.

Characteristically the house, the farm buildings, the sheep folds and the field walls were often made of the local granite. And all built with the same drystone walling technique, and so look as if they were constructed in the same era. I do not have a date for the formal field enclosures in Eskdale. (In England some enclosures came quite late and as a formal movement.) Presumably the granite used at Paddockwray came from its own quarry behind the stable, and I was told by a farm man that granite from this quarry was also used on the main road going up the valley.

While Paddockwray was predominantly a sheep farm like its neighbours, in the past, it also had to provide all the necessities of life for the family and the stock. It had to have buildings and fields suitable for cattle, horses, pigs, poultry, sheepdogs, and the cats to control rodents, and possibly other stock. The farm had to have both grazing and arable fields, a vegetable garden and an orchard to feed all its inhabitants. The water supply came from a stream off the fell. In our childhood Paddockwray was somewhat in decline from such maximally productive days, since it was run as an adjunct to Woolpack which saw most of the farming activity. While we still had sheep, poultry and the kitchen garden, the byre and the stable were empty as the cattle and horses were normally housed at Woolpack.

We had a small enclosed flower garden along the front of the house, circled with a red sandstone wall. The sandstone was from St. Bees, not far up the coast. Hollyhocks did particularly well. Later on Auntie Gladys was to remark on them blooming heedlessly while Granny Armstrong died in a room above. The vegetable and soft fruit garden on the bank was a serious undertaking. On the other hand the orchard was old and so not so productive in our time; it needed re-planting.

The façade of the house showed the main house in the middle, an add-on house to the right, and the stable and loft to the left. This was the old medieval pattern and called the longhouse: the animal quarters and hay loft were directly attached to the house. This use persisted in Cumbria in my time, but I understand that the pattern had been lost in the rest of Eng-

Paddockwray from the fellside above.

land. The longhouse style had been common from the thirteenth century onwards. The hay loft was conveniently above the stable, there were large doors into it at the rear of the building, on the second floor. Hay had to be forked up and carried into the loft. The stored hay was then handy for the stable below, it was pushed through a hatch and dropped into the manger. In addition to the longhouse Paddockwray had a huge free standing barn. While it was used mostly for crop storage and equipment, it also had a section for the byre with its stalls and cobbled floor.

It is tempting to think that the animals living within part of the longhouse would keep the house warm, but since the walls were thick granite this is questionable. The granite walls were very wide and double, and infilled with something akin to clay. In the winter as the water-level rose the water was wicked up the wall and one could see the the damp rise up the papered walls inside the house the 'rising damp'. One can see why such wide and solid walls have survived the centuries as any renovation would have been a major undertaking and expense.

I imagine that the add-on house would at one time have had two rooms down and two up. In our day the downstairs was used as two kitchens, and the upstairs a bathroom (indoor bathrooms may not then have been universal in the valley) and a loft. The main house section had four bedrooms, two sitting rooms and a large larder called the dairy. The dairy and the kitchens had slate floors, and the dairy slate shelves, called sconces, kept food cool. These were of the same blue-gray slate as on all the roofs. The slate was from the eastern Lake District where the style of building construction was entirely in slate.

We used paraffin lamps to light the house, and candles to light one to bed. Even as small children we walked upstairs carrying a candlestick. The lamps and candles cast a soft light, much in contrast to the harsh electric light to which we later became accustomed at Woolpack. We sometimes held family concerts by lamplight with grandparents, aunts, uncles and cousins. Such concerts were customary then, but it was mostly the children who did the entertaining, so we had to have some party pieces ready. With the lamplight and firelight, everyone appeared to loom out of the darkness – chiaroscuro; we moved around as in a painting – with depth.

At this time there was no central heating but most rooms had open fireplaces that could be used as necessary. Before the Second World War Paddockwray meals were cooked on the open fire in the back kitchen. The kitchen fireplace had an iron arm that swung out, with a chain and a hook at the bottom, onto which one could hang the kettle or a pan, and then swing it back over the fire. There was an iron oven built into the side of the hearth. Somehow this arrangement heated our water, cooked our food, and warmed the house somewhat. We made toast by skewering the bread with a long toasting fork and holding it up to the fire. The fire had to be 'banked' at night. That meant arranging embers to be kept alive till morning; failing that my mother would have to build a new fire.

We burned wood from two parcels of woodland and bought coal. The latter was delivered by the coal lorry in sacks from Whitehaven, where there were coal mines. Delivering coal was a heavy and dirty job, and the delivery man was blackened like the miners one sometimes saw on the street in Whitehaven. He picked up the hundred weight sacks and carried them on his back into the coal house, dumped out the coal, and took the empty sacks back to the lorry. Later there was an Aga range, or possibly an Esse, put into the back kitchen, and this was fed by anthracite, a high grade coal. The range was much more convenient and presumably much more efficient and easy to use. It had a hot plate and ovens of differing temperatures.

The range heated the water for the bathroom and did something to warm the large house. Since there was no mains electricity at the time, there were few household conveniences. The laundry was dried outside and put to 'air' on the pulley rack that was overhead in the kitchen. You had to choose your day to do laundry by the weather, and it was important to get it outside on the line early enough to have a chance of drying over the course of the day. But that was true of everything on the farm. The weather decided, by and large, what you were doing and when, and you had to be ready to take advantage of sunshine or wind. Getting enough rain was never a problem.

It was rather dark at the back of the house. In fact most of the farm houses of the era were dark, and most often the ceilings too low for taller men. It was inferred that in earlier times people had been shorter. The rear kitchen where we spent most of our time faced north. The kitchen window looked out onto the fell but there was a narrow trench there luxuriant with royal ferns. The second kitchen, called the back kitchen, actually was at the front of the house facing south and in our day was used for purposes and chores other than cooking. It had an ancient free-standing flight of oak stairs going up from it to the loft. Outside the kitchen door there was a sandstone sconce for outdoor jobs, like cleaning vegetables or gutting game. We children were sometimes bathed in a tin laundry tub out there.

Farther down the long house was the front door proper. It led into a long passage with very dark, almost black, panelled oak on both sides, with similar dark oak doors into the two sitting rooms. The doors had ancient iron 'snecks' (handles), and there were worn decorative coloured tiles on the hall floor. I don't know if any of it was 'bog oak' but the term comes to mind. Bog oak was oak that had been in a bog for a very long time and had so changed to a distinctive grayed colour. Such oak was spoken of as being valuable, but it was not clear if this was due to it being different to work than normally aged oak, or if it was the colour, or just the curiosity value.

The two sitting rooms and three of the four bedrooms faced south so that they made the most of the sunshine, and the stunning views over the valley. In the past Paddockwray had been two separate dwellings. One assumes that one of the sitting rooms would have been the original kitchen, possibly the one on the left, next to the stable, as it had a large cupboard inset into the wall with an old dark oak door. Where the original oak in the structure of the house was exposed, and had not been treated in any way it, it looked very old too but in a different way; it was bleached and thinned – sinuous in following the grain – but still enormously strong. This was most readily seen in the thinned steps of the open stair going up from the back kitchen to the storage loft, or in the attic itself under the slates. Now and again one would find beetle damage in the old exposed wood, or in the furniture, or find the tiny brown beetles themselves, scurrying along.

What do I remember of living there before I was six? Mostly alarming and unusual experiences: being pecked by a hen, getting burnt by the open fire, having to occasionally sleep in odd places like in the attic with its low roof, or in the wooden cabin in the orchard when the bedrooms were given over to summer visitors. One Guy Fawkes Night was memorable. We watched Catherine wheels set into the fellside behind the house, through the kitchen. Guy Fawkes was part of an attempt to blow up Parliament in 1605, in the time of James I. Guy had stockpiled gunpowder under the House of Lords, but it was discovered the night before the planned detonation. It was never clear to us why Guy had to be celebrated, whether it was the plot, or the foiling of it. Guy Fawkes Day was close to Halloween and for us it took the place of Halloween. Just once we had a huge roaring bonfire in the field and roasted potatoes in the embers at the bottom.

Playing in the stream at the bottom of Christcliff meadow was a natural attraction for children. It was quite close to the house, through the yard gate flanked by two Cypress trees – possibly Mother had planted the trees. It could have been her signature, we had an identical pair at Woolpack later. The Christcliff meadow stream was of the size locally called a 'gutter', but this was in no way a drain for polluted water, as might be supposed from the word. A 'mac' (raincoat) with ingrained dirt could be washed clean by anchoring it under a stone in the running water; it was an an old way of cleaning things.

This gutter water was pristine; in fact a paradise of freshwater biology. As children we played with the minnows and water beetles, the caddis fly larvae, the water plants and a lot of other small things. There were

tiny black caterpillar-like creatures, very active on water plants, but frag-
ile – they died quickly in jam jars. We could always find plenty of small
life for entertainment. Much later I was told by a city boy, rather older
than me, that I had introduced him to the attractions of earthworms. He
had stayed as a visitor at Paddockwray, and said he had been astonished
at the lessons. It had been a novel and foreign experience for him, worthy
of reporting years later.

Our play all had relevance, as it was all part of learning about farming
and natural history. Indeed I do not recall a lot of toys, or dolls, or even
many books for that matter. But my mother found the time, at bedtime,
to read Beatrix Potter to us as very small children. The story of *Pigling
Bland* was frightful, since we knew all about the threat hanging over him.
We had an early acquaintance with the origin of meat. Beatrix Potter herself was an 'incomer', originally from London, and she had become part
of our lives since her stories were about our own kind of farm and animals, and set amid our own fells. And Beatrix lived on a farm not so far
away at Hawkshead.

As sensible young children we used to go on outings by ourselves.
Alastair and I walked from Paddockwray to Woolpack, just the two of
us – perhaps sent to post letters and to stay to have tea there. At most we
would be four and five, possibly younger, going over the fields for most
of the way. We posted the letters in the bright red box set into a stone wall
with GR engraved on it (for George Rex) at the lane into Woolpack farmyard. Then walked around the yard behind the inn, to the top of the steps
leading down to the back door and the large kitchen window below.
Someone was always at the kitchen sink there so that we would soon be
spotted and summoned for tea time.

My mother had a good story from the Paddockwray years. She sometimes felt isolated down the lane and Alastair cried a lot as a baby, without
any discernible cause. Naturally she was exhausted and distressed by having to listen to it. For a respite she had wheeled him in his pram, still crying, into the stone Stick House, which would have had a few hens perched
about – giving herself a harmless break she thought. One day there was a
knock on the kitchen door and an indignant-to-outraged farmer, without
introducing himself, accused her. 'You don't spoil your babby, missus!'
He turned out to be the neighbour, Ted Sim, from Ghyll Bank Farm above
us, half way up the fell. He had come down the path from Ghyll Bank.
He was the very man I later refused a ride in his cart, but we didn't know

him well in the early years. Ted was very much on the child's side in all things, and only had one of his own, Betty, we eventually got to know her at school.

We referred to paying guests as visitors. By the 1930s it was quite common for 'marginal' farms to supplement their modest income by taking visitors in the summertime. These were guests by the week, not so much bed and breakfast, since at the time there was little through traffic. This trade was made possible by the popularizing of the Lake District by the Victorian poets, such as Wordsworth, Southey and Coleridge. There was no advertising then, it was all by word of mouth. City people looked for fresh farm food, fresh air, walking holidays, and perhaps some contact, I am guessing, with a style of life that was well in the past for them. It was an opportunity for their children to spend time on the farm with animals. They came by train up the coast to a station, usually Drigg, seven miles or so away; and our visitors were then met by the Woolpack's car. Paddockwray got the spillover visitors from Woolpack which was always a busy place.

Paddockwray was on the sunny side, and this far up the valley was quite narrow. The farm had, and presumably still has, five valley fields on the north side of the road, three of which would qualify as meadow, one as rough pasture and one as arable. The enclosed rake was to accommodate the sheep when they were going to the fell or coming back and the folds were for sorting and attending to sheep. The very large 'intack' on the breast of the fell, was rough grazing and notably full of whins (gorse). On the east side of the main road there were two more grazing fields and an evergreen plantation on a slight rise. Paddockwray's acres were not anywhere near prime agricultural land, but had still managed to feed a lot of people over the centuries.

The upper valley had its maze of pathways, connecting farms or leading to important venues. These were the ancient 'rights of way'. Paddockwray had four such paths going out from it: up to Howes Farm, up to Ghyll Bank, up the Christcliff field and on to Woolpack, and the one straight over the Big Meadow, through Rake Ring to the main road. We used all of these paths, the one to Woolpack most regularly. These paths were hardly noticeable to someone not familiar with them and there were no sign posts. A stile was a clue that there was a path. Knowledge of, and use of the pathways, was passed down the generations.

While in Eskdale it was customary to be cooperative with neighbouring farms, and indeed the farms were to some degree interdependent. Unusually, we had a bad history with one neighbour, Vickers (or Vicars) of Christcliff, and most unfortunately Christcliff was sandwiched between Paddockwray and Woolpack. The story began in Father's childhood when the family had a much admired horse called Biddy. Her leg was broken by a wild and unruly horse from Christcliff and believed to have been put into the Paddockwray field with Biddy in order to cause a problem. Then there was Mother's cat, thought to have been poisoned by the same farmer. Vickers himself was certainly not friendly; he was reported to have expressed the hope of the Armstrong family, that 'their backs will git them aw.'

He was ever on the look out for people who were in his view trespassing; to do this well he was said to use binoculars from his house. As children we were terrified of being seen through the binoculars or, even worse, of meeting him. Nevertheless, we were ordered to use the path going through Christcliff when walking to Woolpack. It was thought important to maintain the right of way as well as save time with the short cut. Fortunately Vickers did not come after us as children, and we were clearly visible when climbing the stiles, and there were two of them en route. A bit of the path went down his lane and that was the most scary

Paddockwray haytime.

section, we imagined a crazed figure like Mr. McGregor chasing Peter Rabbit while brandishing a raised garden rake.

The designation of marginal land meant that nowhere was the soil very deep, and there are frequent rocky outcrops. In fact to get a field that can be ploughed was a tremendous achievement and a most valuable resource. These fields must have had man-years in clearing stones alone and in the cultivation of the soil. Clearing the stones accomplished two ends – rid the field of stones and create walls to confine the stock. This kind of dry-stone walling does not depend so much on dressing the stone as much as selecting the right size, and knowing how to fit them together so that they will stand. Cross stones were essential: they went through the width of the wall and gave stability. The cam stones at the top of the field walls jutted out a little bit in order to discourage sheep from trying to jump walls. Sometimes a jumping sheep can cause a 'rush' where the stones may come down as a cascade, or they might also come down as a result of a hard frost. What is astonishing in Eskdale is how far up the fells these walls can go, enclosing the intacks. It must have been years of work. The grass in the intacks was a little better nutritionally for stock than the open fell, because of the manure left there by the stock. Nowadays where these distant walls develop a wall-gap, they are often just left down, since in-takes are not so often used for cattle. Walling took real skill and was heavy work.

As mentioned previously, sheep were heafed to their own bit of pasture on the fell. The lambs accompanied their mothers to the fell, and so learned where they were supposed to go. In a sense all of the farmer's family were heafed as well, becoming familiar with their allotted fell graz-ing, and the way to it. It cemented their feeling of ownership. One reason why the recent foot and mouth disease and the government solution to it was so devastating was that, if a whole flock is destroyed, then future sheep brought in will not have the knowledge of where they are supposed to be. Untrained sheep will wander.

To aid in the identification of sheep and to distinguish them from the neighbours' flocks, they had to have an earmark, cut into the ear when a lamb. Thereafter a red oily 'smit' (ruddle) mark was applied to the wool, and re-applied as necessary. Smit was something local. There was said to be a place in the Wasdale Screes where pure smit could be found; it was red due to the iron content of the earth. Smit marks enable you to recog-nize your sheep at a distance, so you can send the sheep dog around to get them. The distinguishing factor being the location of the mark on the animal. Paddockwray's mark was a pop (a dot) behind the head and a pop above the tail. At gathering time, farmers exchange those from other flocks inadvertently gathered. Sheep stealing, I don't need to say, was spoken of as the most dreadful crime as trust was everything. Ear marks were final identification.

When we moved to Woolpack in 1937, I had to leave for school from Paddockwray in the morning and walk back to the Woolpack in the afternoon. It seemed a remarkably odd day. Thereafter we only visited Paddockwray, carried milk in cans to the Armstrong grandparents and Auntie Gladys, or we went there for a holiday with our cousins John and Shelagh Bulman and Michael Black. Then there were the obligatory piano lessons with Auntie Gladys, engulfed in the fumes of Lapsang Souchong tea, as the metronome ticked. On a nearby table she had a snarling black porcelain Chinese dog which had been used for some kind of incense we were told, and it had another ghastly smell. Meanwhile Granny Armstrong endlessly knitted socks in the sitting room, beautifully turning heels.

Granda Armstrong was a great tease, he really carried it a bit further than teasing, he called it 'putting one on one's mettle'. One was not to say that Auntie Gladys was putting on weight, or she would stop eating porridge, obviously a prelude to disaster. Helen's hair was 'beautiful'; the subtext was that it was the regular unsatisfactory fly-away Armstrong stuff, even if it was blonde. It was all a bit edgy, but we were polite, and it was generally entertaining. There was one regrettable incident in which I felt the teasing was over the top and I rebelled, an incident over sharing a bicycle, and I got into trouble over that at home. It was just not acceptable for children to argue. After Granny Armstrong died Auntie Gladys and Granda lived on at Paddockwray for many years. Much, much later Auntie Gladys retired to a cottage at Eskdale Green and Alastair married and moved in, and we were into a new generation.

3

Woolpack Inn

It was about Easter of 1937, when we moved up to Woolpack. It was a bigger farm, and long ago the living quarters in the longhouse had been made into an inn. My parents took it over from Granda and Granny Armstrong, while they, and Auntie Gladys, moved down to Paddockwray. Since Woolpack and Paddockwray were run as a unit, poor Mr. Vickers of Christcliff, sandwiched between them, saw a lot of Armstrongs and their helpers taking the short cut over his property.

Many years later Alastair said when he was on that path in the morning going from Paddockwray to Woolpack, he sometimes thought about city dwellers and their commute to work, about the concrete and the asphalt they had to negotiate – dead places like car parks. Then there was the unproductive use of the commuters' time. He felt he was privileged in his walk to work, he enjoyed everything: the sights, the sounds, the air, his feet being in the grass and being able to check on farming matters as he went.

Since we moved to Woolpack just as the visitor season was beginning there was not much time for Mother to adjust and to get organized. And Helen was only a few months old. She sometimes wryly told how she had been briefed by Father's sisters, who would well know what they were talking about, that she could expect hard work. Since she already had four small children, was a farm girl herself, had experience of Woolpack's overflow guests, she hardly needed a warning. But it was true, she was going to be a lot busier and Woolpack was more complicated; fortunately for all she had the most enormous capacity for work.

Just before the war there were plenty of staff around for the inn. The names of Ethel Braithwaite, Nan Harrison, and Jean Denwood come to mind, and they wore the maid's uniform of the era. The uniform was a plain frock with a white apron and a white headdress, something like a nurse's cap, then there was the dress version with an embroidered apron and an embroidered tiara with a black ribbon threaded through it. They were local girls from around Mother's childhood home in Waberthwaite.

There was also Mrs. Cowman, the farmer's wife from Wha House. This pervasive help was to disappear in the war, as a consequence of severe war-time restrictions on the numbers of staff.

There was plenty of work at Woolpack. Up to, and, in our time, it was not just a matter of ordering supplies according to demand, and taking deliveries. The farm fed the inn. In this place it was traditional, and had been since time immemorial, to make all that was humanly possible one-self. (I could say from scratch but that might not tell the whole story to a modern person.) Most of the food had to be grown on site; and everything was seasonal. So as well as the inn to look after there was also the farm itself with its requirements, and farm men to feed, sometimes in large groups, such as the big events of clipping and gathering sheep. Woolpack fed a lot of people, food that would be now described as organic, since before the Second World War it was innocent of added chemicals and pesticides. It would be difficult to find such a place now.

Woolpack was a country inn in an expanded farm house. Originally it is supposed that it would have started out as a farm like any other in the valley, but one that had at some time opened an ale-house. In medieval times the Woolpack had been a significant stopover for refreshment for drivers of stock and pack horses that passed by, since it was on the route from the port at Ravenglass, at the mouth of the Esk, to the eastern part of Cumbria. Woolpack was the last hostelry before the passes of Hardnott and Wrynose. This pack horse trade is said to have carried items such as wool, cloth, leather, charcoal, salt, and also imported goods. Cattle were driven along this route to the interior. There is a record of Woolpack being described as an inn in 1759 (under the name of Dawson Ground) but it was not officially designated an inn until 1817. It was still a farm and, like Paddockwray, intended to completely sustain life, with sheep as the principal stock. As with all the land in upper Eskdale, the soil layer was thin; it had been kept productive by good farming practice.

The Woolpack was close to the head of Eskdale, and easily accessible from the main road. In the last mile up the valley, between Woolpack and Hardknott Pass there was first the Youth Hostel (just being built in about 1939), Bleabeck Cottage that overlooked the Holm Bottom, which had a small bit of land, and then three old farms – Wha House, Taw House and Butterilket (Brotherelkeld) – also a cottage called Bird How. Butterilket, at the head of the valley was a notably large sheep farm. It had at one time been known as a vaccary (cow farm): in 1242 it was given to a religious order connected with Furness Abbey, and so had been worked by Brothers; and there is a record of it being enclosed as early as 1290. That puts a known early date on one of our farms.

Also at the head of the valley was tiny Bird How where the well known visitor H. H. Symonds holidayed. He had an organization called the Friends of the Lake District which was an early conservation society. Symonds also formed a Commoners Committee (the forerunner of the Eskdale Commoners Association of 1967). The farmers did recognize his influence, but as a child, one picked their slightly ambiguous attitude to outsiders – even to those trying to help. The threat was that the Forestry Commission had bought 7,000 acres in upper Eskdale and in the Duddon valley to the south, and this included five Duddon farms. The plan was to plant a third of the land with commercial conifers, and it was to be known as Harter Forest Park. Symonds fought against these plans, together with the Herdwick Sheep Breeders Association. Such a large forest would reduce the range of Herdwick sheep and affect farm productivity.

I was very young but I remember being at a public lecture given by Symonds, while I did not then fully comprehend what he was saying, I was struck by his slides, the first slides that I had seen. He showed how

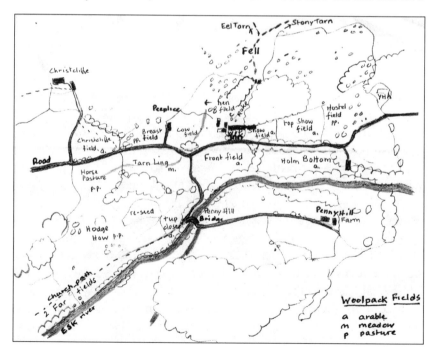

a commercial conifer plantation would look, and how our native mixed deciduous species looked on the present landscape which was a new idea to me. The Forestry Commission's plans for Harter Forest included planting Butterilket. Since we went to school with the Harrison children of Butterilket that had to be important. Fortunately it never happened in Eskdale, although there was some planting in the Duddon, as by about 1943 Symonds had won the battle (and by 1957 the property was bought by the National Trust and so was out of harm's way in that respect). Apart from championing farming and preserving Eskdale, Mr Symonds was also concerned that forestry plantations reduced the access of walkers to the fell. He advanced the idea that the fells were open to all, one could walk anywhere, either on a path or off one. Presumably then, access to the fells was of universal interest.

In 1937 Hardknott Pass was still a significant obstacle to climb, the road was narrow and zig-zagged sharply, and in places still had a one in three gradient, and there was a frightening ghyll (ravine) on the Harter side. In early days Granda Armstrong used to go over the pass on a pony, to visit his daughters in Langdale. (Later when he went over by car he still leaned forward – to help the horse.) Then, during the war, dispatch-riders trained on the pass and created ruts up to our waists. At the top of the pass the road made a steep descent to Cockley Beck Bridge, with its truly isolated farm, and then along a long rocky and deserted valley, called Wrynose Bottom. The Bottom felt wild and other worldly, with just a few sheep and old stone walled intakes. Its rocky aspect and cooler colour contrasted with the green of the cultivated valleys. After this wild stretch there was the rise to Wrynose Pass, after which the road went down steeply again into the easterly part of the Lake District, in what was then Westmorland. A second sign, at the top of Wrynose, said it all about the gradient 'You have been warned'. Going from Eskdale to Langdale one passed from granite country to slate country, and this was immediately reflected in the buildings and walls.

The name of Woolpack was said to derive from the fact that sheep wool from three valleys had at one time been packed there; although it might also relate to the old pack horse trade. If wool from three valleys was packed at Woolpack then one supposes that it would have to be that from upper Eskdale, Wasdale Head and Miterdale, since these valleys shared the fell grazing area of the Eskdale Common where their heafs were contiguous, and sometimes overlapping. The farmers in these valleys were still obeying the ancient decisions, and directives, relating to usage of the Common, the numbers of animals for instance. It could make sense to co-operate over packing the wool and perhaps its transport out as well.

The walk to Woolpack, from both Wasdale Head and Miterdale was over Burnmoor, then south by Eel Tarn, and finally the drop down into Eskdale. There was an old right of way, a public path, from Eel Tarn down to the Woolpack; and in our day this was marked by white crosses on marker stones. If wool from Miterdale and Wasdale Head was packed at Woolpack most likely the fleeces would have been carried over the fell by ponies, and there are Fell ponies indigenous to Cumbria, small and hardy, that were bred for just such journeys. That path from Eel Tarn to Woolpack was also used to bring peat down from the bog around Eel Tarn, and there was a peat house half way down that was once used to store and dry the peat. The same path was designated for taking cattle or horses to graze on Burnmoor.

It is interesting to know something of the past history of the farm and its tenants. The actual date of the oldest part of present day Woolpack is not known. And earlier Woolpack was known either as Dawson Ground, or as Dawson Place (after 1727 the name Dawson Ground was commonly used). Alan Swindale references names and dates at Dawson Ground as follows:

1587 – there is a reference to Nicholas Wilson and Roger Tyson
1635 – Edward Tyson
1661 – William Tyson
1687 – there is a will of Wilson Tyson
1713 – Thomas Hartley married Maria Tyson
1721 – Thomas Hartley dies
1727 – John Vickers has several children baptized up to 1738
1763 – William Dickinson left the property to his daughter Sarah

Tysons, Hartleys and Vickers again … the same family names keep re-curring in the available records. And these families were still around in our day, the first three certainly still in upper Eskdale. There are numerous references to Vickers (or Vicars) on farms in the valley. That the same names persist over the centuries is yet more evidence of the relative iso-lation and of the stability of the population. Indeed Auntie Gladys spoke darkly of the hazards of inbreeding.

In our day Woolpack was one property, but it had been two in the past.

Apart from Dawson Ground (or Place) there was also Peel Place which, to us, was a ruin at the bottom of Woolpack's Cow Field. We pronounced it Peeplice. My niece, Jane Holmes, has uncovered an older family connection with this ruin. In 1692 John Vicars wrote a will and died at Peel Place, and we are descended (twelve generations on) from his daughter Alice, and eventually through Granny Leece. That knowledge is one of the most mind boggling; as children we certainly had no idea of any such thing, as we scrambled and played over what was left of Peel Place, its broken down walls covered with pungent Herb Robert.

The Percy survey of 1587 lists two owners of Peel Place. They were Nicholas Hartley and Nicholas Nicholson, and they appeared to share fields and a barn, even though to us the ruin itself seemed to be smaller than most valley farms. It did still have its own cart track from the main road up to it, and still had the iconic elderflower tree at a front door for elderflower wine and for elderberries. I think Alastair was to try making elderberry wine but making damson wine or sloe gin was more common.

In the past, it was obvious from the records, that the farms had employed more people than in our day, and the families themselves were much bigger. Interestingly farm families were still bigger than urban families in our time. It turns out that there were two families at Peel Place and two at Dawson Ground, so Armstrongs now farmed the land of four former families, a big reduction in man power.

The Percy survey of 1587 gives the names of the fields, and some are recognizable today. The two farmers at Peel Place shared Turn Inge, that must be our Tarn Ling, and they shared Hodge How, the large hill of that name in the middle of the valley. Then there is a Long Field listed, and I do not know to what that refers. Since Peel Place was cut into our Cow Field, that, or Christcliff field could have been the Long Field, or it could even have been somewhere near Hodge How and the Horse Pasture. Peel Place farmers had Croft Close and Garths; these may have been Christcliff field or part of our Bull Coppy. The Bank is also mentioned as belonging to Hartley. It was still the Bank to us, the bit behind the quarry bordering one of the plantings. The 'moulture' and the 'walker' are set out as for Paddockwray. The document Eskdale 24 also gives Peel Place its specific grazing rights on the fell, along with the rules for their use.

All of the land listed at Peel Place must at some point have been taken over by Dawson Ground (or earlier Dawson Place) – the previous names for Woolpack. The Percy survey of 1587 is fascinating over the names of the fields listed for Dawson Place. Again there were two owners, Nicholas Wilson and Roger Tyson, and they shared a Long Field and they had Croft Closes. Again I do not know which was the Long Field, maybe the Cow field or the Show field and beyond up the valley. The Closes, by their name, must have been close to the buildings. Wilson had the Holme, that must have been either the Front field or Holme Bottom beyond it, or possibly both combined since Holme Bottom is down by the river, at a lower level than Front field. They shared Tippie Close, that would be our Tip Close skirting Hodge How, and they shared Brerie Land. The latter is a name that I do not recognize at all, but possibly it was some of the pasture or the intake close to the present day hostel. Brerie Land has the sound of rough ground. The two farmers shared 'certain wood ground in two places', and we did have two plantings of conifers behind Woolpack, so maybe that was it, but there was a third older treed section, but deciduous, up near the hostel. The 'moulture' and 'walker' are listed for Dawson Place. It is fascinating to us that we can recognize some field names, over such a long time period, passed down mainly by word of mouth. It made us part of a long line of residents.

The Eskdale 24 Book also gives Dawson Place grazing rights, about Eel Tarn to Stoney Tarn and beyond on the fell, and the Manor rules for the farm. Again for interest I include references to Peel Place and Dawson Place from the Eskdale Book of 1587, regarding the rules for taking sheep and cattle to the fell. Concerning the sheep drifts to the heafs, that is the paths taking sheep to the fell and the pasture, the rules stated that the tenants of Peel Place, Nicholas Hartley and Nicholas Nicholson, should go:

> ...from their own Houses up at Brownhows toppe, and up the side of Kirkhow, and up through the Whawbottom, and up the Height of Whinny Cragge and over the Cragg at Eller, and forth at the Readmire end, and to the lower With how, and up over the overmer With how, and to the cloven gray Stone.

As for sheep of Dawson Place the tenants, Nicholas Wilson and Roger Tyson, should go:

> ...to the fell up through the Rough Cragg, and up at Horpinhow and up at Whinney Style and up at the Green Cragg at the Eller and to the Hill at Read Mire and on the Eastside, and to the Longrigge above thee Thornehow, and to the White borrand, under Seivie Sta ... and on so towards the Gray Stone.

Both holdings seem to end at the same place but I recognize only a few of the names. One sees the familiarity and importance of all the named markers. It was an owned geography.

Concerning the cattle drifts going to the assigned cow pasture on the fell, there are similar fascinating rules, for Peel Place cattle should be driven:

> ...forth the Broadrake and up over the Fowle Brigges, and to the high Stone and to turn them upon the Southside of the said Stone and up to the Broad Mosse on their own Ground and let them go.

For Dawson Place they should go:

> ...up at Clattergap, and forth at the Evilrakehow and up under the Oak at Brownhow, and up at the Foot of Minigatehow and over the Skale in the Bleabeck Dubbs and so let them go.

Again I recognize only a few names; our farm men would have recognized many more.

While we were still following these medieval rules for Paddockwray, Peel Place and Dawson Place, the Manor Court for the enforcement of rules had itself disappeared. The Whitehaven Records office has a map of these place names, drawn about 1900, giving guesses of their location in the manors of Eskdale and Miterdale, from the Eskdale 24 Book of

Woolpack in the 1940s.

1587. The actual sub-sections of the Eskdale Common have been mapped out for the farms permitted to use it.

The Woolpack (Dawson Ground) was in a similar building style as Paddockwray and so presumably of the same general date. The main building was the basic longhouse. The living quarters at the east end of it were part of the modern inn, and the animal quarters were on the west end. The granite walls were whitewashed on the animal end in the traditional fashion. (Wordsworth hated whitewash, he thought it too harsh on the landscape.) In our time the inn part had a light gray trim and was decorated by its large inn sign portraying a Herdwick ram. I once re-painted over the original design on the sign. Over the centuries some improvements and changes had been made to the inn, in acknowledgment of its public nature and needs, but considering the time span it did not seem to have been much altered.

In our time the animal quarters did not look as if they had changed at all since construction, maybe some cement in places over parts of the original cobbled floor. In the longhouse there was the original byre and the stable, two animal hulls and a storage area and over all of that a long capacious hayloft and general storage barn, the top barn. There were other outbuildings, a freestanding old granite barn with its attached pig stye, and the new byre with its open Dutch barn for yet more hay, and for bracken. I saw an occasional bat around there. The stackyard was the place for the round corn stack; sheaves in the stack pointed in. I remember a stack being threshed using a Victorian looking and clattering machine; it came around the farms. As the threshing proceeded the level of sheaves got lower until finally at the bottom the rodents had to run out and the expectant dogs sprang into action. The quarry was cut into the Bank behind the stackyard. The main yard had the usual dipping tub and attached drying pen, and that opened up into the Rake, and so to the path up to the fell.

There was a later addition to the inn and that was the annexe, built for extra rooms. The annexe was possibly dated as late as Victorian, its walls were not as wide as in medieval building. Behind the annexe there were older, whitewashed, stone rooms for storage: a section for wood and coal, one for an electricity generator with its many impressive glass batteries, and a section for the beer and wine cellar.

The electricity from the generator was used for lights only. In the early days I do not recall any other piece of electrical equipment in the inn or on the farm. The vacuum cleaner appeared in war-time but it was much, much later for the dishwasher and food-mixer. The farm had some machinery that would not have been out of place in Victorian or Edwardian times, none of it, I think, could be driven by electricity. We had a car garage that in previous times was used for horse drawn carriages, and we did in fact still have an old open horse carriage. It was elegant and doubtless of museum quality, but I do not know what happened to it. The tractor was to appear later.

Woolpack was set back a short distance from the road, and fronted by a large raked and pebbled parking area. That was one of our jobs – raking it to keep the weeds down. The front used to have a circular seat around an enormous sycamore tree, intended for patrons to enjoy their drinks outside. We finally cut that tree down, and certainly more light was let into the inn. Out front were more sycamores, horse chestnuts and limes, rhododendrons and blue hydrangeas (they had to be blue because of the acidity), and crowds of snowdrops and daffodils in season. An occasional hedgehog wandered about. There were two dominant evergreen plantings behind the inn and up the fellside, grown as a timber crop. While we were there they were felled once and re-grown. There were two orchards. The one in front of the longhouse that was too old to produce fruit but the pigs rooted around in it, and it had a fenced rhubarb bed. The orchard on the Bank was productive with apples, plums, damsons, graced by one pear tree and one cherry tree. The latter two came down in our time and were missed. Over the road there was the very important large productive vegetable and soft fruit garden, with a greenhouse for tomatoes, and cold frames for salad items.

Behind the longhouse were gates to the aforementioned walled Rake going steeply up to the fell, leading to the grazing rights and to the path to Eel Tarn, with its white cross markers. The Rake had a stone building which was the settling tank for the water supply that came straight off the fell, the intake pipe of which could readily be seen in a small stream not far up the fell. The settling tank was the only kind of treatment for the water. A few feet away from the intake pipe was a large colony of frogs, and very occasionally one saw a toad in the Rake. The Rake had a sandstone grindstone for scythes, sickles, knives, saws – anything that might need sharpening. This was done by wetting and re-wetting the sandstone wheelstone and holding the item down, while an assistant turned the handle. Seaves grew there in abundance, and that might not have been wholly accidental, since at one time they were a valuable crop for thatch and floors and the inside pith was once used as wick for rush lights. Rush lights were a kind of candle, the dried piths of the seaves were stuck into oil or fat which would then wick up and burn.

Below the tank the household water went underground, while another stream came under the wall into the yard through a sandstone trough, providing clean running water for any passing animal, notably the dogs and ducks. It was handy also for small children to play about, a place of endless entertainment in fact, conveniently overlooked by a kitchen window at the sink. Since the kitchen and Boot House were partly recessed into the fell, there was a short flight of granite steps down to them. I am told that a photograph of those iconic steps once appeared in the National Geographic magazine.

Woolpack Inn and its fields were on the north and sunny side of the valley. On the north of the main road there were six valley fields and two large walled bits of fell breast the 'intacks' with their rough grazing. On the east side of the inn was the Show Field, so called because it was the site of the annual Cumberland and Westmorland Herdwick Show, which was an important event for the breed; in fact Geoff Brown in his book on Herdwicks says it was the premier show. The show was primarily to show prize Herdwick tups (rams) for sale, or for rent, and the Show Field was divided up into wooden gate pens for the occasion. The first of these shows was held there in 1864 and there were many shows in our time, but eventually it was moved away. I think that by then it was seen as not consistent with the visitor trade, and we ourselves found it an alarming rowdy event in the evening. I remember as children being grouped at the top of the stairs unable to sleep, looking down incredulously, as farmers drank beer below, and generally whooped it up. Granny Leece stayed with us and clucked her disapproval. It must have been a relief for the family when the show went to other venues in the valley.

All of the fields were different, had their very own character unchanged to this day. Going home one would want to see as many fields as possible, and it would all come back, their specific feel and aspect, their particular trees, rocks, hog-holes, styles, gates, water, any special plants, and memories of our time there. The fields emanate a most definite sense of place: in them you feel a sense of having come back home, more so than in the house really, it flows over one – difficult to put into words. Some fields felt intensely personal, private even, to the observer, some by contrast felt

Woolpack and Harter Fell.

rather bland and empty – and open to all.

Holm Bottom was one of those very personal private-feel fields, it was at a lower level, down a wooded bank with the river along its south side, hardly noticeable from the main road. Its bank had a long curve on the north and road side, presumably the river had, at one time, been wider and carved it out. The Norse word 'holm' means either islet in a river or flat ground by a river subject to flooding. It looks as if our Holm Bottom was named for the second meaning. The field was unusually flat and long, and it was productive. It once had a sizable rabbit colony at the end with the deep pool in the Esk called the Black Rock. The rock jutted out into the pool, black because of its lichen; to us it was a third rate swimming place, we had at least four other places we preferred.

From Penny Hill Corner on the road, Penny Hill Lonnin (a lonnin, or lonning, was wide enough for a horse and cart and gravelled) ran between the Front field and Tarn Ling to Doctor's Bridge. And over the bridge were lonnins to two farms; all part of the medieval maze of paths and lonnins. From the bridge, going down the valley, there was an ancient bridle path, running along the north side of the Esk River, skirting Hodge How. There was another public path on the south side of the river. Both paths led to St. Catherine's Church.

The path to church on our side was a mile of very pleasant beck side walking, and for half the way it was through Woolpack land. It had the feel of a half-wild and forgotten corner and was pretty rough grazing. There were alders, hawthorns, hazel, rowan and holly by the river, and the iconic oaks. The native trees were predominantly deciduous; coniferous trees were normally in plantings. When you look down the valley sides the deciduous trees make characteristically rounded shapes, and in summer you might be lucky enough to hear the magic of a cuckoo calling, and echoing around. Nearer the church there were a lot of whins about, and the pest of the bracken – nothing seemed to eat the encroaching bracken. Just a little way before the church was Arment Hill, and a short way up it was the Holy Spring, St. Catherine's Well. Then it was Gillfuss (Gill Force) Dub, a deep cold pool that was one of our more distant and dramatic swimming spots. The path went on to the church, right by the river, and surrounded by its churchyard.

The farms on the far side of Doctor's bridge were Penny Hill and Low Birker, ('pen' is Norse for hill, 'birker' is Old English for birch). Penny Hill was part of the estate of Beatrix Potter, who had bequeathed it to the National Trust. Low Birker was tucked under Harter Fell range to the south, it was notable for having the sun touch the chimneys at only one time of year. The water at the bridge was quite deep and it was near and our most frequent swimming spot; and it was possible to dive there. We had another spot a few yards downstream by Tip Close, it was more private and skinny-dipping was a possibility. The water there was fast moving but not so deep or dramatic, and a painful walk over the stones, but you could open your eyes under water and see the fish dart about. Swimming in a beck during a rain shower was a surprising treat.

Doctor's Bridge was so called because the original packhorse bridge had been widened for a doctor, who once lived at Penny Hill, in order to take his horse and trap. You could see the join underneath. This was a favourite place of ours, as it had been to a previous generation of the family and was convenient for a quick swim on a hot day. In fact we learned to swim there. Father just threw me in and gave the order, 'Swim over here'. I did, I just had to, the water was deep. He threw in dogs in a similar fashion and they came back for more, so I suppose he expected it to work for children as well; for us it was a partial success. The rush of the water was hypnotic, the roar amplified under the bridge, it had a timeless quality; every stone on the bottom of the river was clear to see. It was alive with small fish. Bigger fish, of eating size, rarely made it up this far since they were caught lower down.

Doctor's Bridge was a very good place to play about, sit, think, read, or swim, to spend a little of one's rare spare time. We all used it for a bit of time out. It was here, much later on, that Alastair came down to think after he had been told that he had six weeks to live, and that an ambulance was on the way to collect him. He had just helped serve a special anniversary meal in the inn for some relatives. Woolpack was always busy no matter what.

While we were at Woolpack the farm supported about 400 plus ewes, in addition to that would be their lambs, the heaf must then have allowed for about 600. In the early days we also had about 40 cattle, two or three pigs, two horses, and the two hen houses, in their specified fields. We always had about half a dozen collie dogs. Also some half wild cats who had learned not to bring their kittens home until they were grown.

Before the war the staffing situation on the farm was generous. In our time the Woolpack Inn had eight double guest rooms and two single guest rooms, six other bedrooms and the attic being taken up by family or staff. For a while we slept in the attic due to space concerns; the hay was through the other side and now and again a caterpillar might get through to remind one. To begin with, in 1938, we managed with only two full bathrooms and two separate indoor toilets; it would be inconceivable today to have so few, but we made it work. Practically all the bedrooms had wash-basins, but early on there were no space heaters. Three of the bedrooms had fireplaces. None of the rooms had locks. Only the front door was locked at night and that as a signal we were now officially closed to callers; the many back and side doors had no locks, only snecks. I expect that the general lack of locks was customary in Eskdale.

When you entered the front door of the inn there was a coloured tiled hallway floor leading to the kitchen and the stairway. On the left was the dining room, on the right the smoke room. That was an old name, it was just a sitting room; in our day people smoked anywhere they felt like it. Most older men smoked pipes and blew smoke rings to entertain us. Leading off to the left was a passage past the original bar, to another sitting room and the dairy. Leading off the right was a passage to the snug, and a path to the annexe. In the right passage there was an interesting very old dark oak door let into the wall. It had a date on it, was it 1607? I believe that the snug had originally been a kitchen, and it was quite small. In the summer it was a place for drop-ins to the bar, in the winter it was our sitting room with a fire going for warmth.

Our kitchen was large and at the back of the house recessed into the fell side with doors and windows at either end. The kitchen was an add-on to the original longhouse, and had bedrooms above it. It boasted a large anthracite burning Esse, a range similar to the better known Aga, that did sterling work. The Esse had three ovens of varying temperature and a cooking top with a lid, with a second section that heated the water for the inn. We added a smaller, but similar, range later. When Mother retired and was faced with an electric stove she was not impressed, said the food tasted of electricity. The kitchen's three large wooden tables coped with all activities, and there was one sink and a lot of cupboard space for dishes and supplies. The kitchen floor was of large blue gray slate flagstones.

Flagstones also covered the walkway to the dairy and boot house, which also had flagstone sconces which were both working and cool storage surfaces. The walkway to the right was covered with flagstones and led to the wash-house similarly done out in flagstone, and with its own boiler and fireplace. The wash-house also had a furnace to heat the annexe water. The annexe downstairs had two large rooms initially, one very big sitting room and one a store and workroom, and the bathrooms. Upstairs there were five bedrooms for guests or family. During our time, considerable changes were made around this area, mostly to increase the number of bathrooms, and to create extra bar trade space.

It was certainly a formidable challenge for a mother of four young

Old barn and Birker.

children, and later five. Father had been there since he was a boy, so he was familiar with the constant activity and to sharing his home with a constant stream of visitors. We believed he was more interested in the farming side than the catering. Woolpack was a property that demanded constant forethought and attention year round, it needed and formed a lot of different skills. Not that the planning was visible: it was all done in the head.

I recall a visitor advancing the thought that the Woolpack was possibly the last inn in England to be fed off its own farm, a left over from previous era. It was a most important observation and we really should have paid attention to it. We were so busy and absorbed that the thought hardly registered; it was visitor talk to us.

4

The early years at Woolpack and Dyke

We had only been at Woolpack for about eighteen months when World War Two was declared. I had brought my charges, the younger children, into the kitchen to find Irene Dawson, our help, weeping hysterically in a chair by the stove, and that most certainly got our attention. The explanation given was the announcement of the war; it meant nothing at all to us. If it hadn't been for Irene's distress, I am not sure that it would have been mentioned at all, even though Uncle Benny had been a soldier in the First World War. There was an ages old tenor to our life, and very likely we had a false sense of our own security: the rest of the world seemed far away. It may also be relevant that my mother had the idea that uncivilized or disgusting things were just that – uncivilized and disgusting, and so not fitting as conversation, or even to be in the press. Later on, *Picture Post's* portrayal of war atrocities was to particularly upset her.

Our early years at Woolpack seemed to be entirely occupied by activities on the farm and in the inn: farming and feeding people were our business. National affairs were somewhere else, and pretty much the modern world, even political parties. For us there was little difference between the pre-war and war-time situations; our lives were consumed with our work. We were so self-sufficient that in important respects we would hardly notice the war, our diet for instance was pretty well unchanged.

Since I was the eldest child, my responsibility was to babysit the other children, although it was not spoken of in that way. I was just held accountable for their safety and for marshalling them around. It was my job to take Alastair, Hughie and Helen, and later Barbara, outside during the day, from spring through the autumn, and to bring them into the kitchen for meals only. Should we appear between meals we were invariably asked, 'What are you doing in here? It's a perfectly nice day outside.' They were all busy. The most important bit of time-keeping was to be in promptly at six for supper, since we had to have eaten, be bathed, all four of us in the bath together, and in bed by seven, since that was the visitors' dinner time, the big and final push of the day. Because we were living in a hotel situation, in close proximity to the guests, sharing bathrooms, there was to be no unnecessary noise. So successful were we at this that occasionally Mother would say that a visitor had expressed surprise to hear that she had any children at all! But then, in those days, our guests did not expect impersonal service.

To begin with we walked to school, but later on we got two bicycles and Alastair and I carried Hughie and Helen on the handle bars, along with the lunches, fortunately we had no homework books. I do remember getting home at tea time, sometimes exhausted because there were hills to push the bikes up, notably Cross How and Peeplice, and it often seemed hot. The treat of Shrove Tuesday pancakes I particularly recall, thin Swedish pancakes with lemon juice and sugar, and rolled; it was an indulgence. After tea there were the hotel dishes to wash, particularly after staff was restricted in the war. Then a bit of time outdoors with farming chores.

Babysitting children on the farm was not so bad; there were plenty of diversions around the farm and in the fields. If it rained we found shelter in a building or under trees. We got remarkably few instructions about what we should be doing, to be honest I cannot remember any, and no

Granny Leece and the author at End of a laundry day in Woolpack kitchen.

one formally checked on us. I think that early on we were not supposed to go down to the river, but we inevitably did, water being an irresistible draw. How then did we spend our time? Well, whatever took our fancy at the moment or what the major activity on the farm was for that day. There were plenty of places to explore, and plenty of animals to view. We trailed about after the farm men doing jobs, like feeding this and that: cows, calves, pigs, dogs, hens, an occasional pet lamb. Then there was milking, by hand, and it was a time consuming job, so the more milkers the better; but we liked milking and being in the byre with the cows. The cats too hung around at milking time, in hope, as just occasionally a farm man might kindly aim a stream of milk at an expectant mouth.

Children were often used to 'turn' animals: you had to stand in a gateway or place where the animals were not wanted, and redirect them, just by your presence. Even a small child could turn stock: you held out your arms to make yourself seem bigger and so more of an obstacle, and amazingly the advancing herd of cattle, or flock of sheep, would turn aside and take an unobstructed route. City children had misgivings about stock turning. We were ordered around turning rather as a collie might expect to be; but in this case the collie would be moving around the sides and back of the group of animals concerned.

We played with young animals of all kinds, and pet lambs were lovely, who could forget those little bodies and the quivering tails. But we got most action out of young dogs: they were always ready for some fun. In one game the dogs chased the girls up the Front Field until we fell down laughing, out-run and exhausted. Then the dogs 'worried ' our heads until they managed to get the hair ribbons out of our hair. With the ribbon dangling from the mouth, they waited breathlessly for some retaliation, recklessly and willingly squandering get-away time. Eventually, we scrambled to our feet and took off in hot pursuit, the aim being to get the ribbons back, and so on ad infinitum.

Fortunately for me, nothing too serious happened on my babysitting watch. The worst episode was when we were all sitting on top of the last hay cart coming in from the hay fields, the one with the 'rakings' – the left over hand raked bits. It was an unstable load. Without any warning the top layer suddenly gave way and slid off, carrying all of us and the farm man onto the stubble. We landed in a heap, and somehow I was under the farm man's heavy studded boots. It goes without saying that there was no unnecessary crying, but I had to get my charges to swear that they would say nothing of this incident in the kitchen. My judgment could have been seriously questioned. The farm man would not be in a hurry to report the incident either, and for exactly the same reason. I just tried to avoid the bath tub until the boot bruises started to fade.

I know that animals have an emotional life. I am constantly amazed by urban thinkers and scientists finally finding proof of this. Any five-year-old on the farm could tell you that it was so – you only have to look into animal eyes (mammalian eyes, that is) to understand that there is an emotional connection. A few things that we observed as children might influence a city skeptic. When the cows were first let out into the field in the spring, after a winter of confinement in the byre, they skipped around, in spite of their lumbering size. Lambs gathered together as a group in the summer evenings, as the sun was setting and they all jumped up and down together like jumping jacks. It was pretty obvious they were having a good time. A pregnant, or a recently delivered animal, looks and acts motherly, just like a human mother. Then there was the awful upheaval of getting lambs and ewes back together again, into the right pairs, after the ewes had been dipped. The desperate blaring and the answering bleats came through the bedroom windows for much of the night, until they were all reunited. I hear them still.

Then there was the cunning of the neighbour's Shetland pony, Bonnie, that we pastured and got to ride now and then. Bonnie was apparently compliant while the saddle was being put on, the girth tightened, and the rider mounted, but she had a secret plan. She had blown out her belly, and was holding her breath. Suspecting nothing the rider started to move, but then Bonnie suddenly took off, unbidden, like a rocket up the field. At the same time she let out her breath, so that the saddle was suddenly loose and slipped around the belly, and the rider was thrown onto the grass. Bonnie immediately got back to serious grazing, one irritation the less, no doubt, completely ignoring the saddle draped around her middle. An alternative trick of hers was to walk slowly and deliberately sideways right up against a stone wall, and so attempt to scrape off the rider in a painful fashion.

Certainly animals have an emotional life. We had one collie who had at some time been frightened by a gun. Should it see a man with a gun on the farm, she flew down the steps at the kitchen door, and straight into the kitchen and hid under a table. She was ready to stay there for hours and it was difficult to coax her out. Dogs never, ever, normally came down

Swaledale tups at Woolpack.

to the bottom of the steps, never mind into the kitchen. Sometimes they came half way down and stood in a way as to block a small child falling down – or so it seemed to us. Presumably, the frightened dog felt safer among women; in fact our dogs were always delighted to spend time with women and children. Men ordered them about; with women and children it was all about affection and play. Then there is the desperate business of having to shoot an old suffering dog – they know. Alastair told me.

We had an incident of the cow in the annexe, after being spooked by a truck. She bolted and also, like the dog, aimed for the house. She thundered into the annexe and up the narrow flight of stairs into number nine bedroom – fortunately the guest was out. Since the cow is a large animal she inevitably got wedged between the double bed and a chest of drawers with a mirror. Meanwhile the men panted into the room behind her. She looked at herself in the three way mirror and it was one that gave multiple images. She may have felt momentarily better and back with the herd so she made a cow plop on the rug. The men managed to get her turned around and into the hallway. Unwittingly, the guest in number ten stuck his head out of his door to see what the commotion was about. He was yelled at to shut the door. Fortunately the cow chose the stairs and they got her down head first and safely out of the building. This cow was panicking and I know how that feels. The incident also illustrates our dual nature as hotel and farm.

About this time Granny and Granda Leece came to live with us, and took over the annexe ground floor. This was a very good thing for us as children since we now had a readily available inside place to go to in the summer, particularly in the evening when all the rooms in the inn might be taken over by the visitors, or the bar trade. Granny and Granda were totally tolerant, completely accepting of our presence: the comings and goings, the constant piano practice, the only refrain was 'Shut the door'. As a couple, they deplored complaints and had a definite stoicism. Granny was sometimes heard to mutter 'Sic a fuss!' in response to some unnecessary outburst from one of us, or even from a guest. On the other hand she was onto real problems; she was about the only one who thought I carried a lot of responsibility. Still Uncle Tony once said to me that they might not have been so comfortable in their new life in the annexe.

Before Granny and Granda came to live with us, there were the holidays at Dyke Croft, on their farm, near Waberthwaite village. Well, rather less than a village, since the church was some distance away from it right at the estuary of the Esk, and facing Muncaster Castle, and with its stepping stones for church goers in the river.

Dyke Farm was probably less than ten miles away and on the flat coastal plain, where the Esk poured into the sea. The fells were in the background. The farms here were on better land than existed in the upper valleys. It was where Mother had grown up; the family had moved from Skellerah farm, on Corney Fell, to Dyke when she was seven. She admitted that when she first went to live in Eskdale she felt hemmed in, oppressed even, by the fells rising steeply all around. The coastal plain was closer to civilization. The main road was the Coast Road and went around the Cumbrian shoreline up to Carlisle and the Scottish Border. So there was through traffic. There was even a sort of bus service, a breezy, summery one with no roof comes to mind, we must have tried it.

The locals were possibly more mixed ethnically and socially than in the upper valleys. The story goes that Celts and Anglo-Saxons got the better coastal land before the Norse arrived from Ireland; therefore the latter had to take the less fertile land at the heads of the valleys. One might find it hard to picture the Norse being so obliging, after their fearful reputation on the east coast of Northern England. People were a bit more mobile on the coast: moved around more readily. Granda Leece's three sisters had done a spectacular thing, in that they had emigrated, all together, to British Columbia. The reason given was that one of the husbands was asthmatic, and the climate in British Columbia would be beneficial. Granda Leece was tight lipped about it all; he regarded it as an unforgivable desertion. And it was certainly final, since it was very expensive and time consuming in those days to go home for a visit, and I don't believe that they ever did.

Mother had two younger brothers, Tyson and John, who both died tragically in their twenties within two years of Mother's marriage. Tyson drowned himself in the river, and John died of an inoperable brain tumour. These deaths were preceded by another tragedy: Dorothy, the girl next door from the main house at Dyke, had accidentally drowned in the river while out swimming with a girl friend. Dorothy and the three Leece children had been young together and quite suddenly, over a short time period, there was only Mother left, and she had married and left home. Understandably these happenings were never, ever, talked about; I was only alerted to the existence of the uncles by a photograph of the three children on Granny's dressing table. It was logical then for the grandparents to finally move to Woolpack.

We were oblivious to this tragedy, and on holidays at Dyke we had a wonderful time. It was a small farm but had a large three storey house and a large kitchen garden. Granda had cows and hens that I remember, and some sheep. We walked to the hen field to feed the hens, and on the way back swung the cans of collected eggs in circles over our heads and shoulders without spilling any. Granny's home help showed us how; we certainly would never have tried such a risky thing at Woolpack. We watched the cows being milked while the farm man doing the milking taught us a bawdy song that went 'Sam, Sam, the dirty old man, washed his face in the frying pan, combed his hair with a donkey's tail and scratched his belly with his big toe nail.' I doubt that would have gone over well at Woolpack. Granda had one horse, and we walked with it at hay time. The horse seemed to ignore the fact that it was hitched to the cart being loaded with hay, and grazed its way over the stubble in a relaxed fashion. The whole farm seemed relaxed to us, and Granda did not have much help.

The Dyke farmhouse was not anything like as old as other farms close by or those in upper Eskdale. It is quite possible that Granny and Granda

Granda Leece ploughing at Dyke.

were the first occupants. Although the house was not old I do not recall any electricity and there was no indoor bathroom. There was running water in the kitchen, but I am not sure how it was heated; we seemed to rely a lot on kettles of boiling water. The outside earth toilet was a wonderful novelty to us – in fact, we were completely delighted. You had to walk through the long garden to get to it. When we had a bath Granny took hot water up two flights of stairs to the attic where she had a large round papier-mache type bath with low sides, rather like a modern day child's wading pool. Then, of course, it had to be emptied. Fortunately she had the home help, Annie Denwood, our instructor on centrifugal force and eggs. In those early days, certainly before the war, it seemed that help was readily available, which was just as well given that there were few home conveniences.

Once there was a birdwatcher staying at Dyke, Edgar Haines, so we got to go out with him at night into the woods to observe owls. He photographed baby owls as they sat motionless on branches looking just like gray skeins of wool. We had to be very quiet since the mother might return at any time: if alarmed she could attack. He warned us that she could come down and beat us with her wings. Fortunately the adult owls appeared to be out hunting while we silently crept about under the trees. In the course of our growing up we did receive cautions on how to treat animals, wild and domestic: we learned to give space, be respectful, not to intimidate, not to show fear, learned what to avoid, all of it important when you have a great deal of unsupervised time in the country.

Other excitements at Dyke were the visits of the grocer's and the butcher's vans delivering Granny's orders. The grocer was from the Woodall business in the village, he brought special bags of sweets as gifts for the children, done up in a paper cone. I was afraid of the butcher and most particularly of his knives; as by now I was part vegetarian, though I did not know there was a name for my distress then. I refused outright to eat beef or mutton. In my mind I could see the animal looking at me, and sensibly no-one in the family forced me. Illogically I felt that bacon and gravy were alright, sufficiently altered perhaps. I suppose they picked out the pieces of meat in stews, if not, I would do it myself. I do not recall being frightened by any particular incident, although that was certainly a possibility. All the farm men were careful not to alarm us; but I had most certainly connected the dots. I knew where meat came from, and I was horrified. Really, there was no shortage of protein on the farm: milk and eggs were free at the point of consumption. We had yet to learn that the situation in the industrial towns and cities was very, very, different, especially in war-time.

One of Granda's indulgences at Dyke was to cut our hair in his shed, in the yard. It was a doubtful privilege since he sometimes nicked an ear by mistake; but his intention was the best. When the day came for us to go home, Woolpack's car would appear in the evening. It was Granda's custom to get into the car with us children when we were ready to go, with his lantern, and sing to us in the gloaming. Very, very atmospheric. The songs were, as I remember, all sentimental, 'When its springtime in the Rockies I am coming back to you, when its springtime in the Rockies ...' and, later on, something about 'Shining eyes of blue'. Then there was 'It was only a beautiful picture in a beautiful golden frame' and 'If those eyes could only see, if those lips could only speak, if those beautiful golden tresses were there in reality'. They must have been popular songs of the previous generation. When the concert was over and we were half asleep, then the parents came out of the house for the drive home. Granda did not often sing at Woolpack: he reverted to a sterner self.

Holidays at Dyke ended when Granda and Granny came to live at Woolpack, and they had plenty to do there because of the war-time staff shortage. Granda ran the vegetable and soft fruit garden for the inn, grew the table flowers, and looked after the hens and the orchard. I really think he was more interested in gardening than in farming: his father had been a professional gardener. Granda was a bit of a joker; on his marriage certificate he had put himself down as rabbit catcher. They had lived at Mount Rivers, not far way, and it was true it was not a farm and, as he told us, he did catch rabbits, and put them on the early London train. Still to describe himself as a rabbit catcher was depreciative and typical. He liked to be a little obtuse. At Woolpack he kept his own dog, a terrier, and he was careful to provide it with its own kennel, away from the other dogs. He was extremely concerned about the quality of animals' lives. One of his admonitions was 'Don't make a fool of an animal'. He did not expand on exactly what he meant. We definitely got the guilt of destroying a plant from him. He did not talk about much at all, simply worked alone all day, and inside he sat in a rocking chair in front of the annexe fire and read the local paper with a magnifying glass.

On the other hand, Granny's day was full of conversation, since she worked around the kitchen. She hand washed the pans and dishes, and prepped the vegetables at the back door outside, on the sconce. She wasn't put off by a bit of rain; if she needed a slicker and boots then she got them. She also baked the bread. At the same time, and looking back it is obvious, the grandparents did oversee us as children since we spent more time with them than we did with our parents, who were forever working and preoccupied with customers.

The war brought changes, a significant one being allowed only one farm man and one hotel maid. It was all to do with government regulations on the exemption of personnel from the forces or essential war work, so family members had to do more of the work than in normal times. The visitors changed too. Without being requested, they started making their own beds and clearing the tables in the dining room. I recall them drying dishes, even bringing in laundry off the line. Occasionally we would have someone lend a hand outside. There was a palpable feeling of solidarity in war-time: people pulled together. War-time visitors, I suppose, were only too happy to be in the country and away from the bombing and the shortages, the rationed and not so fresh food in the city. The infrequent and stale eggs, with the lions stamped on them, come to mind.

My mother would occasionally get a phone call from London during the war, from previous guests, and she might have to explain that she was

Margaret and Helen and the Esse range.

fully booked. They said things like 'No matter, we're coming anyway, we'll sleep anywhere', and they did. Once doing my piano practice in the annexe I was startled when a figure suddenly arose from the floor behind a table, I had interrupted a much needed sleep. Some slept in the hay in the top barn. Londoners worked around the clock: after the normal day at work they had turns at fire watching duties at night. It was no wonder that they were desperate for a break from it all.

Although our life was not much changed in the war, there was the obligation to produce more food, and one unusual thing was that farmers were required to give up to the government half of any pig slaughtered. The local butcher himself had a constant drama going on with the meat inspectors. He stayed for lunch in the Woolpack kitchen while on his delivery round, and entertained everyone with his tales of deception. The narrative was that he had to be one step ahead of the inspector, moving his illegal cuts of meat around the countryside, in order to evade government eyes. At this time there were small local abattoirs. He had informants all over, and was constantly checking with them by telephone and with his assistant back at base on the inspector's progress and exact location, then making adjustments to the plans for the day. He was determined to keep his customers supplied as in normal times. It was a comedy and the only person in ignorance of it all must have been the inspector.

If bombs were dropped near us, it was because the planes were unloading on their way back to the continent, lightening the load to make a faster getaway. We did get a few craters this way, mercifully on the fells, but one landmine did come down in a field right in the middle of the village of Eskdale Green, four miles away, and knocked out windows. Once Auntie Gladys had us hit the ground in the school field when two planes overhead appeared to be having an aerial battle above the vicarage, and once, when we were shopping in Whitehaven, a plane just blew up over our heads, we heard a large explosion, then little bits of it rained down. One night at Woolpack, we all went outside, as the sky was red, and were told that the shipyard at Barrow-in-Furness was burning. The searchlights could be seen and the explosions heard. Then there were some crashes of Spitfire and Hurricane planes on the fells. We walked up to two crashes on the Scafell range; at least one was a Polish pilot, presumably from the base at Silloth on the Cumbrian coast.

Alastair was a sensitive boy, and since we spent most of the day together, and slept in the same bed, in Back Nine over the Boot House, I was the recipient of all his fears. Most of the time I just listened, or we play acted; for instance we had to cope with pig killing days. Occasionally as an older sister, I felt I was called upon to make him feel better about something. One such time was when we had an army unit camping and soldiering in the Hostel Field, their dispatch riders tearing up and down Hardknott. We wandered amongst the soldiers and checked out their gear and cooking arrangements just as we would anything new on the farm, and saw nothing particularly alarming. It was the word manoeuvres that we overheard that caused Alastair extreme anxiety. This unit were about to embark on manoeuvres. Well, of course, I also had no idea what manoeuvres were, but I told him that it meant that they might, or they might not, do something, whatever it was, and this put it in a 50/50 category. It seemed to help; figures easily mystify. The astonishing thing is that we felt we were on our own about pretty much everything; we didn't ask adults a lot questions, they were always busy, we had to work it out between ourselves.

About the start of the war Alastair and I did have a memorable full day's hike when we were about seven and eight. We walked by ourselves over the passes, Hardknott and Wrynose, to Langdale, to stay with our cousins the Bulman family, who ran the Old Dungeon Ghyll Hotel. This walk was done by the family for several years. It would be considered today to be a big deal to set off such young children on an all day walking trip where they were going to have to navigate by themselves, and be totally on their own, with no telephone en route, or even half way house to call at. It involved the climb up to Hardknott, the steep and long pull, then over the top and steeply down to Cockley Beck, turn east and go up the deserted valley of Wrynose Bottom and then up Wrynose Pass, past the Three Shire Stone which at the time marked the boundaries of the then three counties of Cumberland, Westmorland and Lancashire. Then down the other side of Wrynose to Fell Foot, turn left and climb up again to Blea Tarn, go around that, and then head for Langdale. On looking down into Langdale, we saw cousin John, he was a few years older than us, and had been sent out to meet us. He was the first person that we had seen all day.

Then of course after our stay we had the return journey to do, with our sandwiches. It rained hard about the Three Shire Stone, so we rested under a rock until the worst of it had passed and ate the sandwiches. They were tomato, something we both hated, but we were so hungry that we ate them anyway. There were a few occasions on the fell when we were tired and wet, and maybe cold. Then food felt life-saving and enabled one to go further.

Eskdale showed few signs of the war; it seemed far away, but there were certain government requirements. There was a Home Guard group and a Harrison brother from Butterilket occasionally biked past with his rifle strapped to his back, on his way to training session somewhere. Mother and Father were wardens for the distribution of gas masks in the valley; and children were instructed to carry them to school. Barbara was born in 1943 and so had a crib size gas mask. Masks were issued to everyone on the off-chance that a gas might be used on civilians as it was in the First World War on the continent. The war was accepted as an inevitability, something over which we had no control. Granda Leece was the only one heard to express himself politically on the war, he had no time for it at all. He said that Germans were the people 'the most like us' and it was all a ridiculous idea. There was a story that in the First World War he had chased off a recruiting officer with a pitch fork, and that the officer had not dared to go back. The story was entirely in character.

Granda had his own opinions about things and once, for instance, cautioned me about reading books: 'Just because it's written in a book doesn't mean it is correct.' Well, good point. He had my number then – reading – the over-riding preoccupation and sin of a lifetime, as it transpired. Not that there was a great deal to read there and then; we had a few childrens books, and some works on the proceedings of the Cumberland and West-morland Antiquarian Society. Nevertheless, the signs must have been there.

I do not know to what degree the adults followed the progress of the war. It was not discussed in the kitchen, the radio was not much listened to, and the daily paper was not a 'serious' one, and in any case seemed to be read only by the men. We hadn't heard of television yet. Sometimes we did hear war planes going over at night and cousin Michael tried to teach us what they were: ours or theirs, he recognized them by the sound.

Michael dipping sheep at Woolpack.

When he heard the planes inside the house, he would take us out to gaze overhead at the shadows and the shapes. Enemy planes were on their way to bomb the shipyards. We had the 'black-out' too: windows had to be completely screened at night, no light must show that might give any geographic information to a bomber.

Our war experiences in Eskdale were not much compared with the frightful goings-on in the cities, and the mass mobilizations. We were very lucky in our relative isolation. Michael was our only close family member who was conscripted. He was taken out of his school before he graduated and put into the Fleet Air Arm, and from thence sent to Corpus Christie in Texas to train as a pilot. Fortunately, by the time his training was completed the war had ended; he became a test pilot at Lossiemouth for a few years.

As children we got no regular rundown on the progress of the war from anyone, we did once happen to see a shocking news reel in Whitehaven while on a shopping trip. It was early on in the war, and the report was from Dunkirk on the French coast. The British Expeditionary Force and the French Army had been cut off and driven into Dunkirk, in enormous numbers. The call was made for anyone with a boat, a fishing boat or a yacht, to go and pick up as many soldiers as they could manage. The newsreel showed the soldiers wading out into the Channel towards these boats; then they were photographed disembarking in England, and a demoralizing detail was that the army was not completely clothed – bits of uniform were missing. The newsreel conveyed the scale of the disaster. I think this was when Churchill made his most memorable rallying speeches on the radio, about 'fighting on the beaches', but as children we did not hear them. Though we were protected from a lot; we certainly had the gravest of misgivings about what went on in other places away from our fells. However, at the time of Dunkirk, there was a palpable fear abroad that reached even Eskdale. 'They could walk right in,' – that phrase sticks in the mind. (As it turned out Hitler's astrologer felt that it wasn't an auspicious time to go past the Channel Islands.)

Then there was the arrival of the evacuees, overnight the number of schoolchildren doubled. They were mostly from South Shields, on the south side of the River Tyne, and came with their own teacher, Miss Hately, and there were also a few from London. The morning that we got to school and found all these additional children, and Miss Hately as well as Auntie Gladys, was a fearful shock, it felt like the whole world had changed without warning. One inexplicable detail was that the new children were wearing our clothes. I suppose that there must have been a quick round up, since the children would have come with very little, only what they could easily carry themselves, and they would have been burdened with their gas masks. No-one had thought to tell us of this invasion, or if they did we had failed to understand. Let us hope that the evacuees themselves had been better prepared. Here they were suddenly away from home, family and the city, into what, to them, must have seemed like the back of beyond. But what an inspired stroke it was to send a group with their teacher, making it into a kind of unexpectedly long school outing. I am not sure of the exact date of their going home, but our send off for Miss Hately was memorable.

The day Miss Hately left, Auntie Gladys had us on a school outing at the Roman Camp half way up Hardknott, we would have walked over two miles from school. It was there that the intrepid taxi driver found his fare, Miss Hately (the road must have been somewhat repaired after the dispatch riders). We sang to her 'Will you no come back again, better loved ye cannae be ...' as she was driven off – the song written for Bonnie Prince Charlie, after his failed attempt to claim the throne, and we felt our nearness to Scotland. Well good for Auntie Gladys: history and archaeology, the not unusual ambitious walk, and a dramatic send off that Miss Hately would not forget.

5

The seasons on the farm

On the farm, in this place, at this time, everything was seasonal. Spring with the sun, the warmth and the growth was a relief and a new start. It meant planting and lambing. Summer was fully leafed out, the days longer and hopefully hot. It meant tending and growing. Towards the autumn when walking down a lane with the leaves starting to turn, one knew why one was present. It meant reaping and storing. The winter was all about 'hanging in' and waiting it out, doing the repairs. This was so for all: the stock, the land and all who worked on it. All this was done without a re-frigerator or a freezer; and mostly with equipment that would have been familiar to a Victorian. We were dependent on what we produced.

I am at a disadvantage when talking about what went on outside, indeed about farming at all, since I was supposed to be working inside, and that was a full time job. My big advantage is that at the kitchen table the men did all the talking, and it was all about farming. Since the entire family and staff, and any visiting locals, sat down together to eat, and there were never less than a dozen of us, there was no shortage of farming informa-tion. And I have to say that what was going on outside appeared to be more interesting and varied than housework, and more important than the visitor trade. So much so, that it was hard sometimes, not to feel like a prisoner inside, looking out into the daylight.

Farming was, and presumably still is, a complicated business. The din-ner table was an ideal place to get up to date: it was an obligatory rest and did not waste anyone's time. The weather was a big topic, and of paramount importance, as it determined what could, and what could not be done, in the short term, and might have consequences for the season as a whole. It was reported to be a 'good year' for this, or a 'bad year' for that. Since the farm was mixed there was always some good news some-where. It could not all be disaster: the advantage of diversification. There was conversation about calving or heifers or bullocks or lambing. Or it might be sorting out some groups of sheep: hoggs, twinters, gimmers, wethers (the names refer to ages and types of sheep). And more ominously – what was to be sold on? Then there was planting and where, picking, harvesting, cutting, drying and leading. All the specifics relating to stock and crops were gone over at the dinner table. Conversations like these had been going on at Woolpack certainly for 800 years, perhaps a thousand, maybe more.

A hay day was a busy time, and for it the weather was crucial. Good hay weather had to be perfect – sunny and dry. The aim was to mow as early as possible in the morning, and then to turn the cut grass and turn it constantly as it dried in the sun. While there was a mowing machine and a side-turner there was still plenty of hand raking. All could be jeopardized with a heavy and continuous rain, a bad summer was a disaster. You had to know when to get the damp cut grass off the ground to avoid mould. When the hay was dry enough it was piled into haycocks or pikes using hand rakes and forks.

Haycocks or pikes minimized the damage done by rain. As children we were able to rake hay into haycocks since they were small and low. The hay lay as cut in rows, it had been hand turned with a rake to get the sun, and so it turned from green to more of a Naples yellow. When dry and yellowed then it could be assembled into haycocks, still in the rows. Pikes, on the other hand, took hay from a larger area, were large and high and so a job for farm men. Pikes, being much larger piles might generate more heat inside and that itself could dry the pile from the inside. The earlier cut grass was more nutritious but took longer to dry and that could be a relevant factor when making decisions on what to build prior to 'leading'.

It might be a day or two before it was judged time to 'lead' the hay, it all depended on how good the drying had been. When the hay was judged ready it was hand forked from the cocks or pikes onto the wagon and taken to the barn, there it was unloaded and stacked again into a 'mew' (a wall to wall stack in a section of the barn). Standing on top of the mew in the barn receiving the forkfuls of hay, and positioning it all, was hot and prickly, and it could be a dusty job. When the stack neared the roof it seemed harder to breathe and was even hotter. And it was a job for a man really, as children we would be sunk up to our waists in hay so had difficulty moving about, so for us it was more about flailing about, packing the hay down, and generally having a good time. But no, we didn't play much throughout the year in the haystacks, it was discouraged – hay was too valuable to be endangered and it could be dusty and could even grow mould.

If the crop was corn, the sheaves were stood into stooks (groups) to dry in the field – the grain uppermost. When judged dry, the stooks were led into the stackyard and built into a corn stack or two – stalks facing out and waited for threshing. The top of the stack was shaped so as to direct the rain off. Our corn then, unlike the hay, was kept in the open for a while before the threshing.

One of the more dramatic farming events was taking the sheep to the fell and leaving them there to graze, and subsequently gathering them up and bringing them down off the fell. Hill farming involved a lot of walking and climbing; all the men on the farm were fit and strong. At table there were references to known markers on the fell: certain crags, hills, tarns, mosses, or becks. Certain names came up constantly: for instance Eel Tarn, Stony Tarn, Bleabeck, Burnmoor, Black Apron, Great How, Slight side, Cam Spout, Mickeldore, Scafell, Scafell Pike. There were recurrent references to other farms up the valley: such as Whaes (Wha House), Butterilket (Brotherelkeld), Taes (Taw House), Penny Hill, also to the families in them – Ellwoods, Harrisons, Cowmans and so on. The farms and families of Upper Wasdale and Miterdale were also frequently mentioned. There were connections, coming and goings, and a lot of mutual help.

Often we had visiting farm men for the big events of the farming year, notably clipping or gathering. At hay time women and children were the extra hands, and we were good at it, it was our pleasure. At clipping or gathering, any visiting farm hands came in at lunchtime, and again it was a social occasion around the kitchen table. There was the custom of helping each other on busy days; it was a reflection of the historic relationships between the families. The air was wreathed with the scents of perspiring men with hints of both their animals and the crops. As a consequence, I do not now ever notice farm odours. They seem natural to me – going further than that they give information – so I am surprised to find that such odours may drive some urban people wild with distaste, even outrage. Ugh, cow dung! But then the kind of farming we did was very different to some modern farming. Our animals had space and dignity.

Fox hunts were exciting events in the valley; it was what the men did for relaxation, and again it was dissected at table. The ostensible reason for hunting was to keep the numbers of foxes in check, on account of their depredations, but it just so happened that it was an enjoyable day off. Stoats and weasels might be hunted too for much the same reason, but

Piking hay in the front field – Tyson and Alastair.

that did not have the same glamour. As children we accompanied Granda on stoat hunts, which seemed to be all in holes in the ground, and I think that Granda had his terrier and possibly even a pet ferret. I don't remember organized bird hunts although they could do a lot of damage. Crows and magpies could be horrible – I don't like to think of them. They just peck, no clean killing, and they can go for sheep eyes. Just now and then a man would have to go out with a gun to sort things out.

A foxhunting day was really not much different from sheep gathering days, it involved a day long energetic walk and even more energetic dogs, in this case the entire fox hound pack and a few fox terriers. It had to be a walking hunt since fell country was not suitable for horses. In fact we no longer kept riding horses as we had a car, but the curious thing is I do not remember riding horses on any farm without a car. I never knew how the hunt starting points were chosen, maybe it was by hearsay of a sighting. In any case the hounds soon picked up the scent of a fox and were off after it, baying as they went, and that was a sound that echoed from the fells around the valley. It was tough for the hunters to keep up with the dogs on the fell; luckily, they were able to take short cuts by taking educated guesses on the fox's route. Father cheated by taking the tractor, he had a hip and back problem, as he had been thrown from a horse in his youth.

We had our own Eskdale Foxhound Pack and a huntsman in charge. The traditional uniform was a bright red coat and beige riding pants with highly polished leather gaiters and a black peaked cap. The huntsman carried the horn to announce the sighting of a fox. The pursuit ended in the kill of the luckless fox, and this was likely to be when it was exhausted and had 'gone to ground': into a borran (a hiding place under some rocks). The frenzied mass of hounds and terriers soon had the fox out and it was instantly in shreds. A macabre note was struck by the rescue of the brush. A kill was not a great draw for girls or women; like me, they likely saw it once and that was more than enough.

Still as children we sang about the Cumbrian huntsman John Peel, an eighteenth century ballad that went:

> *Do you ken John Peel with his coat so gay?*
> *Do you ken John Peel at the break of day?*

We sang about Joe Bowman, the Ullswater huntsman of early in the twentieth century. That ballad went:

> *For we ne'er shall forget how he woke us at dawn –*
> *With the crack of his whip and the sound o-o-of – his horn*

Since what happened inside the inn got very little attention at table, one had to assume that it was of secondary importance. Strangely, absolutely no-one was interested in what women did all day, how many meals had been served, how much laundry done, how much bread baked, what cooked, how many floors scrubbed, or even who had called in. It was very definitely a man's world, and a farming one. In that regard I now comprehend that in our left-over bit of the pre-industrial world the strength of a man was critical to survival.

There was one exception to the prevailing patriarchy at table: Granny Leece. She often expounded on genealogy, which was her consuming interest. It seemed that she could supply the genealogy of any neighbour or of any family. She could tell you where someone was born, married, where they had farmed and when, around Eskdale, Wasdale or Miterdale, and very possibly in other valleys or their villages. Although most of her married life had been a few miles away at the coast, one felt that she was happy to be back on home ground. She sometimes ended her histories by saying, somewhat wistfully, 'Like, what I am speaking of is 60 years ago.' Adding that to my age now would take us back to about 130 years ago.

All the adults in the family and the local hired help and anyone who had dropped in, were delighted to add to their knowledge of their personal local history. 'Oh aye!' 'You don't say!' 'Is that so?' These were common refrains, signifying the discovery of a new fact, something added to local lore. And Granny was questioned; she was one of them, a true native, and was obviously carrying around a gold mine of local history. As children, it went right over our heads: the endless stories seemed not to be about much of anything and of the impossibly long ago. But, as always, we listened politely. Of course what I should have been doing was getting pen and paper and writing it all down, asking the right questions myself.

And so an opportunity to learn more was lost for ever. There was obviously a vast oral history which should have been recorded, and now there is no-one for me to ask. The locals, did not write down much of anything beyond bills or letters. In spite of generations of formal elementary school education they did not often read books, and the national newspapers not very much. The only thing perused, from cover to cover, was the local paper – the *Whitehaven News*. It was passed from hand to hand; it was full of chatter about people they knew, and of meets and events. The locals did not appear to be much interested in the wider world: of politics – beyond a certain rural conservatism, of world events or the arts or literature.

It often seemed that, in our corner of the world, there was very little interest in anywhere, or anybody, that wasn't immediately local. Even travellers' tales might not get much attention. We had a visit from a rare Eskdale man, a local farmer's sibling, who had emigrated to California; one might have thought that he would have received some interest and emigration from the valleys was not common. He was back for a visit on the family farm, possibly the only time that he would come back, and he had come into the Woolpack for a drink and chat. He brought his beer into the kitchen and sat down under the kitchen clock, and I quote him directly… 'Hanestly, we've gat everything in Calafornia.' He had adopted the accent; and then we did not have experience of American movies. Admittedly it was a brash opening, even I as a teenager could see that, but the kitchen emptied instantly, not even California rated courtesy. I alone was polite enough to hear him out. I must have been clairvoyant, since, years later, I myself was to come back from California. But then I had the advantage of knowing that no one would be even slightly curious, even particularly about the farms, on good land, in a place with a fabulous climate but a shortage of water, and all that fruit...

My time at the inn is roughly during the war, 1939 to 1945, and shortly thereafter. Up to this time, work on the farm was still traditional. Our farming was what we now call 'organic', and it was local, labour intensive and family oriented. The mixed stock and crops were interdependent: the crops fed the stock, and the stock provided the fertilizer for the fields. The style of farming was not too ecologically damaging; it had been going on for centuries. Most certainly there had been a thousand years, or more, of grooming the land, and farming in some form going back much, much further. The pastoral landscape that had developed was visually pleasing; the farms were still viable. I feel sure it was expected that the style of life would be much the same for future generations.

However, the war was a time of change in Eskdale: new ideas came in. As a consequence of the war, the government sought to increase productivity in the country in general, to protect the food supply and the farming way of life, since it was not easy to import food. Ships bringing food into the country were being sunk so farming became an essential part of the war effort. Rural depopulation had to be prevented, and a certain number of agricultural workers were exempted from call-up into the forces. This was the time when the government first paid hill farmers to keep sheep or cattle and there was a subsidy for each individual animal.

Woolpack got a war-time agricultural adviser, and he made periodic visits to dispense official advice. He inevitably stayed for lunch; like anyone else who came to Woolpack, he became a friend and lifelong acquaintance. He riveted our attention as children because he had stomach ulcers, so Mother had to be careful what she fed him, milk puddings were much desired. I suppose that we weren't used to people being sick and were learning about good nursing.

One thing that our adviser encouraged was the idea of chemical fertilizers – nitrate, phosphate and potash – familiar to us today as NPK. They were to be grafted onto the organic farming that had previously been the norm. Bags and heaps of these things appeared, particularly nitrate. Pollan refers to a Question being asked in the House of Lords in 1943. 'Did the

House know that farmers were complaining that there were more plant nutrients than the NPK being prescribed?' Since there were seventeen or so plant nutrients that had been identified – could there be some problem with concentrating on three only? A pertinent question that has reverberations today in the discussions, clash even, between industrial type farming and the present organic farmers and their customers. How to look after productive land: short term gain or long term soil quality?

Science was coming to influence traditional farming in Eskdale and Father was generally positive about 'progress', the modern ideas of using chemicals as nutrients and getting rid of pests. Years later, when I gave him Rachel Carson's *Silent Spring* to read, he was incredulous, said he didn't believe it – the bad news about DDT and its drastic effects on all living things, not just pests. Indeed, there were possible implications for chemicals in general. This, in spite of his usual environmental stance, it was a step too far for him. As far as I know, he had followed all the wartime advice.

Our agricultural adviser came from what was referred to as the War Ag office set up by the government to boost productivity. Probably it was this office that sent out prisoners of war to this end, since the normal number of agricultural workers was down because of the 'call-up'. We got the gang of singing Italians to drain excess water from the Big Meadow at Paddockwray, and that was a relaxed affair. There was a German camp near Ulpha, on the other side of Birker Moor, and very likely men were sent out to farms from there as well. We heard the story of one German prisoner who made headline news by escaping and evading an attempt at recapture by immersing himself in water, I thought on Birker Moor – then presumably that was Devoke Water.

In our story, he breathed through a straw until the search party gave up; we were told that the dogs lost his scent at the water. However, the escapee somehow got to Canada, either under his own steam or by being recaptured and then shipped to Canada was not clear. Once in Quebec he rowed himself over the St. Lawrence Seaway and made his way to either New York or Washington, I don't recall which. He made political points that got a great deal of media attention; this was before the US entered the war. It is likely that this was our version of the Franz von Werren story, a downed pilot who had been interned at Grizedale Hall used for officers. In the 1950s, a film was made of it entitled 'The one who got away'.

As part of the productivity drive there was the war-time force of the

Land Girls. They wore a uniform with riding pants, and were sent out in groups to do certain specific farm jobs. I have a vague memory of seeing some at Wha House. Many women who had not gone out to work before the war were offered a choice of jobs. Being a Land Girl must have been the best option, a real adventure for city girls.

The vet became a war-time fixture on the farm, he too became another long term family friend welcomed around the dinner table. He was the one who had the job of introducing DDT for dipping sheep. And it must have looked like a godsend at the time, for sheep had plenty of pests, and nasty ones: ticks, keds, lice, scab and blowfly larvae. We all know that DDT finally turned out to be environmentally disastrous, especially noticeable for its effect on wildlife. It must have done significant harm in Eskdale and on the fell, but I have not ever heard this quantified or even discussed. In the early days robins nested above the dipping yard. Dipping was hazardous, too, for the farm men, they breathed in the fumes of the dip and got splashed all over. I am not sure what farmers used before DDT. Derris powder was still much talked about; it came from a plant in India, but the supply of it was interrupted in the war. Derris was still used for warble fly in cattle and horses. Warbles were horrible grubs that grew underneath the skin. You could see the bumps and they must have been uncomfortable for the animal, they just had to come out.

Alastair and I were early witnesses to the arrival of DDT. It was on one of our long hikes, when we took some fresh pork to Uncle Benny's family at Cragg Farm, down Birkby. 'Oh Lord, pork!' exclaimed Aunt Janey as we walked in. Fresh pork was routinely handed around the family and neighbours and Aunt Janey had received a lot already. We had lunch and Uncle Benny took us into the orchard to fill up on his very delicious, and falling, greengages. Alastair and I then thought to make a social call on the vet, at his home at nearby Cragg Cottage. The vet was delighted to see us and showed us his lab which was a wooden shed in the middle of one of Uncle Benny's fields. He told us about this great discovery of DDT, and of the remarkable effect that it had on flies and bluebottles. He had a bottle of liquid DDT and he demonstrated its power. He dipped a screw of paper into the liquid and touched one of the horde of flies on his windowpane. It was instant death. So we had a turn – touching flies with the charged paper. We had not seen anything so dramatic in its effect. I have no recollection of washing our hands after handling it; we were all to get a dose of the poison, one way or another.

So what was going on during the seasons on the farm? I will attempt a brief overview starting in winter when the hoggs (one year old sheep) were sent to 'winter' at the coast. The ewes had been mated and sent back to the fell to forage. The cows had been brought into the byre, they were bedded on dry bracken and were fed hay, and a high nutrient content cow cake that was largely linseed. It didn't taste too bad – as children we snacked on a fair bit of animal food. As mentioned wall gaps were repaired. Fields were rested after being grazed, planted, or reaped during the summer. For us it felt like a closing in, the valley was ours again, the visitors gone. There were still jobs to do but we stayed close to home, were focused more narrowly on the survival of everything in the cold.

Not many sheep were kept 'in-bye' (the valley fields or intacks), only those that needed to be looked after, and they got supplementary hay and turnips. The in-bye was used to grow fodder for cattle, and for some ewes and tups in the winter. Generally speaking it was thought that, in winter, there was actually more nutrition in the grass, sedge and heather, on the fell, 'marginal' though it was, and higher up, therefore more exposed. The hoggs chosen to winter at the coast were the best looking female lambs of that year, the less promising ones and the males were sold on. Our hoggs wintered at Walney Island, not far from Waberthwaite, where there was more grass. Also at the coast the presence of salt on the coast meant that the liver fluke (a little parasitic flatworm that caused anaemia and weight loss) in sheep could not complete its life cycle, since the secondary host, a snail, could not tolerate the salt. The fluke needed the freshwater snails on the fell. The wintered hoggs got a good start, more nourishment, since life on the fells was tougher because of the lower quality of the diet there. Wintering was a kind of transhumance, an institution coming down from neolithic times, where the lowland was for stock in winter, and the high ground in summer.

The medieval manorial terms of levancy and couchancy (literally getting up and lying down, a day, and relating to allowed grazing time) still had relevance to us. The historic medieval Manor Court had rules on the carrying capacity of the land, and that of each individual farm and its allowed grazing on the Common. The court dealt with complaints and enforced its rules – they gave fines for transgressions. This meant that the farm was restricted to keeping the number of stock that could be completely maintained on the farm, on its 'in-bye' and on its allotted common grazing. The rules at the time said that one could not bring in feed, one could only keep stock that could be provided for on the individual property concerned. Technically then, wintering hoggs on the coast was a violation of the rules. A 'stint' was an ancient word used for a stock allowance. Although by our day the Manor Court was no longer in existence as such, to a large degree we were still living with its provisions. The law was still there, even if somewhat forgotten or ignored. We were in fact just on the cusp of massive change to hundreds of years of traditional practice.

The Manor Court also controlled the turbary rights (for peat) and estover rights (for wood, bracken, heather and seaves) for the individual farms. The peathouses, once used for storing and drying, are still dotted on the fells. Woolpack may have used the peathouse that is part way down from Eel Tarn, although there is another at Stony Tarn. Eel Tarn itself is surrounded by a vast bog. Presumably it was from that bog that Woolpack took its peat, and Paddockwray also. The Manor Court directed the manner in which peat was cut and how the ground cover had to be replaced, since valuable grazing could not be destroyed. We took wood only from our own in-bye, and by our day heather and seaves were not needed for thatch as they had been in previous centuries.

Bracken was still a crop that we cut, but usually from not much further up the fell than the top of an intack. It was still used for bedding stock, and ended up with the manure on the fields and as a thick cover on the vegetable storage heap. Cutting bracken was a dangerous job, done with a 'leigh', which was a formidable, large, two handled scythe, that cut a wide swath. It was safer to handle in a field but on the fell, or upper intack, it was hazardous to swing it into bracken as there were concealed rocks and Alastair once got a bad cut. I assumed he had hit a rock and that the 'leigh' had jumped. In the past bracken, had been harvested on a more commercial scale, since the potash in it could be used in glass making, and that was another violation of the Manor Court – selling a crop.

Angus Winchester, author of the *The Harvest of the Hills*, raises the situation of the cottagers in medieval times. Those families who did not inherit one of the historic farms did not do so well with the Manor Courts. The Courts' representatives were farmers who were interested in the viability of the farms first, and not particularly of cottages. Cottagers might find problems in keeping stock themselves. There was another way that the farms were kept viable and that was by only one son, or possibly two, inheriting the farm. Other siblings might live and work on the farm, and

Lambing time, Alastair and Margaret.

possibly not marry. One can see that the landless, in general, were disadvantaged; but the farms themselves were kept viable over the centuries.

As well as the paths from farm to farm there was a network of paths on the fells, called sheep trods, mostly to get sheep and cattle to their heafs and back again, and to bring down the bracken or other wild crops. The path up the fell behind Paddockwray went through the rake first, then past Ghyll Bank and on to Burnmoor, Eel Tarn and beyond. Behind Woolpack the path went through the rake and out on top it divided. The path to the right was the drift road to the sheep heaf, towards Stony Tarn, and the path to the left, to Eel Tarn, was originally for bringing peat or other crops, and for cattle and horses going to Burnmoor and back. From Burnmoor there were paths down into Wasdale and into Miterdale. We were in the semi-wild on the fell but we felt at home. We knew where to go and how to get there – rather like our heafed sheep. We too were liberated and free to wander over what felt like our place, checking that all was right with the world. Honestly, it took me years to realize that not everyone lived like this.

In the spring things came to life. The milk cows were let out permanently from the byre on to the new grass. The ewes were gathered from the fell and brought in for the lambing in late April. The men patrolled the fields at lambing time, most urgently if it was raining, and we might get a too-cold lamb or two, not doing well, in the kitchen to warm up and feed. We kept them in lined cardboard boxes either on top of the range or up against the front of the ovens. They got milk and sometimes brandy. It was awful to feel them so cold. You might come down in the morning to find a recovered lamb out of its box and wandering around the kitchen bleating for its mother, or one might have died in the night. I recall a visitor thinking we should be distressed over a death as children but we took it in our stride: there was a tough side to our lives, we had a long view.

There might be a spring dipping after lambing. Some time after lambing the lambs got their ear or lug marks and dripped blood for awhile, shaking their heads with the irritation of it. The fell-going sheep got their red smit marks. The chosen fields were ploughed and seeded. In spring the collected cow manure and bedding from the winter was used on the crops and on the pasture as well. The cart went around full of manure and the farm man stood in it at the back, working with a special fork, with right-angled tines. Thus he pushed off bits at intervals as the cart went, and so the manure and bracken mixture was distributed over the fields. That was the old way of fertilizing the land and the basic one.

In the summer the sheep were sheared and might be dipped again. Following the clipping the individual fleeces were rolled and baled. Then grass intended for hay was allowed to grow in some fields, and animals were kept out of it, since they constantly crop wherever they are. Hay would be cut in August.

In the late summer and early autumn the crops came in and were stored – corn, root crops and vegetables. Our word 'back end' is more descriptive of this season since it incorporates the weather and the closing in. Surplus stock, sheep or cows or calves were sold, generally speaking to lowland farmers who would fatten them up and sell them on – animals from the fells were thought to have a hardy start. There might be a 'back-end' dipping of sheep. The times of dipping were not cast in stone, but rather depended on what pest was around and when; it might be required by some authority.

Now was the time that any pigs we had reared were slaughtered and that was a big day for everyone, both inside and out. The meat was sectioned up. While most of it was to be cured, some was put aside to be eaten fresh or given to neighbours. The flitches (sides) and hams to be cured were laid on the slate sconces in the dairy and packed with an enormous amount of salt. For a few days it seemed that water dripped out of the meat, off the sconce and was collected on the floor. After this the flitches and hams were tied up with string and hung on the hooks on the kitchen ceiling to continue drying.

Pig blood was saved for black pudding; chopped fat and spices were added, and maybe oatmeal, and then poured into baking tins. After baking it could be stored for a long time in the tins. It was cut as required and fried for breakfasts with bacon or put into stews. Sausage making was a big item. The pig gut had to be cleaned as it was used for the casing. Brawn was made from the left over parts and set in aspic; it was eaten cold. Then there was the crackling, nothing was wasted. I don't have all the recipe details since those days were hard for me – in my semi-vegetarian state. It is possible to do all this without refrigeration if you have a cold enough room. The dairy was cool, not quite four degrees like a refrigerator but considerably below room temperature. No-one ever checked with a thermometer; anyway we didn't have ice.

The seasons all had their flavour and their imperatives. To live on these farms took a lot of intelligence and fitness, and by and large people were very fit. Important decisions had to be made all the time. Life was never humdrum or boring, there was a great variety of work and different skills were needed every day: mechanical, stock breeding, agronomy, gardening, weather forecasting – to name a few – all were necessary to be able to eat. Contrast that variety with the routine factory floor, or routine office work and the pay check.

– 6 –

The stock and crops

I am no agricultural expert but I will go over the stock that we kept in the 1930s through to the 1950s – the sheep, cattle and so on, and the crops that sustained them. I will try to give the feel of it all, though being a girl, and not a first born son, I would not be expected to be a farmer myself; I would have to train for something else.

As mentioned our farms were classed as marginal hill farms: that is, they were not on prime agricultural land – nowhere near it, and the large amount of rain could be a problem. Nevertheless the locals had adapted to their circumstances and made it work. Over the centuries they had successfully fed their own workforce, and produced sheep, wool and cattle for sale. They had been net producers and zero waste managers.

The native sheep were Herdwicks, and they have often been described as indigenous to the hill farms. Geoff Brown points out, in his book *Herdwicks* that while their origin is not definitively known, there is some genetic connection with Shetland, Welsh and Scandinavian sheep. Some say that the Norse brought Herdwicks when they came into Cumbria. The name Herdwick is itself curious as it is Medieval English for sheep pasture; the emphasis being on the pasture rather than on the breed. The farms and their heafed flocks were a unit. The two were either rented or bought together.

The important characteristic about Herdwicks was that they were hardy enough to survive on the fell for most of the year: they were able to find both sufficient nourishment there, and be able to survive harsh weather. Heavy snow in winter could be a problem, on the fell or in the valley. In a heavy fall sheep will take cover, shelter behind a wall for instance and the snowdrifts can cover them, and that would become a farming emergency. They had to be looked for and rescued or they might suffocate. Still Herdwicks were mostly able to look after themselves and they required little supplementary feeding from the valley fields. They were so well heafed to their traditional grazing allotment that should they be sold to a neighbouring farmer, they might 'home' to their original territory.

The flock going down the Drift Road with Father, Captain Hoys and Alastair.

Herdwicks have an unpretentious look: they are small and wiry. The fleece has a shorter staple and is coloured from white to dark brown. The lambs have a black face which becomes a browny-grey to white with maturity – often a startling white. The rams have modest horns and the ewes have none.

Our sheep at Woolpack, and presumably also Paddockwray's, were not pure Herdwick. They started out as pure Herdwick, but Father had been experimenting by cross-breeding with Swaledale rams. Swaledales were Yorkshire sheep and bigger. They had black faces and whiter wool. Pure Swaledale ewes definitely had horns and those of the Swaledale rams were spectacularly curled and they were branded. The horns curled like cork screws and had to be checked for growing back into the face, in which case they had to be trimmed back. I have to suppose that the idea behind the cross-breeding was to get a slightly bigger animal and more wool. Herdwicks were the most hardy. Interestingly, Geoff Brown quotes a Boot schoolmate of mine, Noel Baines of The Howes, as saying that, in his opinion, the cross-breds demanded more supplemental feeding on the valley floor than Herdwicks, and so they were in fact a threat to the overall viability of the Herdwick breed. Nevertheless, they did seem to have been generally accepted in our day as, on occasion, there were even a few Swaledale rams at the Woolpack Herdwick Show, which was the premier annual event for showing Herdwicks.

The core of our flock was the 400 plus ewes and their lambs (I believe about 600 adults were permitted by accepted custom) and a small number of rams (called tups or tips by the locals). The ewes spent most of their time grazing on the fells, coming in at certain times to valley fields, the in-bye, in April and May, and then again in November. The wool from Herdwicks was tough, and sold, I believe, for carpet manufacture in Kendal. Due to cross-breeding our sheep had a mixed appearance, as they looked like both Herdwick and Swaledale breeds: some more Herdwick and coloured, with white faces, and some more Swaledale with whiter wool and black faces, while some ewes were horned and some not.

We saw the sheep, en masse, together and up close, when they were gathered in for dipping or at clipping time or lambing. Since we ran Woolpack and Paddockwray as a unit, we kept the two flocks together for these events, but the sheep themselves still had to be identified as either Woolpack or Paddockwray, and their smit and lug (ear) marks applied appropriately. If the previous smit mark was not clear, there was always the earmark to go by. We had an antique book illustrating lug marks and smit markings for the central Lakes that might be consulted if we found strays in the flock. There were a few valley head fell grazing areas around Scafell from which sheep might stray.

The ewes and tups were kept together in the fields through November to ensure that the lambs arrived in the spring. The lambs would then have the kindest season of the year ahead of them. As children we got familiar with our sheep and their lambs, 'turning' them as requested, watching the adults being dipped and then shaking themselves dry, and then reuniting with their lambs. The reunion was interesting. The lamb and the ewe eyed each other and called, and as the lamb got closer, the ewe checked its odour, if it was the right smell then the lamb was accepted and allowed to suckle. If the scent was not the right then that lamb was gently nudged away. There might be many encounters before the right mother and lamb found each other. The importance of the right scent was made use of where a lamb had died. An orphan lamb or a twin would be accepted by the bereaved mother if it was wearing the added skin of the dead lamb. The adopted lamb had to have the right smell. The added skin could be removed later with no problem.

The flock coming off the fell into the Rake behind Woolpack.

Only if there was no mother available did we bottle feed a pet lamb; the reason being that the lamb was imprinted on a human and so didn't quite fit in with the flock. My sister Helen looked after a pet lamb, fed it and played with it, she called it Lavinia. As a consequence Lavinia thought Helen was her mother and followed her around outside and then into the kitchen. It followed her so insistently that when Helen had to serve in the dining room the lamb ran after her, bleating and trying to keep up. Naturally Lavinia was a great hit with the diners. Lavinia did not think she was a sheep and did not want to spend a lot of time with them. As you can imagine Lavinia did not fancy going to the fell with the flock, but eventually she was persuaded. Unfortunately she died at the fell and the farmers thought that was due to her 'pet' status. We loved our few pet lambs but their future was always going to be a problem. I hate to tell you this but they may have finally been butchered when grown up. You can see how, for me, becoming a semi-vegetarian was a better option than eating a friend. And there was one occasion when we all filed out of kitchen at dinner time in protest about the dinner. Mother was good, she understood and it was not mentioned again.

Clipping day was a big occasion and men from other farms might turn up to help, so it became a social occasion as well, and was continued into the kitchen with the mid-day meal. As children we got to watch it all. Like everything else, clipping was 'low-tech'. It was done with hand shears and on a special long clipping stool. The sheep was caught and flipped over onto its back on the stool landing between the clipper's knees. If the sheep was a kicker the legs might be 'langled': tied with a cloth strip, to prevent any injury. The clipping started on the underside and done so as to remove the fleece in one piece, leaving an inch, or so, on the sheep. After being relieved of its fleece, the now startlingly white animal got our smit mark: a stroke over both shoulders and a pop on the top of the tail for Woolpack, a pop behind the head and another above the tail for Paddockwray. Each individual fleece was rolled and tied in one bundle, using only the wool itself, and then tossed into a canvas bale strung up in the Old Barn for the occasion. Wool was sold by the bale, and it was still valuable then.

Sheep always seemed very willing to be pushed around and directed, but at the same time you could see the guarded, alert look: they were observing what was going on and stayed tightly together in a group, keeping as far away as possible from a human being or a dog. While 'stupid as sheep' does have some resonance: they do move as a group and are easily led – but there was an advantage to them in that. I came away with a profound sympathy for domestic animals and their situation, and not just sheep – for any farm animal. I'd like to believe the modern, and sophisticated idea, that domestic animals exploit human protection in order to multiply their genome – hopefully so. While sheep in general had been selected over the centuries for their docility, hill sheep were rather less docile than lowland sheep, since they spent a lot of their time alone on the fell braving the elements.

When the sheep went to the fell, they were driven up their own Drift Road onto their own heafed ground, and at a certain landmark they were let go. The Drift Road was a narrow green path that snaked up through the bracken, the heather and the rocks, kept open by centuries of hooves and feet. A bigger job than taking the sheep up the Drift Road to the fell was gathering them up and bringing them down off the fell. Gathering sheep took most of the day. It was an exciting day for the men and dogs, and a big day in the kitchen too, Granny was always listening for the men and dogs and the flock coming down off the fell, and anxious about a good dinner being ready. 'Them men are coming!' Grammar disappeared in the excitement. It was a command to the women folk to stop fussing over the visitors and to concentrate on the all important farm dinner.

We always had Border Collie sheepdogs. They are a very intelligent and responsive breed, possibly the most intelligent of all. Having been raised with Border Collies, it has been difficult since to take any other breed of dog seriously: after looking into a Border Collie's eyes and registering their attentiveness and understanding, many other breeds just do not appear to be very bright. An outright ornamental dog becomes just another sign of the urban mindset. Just once we had an Old English sheepdog, called Glen, and he seemed exotic. He shambled along and squinted through his mane; I don't know what kind of worker he was.

Father on a clipping day with a Woolpack smitted sheep.

The dogs had a lot of freedom, but not enough to get into trouble. Border Collies get bored easily, they need a lot of activity and a reason for living. Should an individual dog attack a farm animal, or try hunting on its own in the fields or elsewhere, it was a grave matter, since it could teach others to do the same, compounding the problem. Since the dogs roamed around by themselves a good deal of the time there were plenty of opportunities to digress. Farm dogs had to be trustworthy at all times, and in every situation. Farmers were particularly careful about 'bothering' a neighbour's stock, and there were very occasional and serious conversations about an unreliable dog. A dog known to have attacked stock would, unfortunately, have to be shot, as the situation was untenable. Weeding out uncontrollable dogs this way would itself make sure that the breed was maximally reliable.

Some collies would regard just one man as boss, and work only for him, some might work for two or more. One luckless dog that we had would work for just anyone and so got taken to Ghana by a neighbour's family. Nkrumah, the President of Ghana was their personal friend and interested in promoting sheep farming in Africa. Just how did our dog fare, so far from home, away from the cool and the wet into which it had been born? I thought it a cruel thing to do to a dog.

Just occasionally a dog would shamelessly return back to the farm by itself, having deserted a gather, offended no doubt by getting an order from the wrong person, or been reprimanded too harshly by the right person. Granny shook her head in disapproval over a dog coming back from the fell before time; she was ever a good indicator of what was important on a hill farm.

On a gather on the fell, there was a lot of striding about for the men and a serious work out for the dogs. The activities of men and dogs were coordinated. The aim was to get all our sheep into one group and leave

Freshly shorn sheep by the old barn.

those with other smit marks on the common. It was then that the smit marks were truly useful in identifying individuals at a distance. There was a lot of whistling with arm signals and shouted commands to the dogs. 'E Gyp-e-Gyp-e-Gyp, ga-a-a-h by.' That directed Gyp, and not any other dog, to go by: to run around and herd either a group or go after some particular individual errant sheep partially concealed by rocks and bracken. A dog had to have a short name, and the repeated name was interspersed with an e. Other calls remembered were 'e-Moss-e-Moss-e-Moss' or 'e-Glen-e-Glen-e-Glen.' The dogs sailed along through the bracken and heather, constantly responding to instruction, changing tack promptly as ordered. The dogs looked like they were having a really good time, doing what they were good at, and certainly the men were: it was all dissected afterwards at the dinner table with much enthusiasm and laughter. 'When you were there (at so-and-so) crag, I was going after ...' and then perhaps described a certain independent and notorious ewe for going off somewhere. The women hovered about filling dishes, offering seconds. Such discussions on gathers must have been going on for centuries.

When Alastair and I were quite small, we took part in one memorable gather. We had spent the day by ourselves on the fell, following along after the men and dogs, perhaps trying to keep someone in view, certainly tracking the whistles and shouts, somehow keeping tabs on it all. On this occasion when the sheep and men had got back down the Drift Road and were all back into the Rake out to pasture and settled for the evening, I was told that Father went into the kitchen where he was greeted by near hysterical women. 'Where are Margaret and Alastair?' The kitchen had a good view of the gate to the Rake and we had not been spotted coming through it. Father was notoriously absent-minded and he had totally forgotten about us – in short had lost us. He had once forgotten about Mother and left her 22 miles away in Whitehaven. We did not have any extra drink or sandwiches with us, and it would not be too long before it was dark, and so it was thought by Mother and Granny to be a dangerous situation. It sometimes happened that strangers got lost, most often in a mist it is true, and search parties of farmers had to go out to look for them and just occasionally there was a fatality. I wasn't in the kitchen but I know exactly what Father would have come out with, that was a high pitched and stretched out 'Go-o-o-od damn!' It was his response to all problems, large or small.

So Father was sent back up to find us, and was not very pleased about it, unused as he was to correction. As it turned out he did not have far to go. We spotted him as he came up out onto the top, from the Rake. We were quite happy: still skipping about, plenty of energy left. We had not been lost but must have been quite a distance behind the rest. We must have been taking our time somewhere, since we were more than a half hour delayed. Tall bracken can hide children, but we would always have been able to hear the shouts and whistles.

'Where have you been?' demanded Father, in a manner that questioned our common sense. He would then have launched into a lecture of some kind, about how we should be conducting ourselves. Fortunately we were country bred, and we'd listened to a lot of this kind of thing before and obviously there was good reason for it. We knew what we were supposed to be doing, and to what we should be paying attention. We'd had a lot of roaming experience, and had so acquired a good idea of the geography. We had a good idea of direction, of distance, and of time of day. The worst thing that happened to me on this gather was that I had walked into a huge ugly, unpleasantly speckled, spider strung between some dry brown bracken stalks, a particular hazard for me in the summer, and for which I was always on the look-out. Another hazard was sheep ticks latching onto bare legs – but we all got those. Alastair knew to come to the rescue over spiders, that was one thing that would have taken our time, but there must have been other distractions.

It was not unusual to take children to the fell on a gather and we all had early experience of it. Quite young children might be taken up so far and perhaps sat on a rock, with instructions to stay there until collected. Mother says that she once left Alastair and I on a rock, when we were not much more than babies, with such instructions, and we were fine as long as we could see her, however small, disappearing in the distance, but as soon as she vanished we set up a wail, and she had to come back. Barbara too has memories of being left '...freezing on a rock'. Well, they were granite, the covering lichen and bits of moss made it only a bit more comfortable, and the surrounding ground might be too damp. It was all safe enough as long as children did as instructed, and we were all experienced at that.

When I try to remember how many cattle we had then I come up with about 40 head, but it's quite possible I am remembering that figure on the old sale notice in the bar, maybe that was from when the family bought Woolpack. We started out with shorthorns, a hardy breed, but at some

Granda Leece clipping showing the clipping stool.

point switched to Friesians which were bigger animals. Shorthorns were a general purpose breed for both milk and beef, and roan (variable brick red and white) in colour. Friesians were black and white, and produced more milk. Of course cows produce milk for calves.

It is necessary to mention that elementary fact since some city people think that milk is more or less on tap all the time. When the cow dried up then another pregnancy had to be arranged. In the shorthorn days, we had our own bull, but when the Friesians arrived it became a matter of pedigree, the sire was chosen from a catalogue, and the vet was in charge of insemination. With a pedigree, the cattle got an official name and a record of their lineage. Calving was always dramatic and could happen at any time of day or night, and someone had to be on hand for that. The first question asked in the kitchen was whether it was a bull or a heifer. Granny was always anxious to know. Heifers were most desired since they could be kept to adulthood as breeding and milking cows, but the bull calves were maintained only until they were partly grown, and then sold on or kept on a bit longer as bullocks. In the summer, the cattle had a lot of freedom but were always kept down in the fields. While the rules for the heaf did allow for cattle on the fell at certain times, I do not believe that ours ever went.

Our eight, or so, milk cows came into the byre twice a day for hand milking; each one had its own favourite stall and went directly to it. As children we helped out with the milking after school. Milkers sat on three-legged wooden stools called coppies. The milker's head was pressed into the side of the cow, and one had to watch out not to be kicked or stepped on or whipped in the face by the coarse tail hair. Milking developed the forearm muscles, so we all got strong arms. The farm men might sing to the cows as they were being milked, since it relaxed the cows and helped them to 'let down' the milk. That idea would be understood by any nursing mother. The milk was collected in open milk pails and these were carried from the byre around the yard and down the steps at the back of the Woolpack into the boot house for separating. We were once highly entertained by some talkative city boys who passed through the yard (on their way to the public path up the Rake) who stopped to marvel at the sight of milk in buckets. They told us, without joking, that theirs came in milk bottles – being raised on a farm certainly helped to think things through.

In winter, the cows were in the byre more or less full time, presumably they were more productive there than they would have been outside in the cold. The stalls had running water, the cow pressed a lever with her nose to fill her basin. Hay and bracken were brought in from the adjoining Dutch barn. That name was give to barns open on one side. The cows also had a high nutrient cow cake. Mucking out was a big job and the manure

Ewes in the cow field in winter.

pile outside grew throughout the winter.

As children we dared ourselves to be licked by a cow; their tongues were very rough, felt somewhat like the roughest sand paper, and so were surprisingly abrasive on the skin. It was always a pleasure to visit the cows in the byre, especially when it was cold in the winter. The byre was warm with body heat and cow breath. The sound of the cud being chewed was a comforting one, altogether it gave a home-from-home feeling, never to be forgotten.

Much, much later on, when Alastair was in charge, he developed a sideline of breeding pedigree Hereford bulls, something quite new to Woolpack, and did very well with them. He 'topped' a few important markets in the north of England and over the border in Scotland. That meant he got the highest price; the implication being that his breed was getting to be well known and desirable to Hereford farmers. Sale prices and awards in shows were treated with an enduring respect: breeding was a serious business.

Apart from sheep and cows there were the pigs, large whites I think. Their lives were pretty restricted apart from their visits to the old orchard, and if they were lucky a visit to the oak tree for acorns. They were the only animals routinely slaughtered on the farm apart from poultry and rabbits. I'm not sure at what point we stopped keeping pigs, but we did. Pork of course was wanted all year round – that is ham, bacon and sausage. Black pudding was available for a shorter time. All of that was needed to accompany our eggs at the 'proper' breakfasts desired by both the staff and the guests. We bought our beef, mutton and lamb back, as it were, from the butcher van that came around weekly.

I don't know exactly how many Buff Orpington hens Woolpack kept. There were two hen houses, made out of creosoted boards to prevent hen ticks in two separate fields. Our hens had a good life. They were free to wander for supplementary feed from the grassland. They had to be let out of the hen-house in the morning, and in the afternoon fed with grain, and with grit for the eggshells, the eggs collected, then shut up again at night. They were a big commitment in time for Granda, but children might do the afternoon feed. I was not so good at getting eggs from under a sitting hen, they always pecked me but didn't seem to bother Granda. Should a hen go 'broody', that is show a serious inclination to sit around on eggs, then she was given a clutch of eggs to sit and incubate. This required a special hen coop close to the house for security against foxes and stoats,

Judy and Michael in the Front Field.

and for supervision. Then the hatched chicks and the mother had to be fed and watered and let in and out of the coop.

We had the two cart horses named Black Michael and Judy. Michael was of course black and was taller than Judy and not quite as sturdily built. 'He must have some Arab in him,' hazarded Father. They were shod as necessary with iron horseshoes made, and attached, by the blacksmith at the forge in Eskdale Green. Those were dramatic occasions: the blacksmith in his long leather apron, smudged all over by his trade, including a frighteningly blackened face, the bellows driving the fire, the hot metal being flung around and the sizzle in the water when the shoe was cooled. Since Michael was deemed to be too old to work, most of the time that I knew him he was kept as company for Judy – horses, like dogs, being of a different category to the rest of the stock.

During the war we were just coming to the end of the time when horses were crucial for draft and transport. When not working, Judy and Michael stayed together in the field, often standing side by side at a fence, ostensibly to get some human attention. Judy was a handsome bay Clydesdale; she pulled the plough or hay mower or the side-rake that turned the hay into rows. She pulled hay carts, or any other cart with any other load. I have a recollection of the turnip drill as well, but not clearly how it worked. We did occasionally get a bareback ride ourselves, and it was not at all easy to hang on, with that massive side-to-side roll, and the width of the back.

Michael and Judy were the remnants of an earlier, and larger group at Woolpack, of four horses and a pony. Photographs show these horses and the pony with Father, and with his sister Nellie, the latter in a long dress, on I think Burnmoor. One photograph has Harter Fell in the distance.

Horses were permitted on this moor at certain times of the year by the rules on the common grazing. In my time Judy and Michael were always on the valley floor.

The sad fact of the matter was that this was just at the end of the horse era. Even during my early years at the Woolpack we used an old lorry that roamed around the hay fields, a makeover from an earlier Woolpack car, a 1924 Austin 20. While the hay was being loaded Alastair and I might drive the lorry in tandem, one on the seat steering, and the other working the pedals on the floor, since we were both too short to be able to do both together. And then the little Ferguson tractor arrived during or shortly after the war, and virtually took over, in spite of Father's misgivings about the damage wrought by the exhaust on the plant life directly exposed to the tail pipe. The tractor, more than anything else, heralded the changes taking place in farming.

Early on we had plenty of rabbits living wild in the fields and intacks. Then myxomatosis arrived in Eskdale and they were pretty well wiped out. The large colony at the near end of Holm Bottom disappeared. Myxomatosis was brought from Australia where it had been introduced in order to control a huge non-native rabbit problem. I do not believe our rabbits ever recovered their numbers. Until then rabbit was a regular part of the local diet, Granda used to bring them to the kitchen door just as he

Father as a young man with Woolpack horses.

did a hen. It was most often Granny who got to skin the rabbits and pluck the hens, but Father often obliged.

Our fields were classified as to whether they were rough pasture, permanent pasture, hay fields or arable. The hay fields were allowed to grow fodder to feed the stock through the winter. If it had been a bad summer then supplementary fodder might have to be bought from areas with a kinder climate. Stock was rotated around fields, and this allowed the grass to re-grow after grazing. A selected field had to be ploughed for vegetables, mostly potatoes and peas, beans, carrots, onions and turnips for the house, and mangel turnips for the stock. The 'stitches' (furrows) in the vegetable field were heavily fertilized with cow manure and animal bedding.

Early on, Auntie Gladys had raised the subject of crop rotation at our school – no talking down to children there. Crop rotation was basic to keeping the farm productive and everybody fed, especially so in a tough place with a thin soil and a lot of rain. We could not grow barley or wheat, even hay and oats were a struggle. The historic ideal in the area was plough ley (pasture) in year one and sow oats. I recall seeing oats under sown with legumes (vetch certainly) to naturally 'fix' nitrogen in the soil. In year two the crop was root vegetables for the stock, and vegetables for the farmhouse. Year three could be oats again and under sown with a mixture of good grass seed that included perennial rye grass. Rye grass was nutritionally good and could tolerate wet soil. The grass mixture would include white clover, also valuable to fix nitrogen. Year four it was pasture again and kept so for a variable number of years, how long depended a lot on the number of ploughable fields available. Farms in Eskdale had few fields to choose for ploughing so crop rotation was a thing that took experience and judgment. In the war there was pressure to plough permanent pasture for root crops to be able to feed more stock. Also the cover on permanent pasture might be improved by ploughing and reseeding. Altogether, there was plenty to keep young people thinking and active.

Owing to Granda, our garden was a huge success and much admired. It was productive with vegetables, salad components, soft fruit and flowers – again the fertilizer was cow manure and bedding. Strawberries did very well at Woolpack, and we had black and red currants and gooseberries, some raspberries, and loganberries. The soft fruit was used as desserts in the summer and the rest made into jam. We had heavily fertilized heaps for vegetable marrows. Tomatoes were grown in the green-

Front Field, planting vegetables – Alastair and Father.

house at the bottom of the garden. The greenhouse had its own water butt; if that ran dry then water had to be carried in by bucket since Granda did not have a hose. Such a garden was labour intensive and we were constantly in and out. It had to produce something for every day all year round, so we grew some cold weather vegetables as well, an important one being leeks.

Granda looked after the orchards too. He would do any pruning, but I have no memory of spraying. The old orchard in front of the longhouse was no longer productive. There were two rhubarb beds, one in the orchard and one in the stack yard. The newer orchard on the bank was productive; we got a large crop of apples, plums, greengages and damsons. The ground under the fruit trees and on the bank was carpeted with daffodils and lilies in the spring. During winter the cooking apples were stored in one of the guest bedrooms in the annexe, spread out on newspaper on the top of the metal bed springs. The apples were so placed so as not to touch each other. It was cool there, and they were watched and taken as needed. Plums and damsons were used as desserts in the summer or bottled or made into jam for later.

As children, we learned the hard way not to make any noticeable depredations into our own orchards. Granda was watchful. Like Mother, he

Natives of Eskdale, left to right,
Alastair, Hughie, Margaret, Barbara and Helen

was preternatural about our thoughts. If we fancied raiding orchards then we might try the few old ruined farmsteads nearby, they still had possibilities. One ruin near Peeplice Hill, on the Hodge How side, was good for apples, and Underbank, on the far side of the Esk down towards the church, was good for unusually sweet gooseberries, both red and yellow. Underbank's lane end grew very bitter sloes, to be avoided raw but which could be used for sloe gin. Alastair tried making it. An interesting thing was that although we had a bar in the house and a cellar out the back, we practically never had a drink, even when of age. At Christmas Father offered us a modest sherry – not too good a brand.

7

Trinity Hall plus Ultra – More Beyond

Trinity Hall is peripheral to the Eskdale story, nevertheless it was part of my time there. It was an old-fashioned school, of a kind that I doubt could exist today; and for me the beginning of an education that fitted me to live elsewhere not that I ever felt any strong desire to leave.

It was the government's Beveridge report, in the middle of the war, which decreed that all children should be offered free secondary schooling, with some choice on kind of school. The intent was to 'level the playing field' across the nation. This was the first such offer to Eskdale children, and I was just at the required age, eleven, and believe that I was one of the first two pupils in my school to be eligible – later it was a possibility for every child.

Auntie Gladys got us ready to take the new eleven-plus exam for grammar school. This new exam to identify the academically inclined was largely an IQ test and used to select about twenty per cent of the age group. A classmate, Steve Roberts, and I went to Millom for the day to take the exam, I don't recall how. Subsequently the headmaster came to Boot School and he interviewed me. We sat on a bench in the war memorial, our feet in the shillies (small beach stones). He seemed mostly interested in my family – for instance, what did my father do? It was a good time in my life, I was bright and came right back with the answers. He offered me a place at Millom Grammar. Unfortunately, it was miles away on the coast, and it was just not practical: no transport nor boarding option and I was eleven. In addition, nearby Barrow-in-Furness was somewhat militarized, its shipyard being seriously bombed. Millom Grammar looked unrealistic; still, the government's new expectation of a secondary education for all was there.

My attendance was simply put on hold. A year passed. It is possible that nothing might have happened at all; I could have slipped through the cracks, but Auntie Gladys, ever on the side of education, appeared in the Woolpack kitchen and made a huge fuss. After such a fuss she normally went into the annexe and sat with a sympathetic Granny and Granda for a while wondering if she had gone too far. They were always responsive and open with Auntie Gladys in a way that they weren't with my parents. Thus my problem become public knowledge. It was solved by Griff and Nina, the Misses Griffin and Marshall, who happened to be staying; we knew them well, and best of all they were teachers. They suggested that I attend the private boarding school for girls at which they taught – Trinity Hall, in Southport, Lancashire, where Miss Lobb taught English and was headmistress.

Later the same problem for Alastair was solved by another guest, Mr. Ikin, headmaster of the prestigious Public School of Trent College for boys in Nottinghamshire. By the time that Hughie and Helen, and Barbara, were of secondary age, our own county had thought it through. The solution being that children from the isolated heads of the valleys would go to state boarding schools in Keswick. Overall that was less of a culture shock for country children: and so an easier transition and closer to home.

Alastair and I had to travel a lot further to our schools and stay there for the entire fourteen week term. We usually spent the half-term holiday at school as well; only very occasionally was there a visit from parents, since petrol was rationed it was not possible to drive far. Griff and Nina took me out at half term, on country walks around Ormskirk or to the beach. We might have coffee and extravagant cakes on Lord Street, and after the war they bought me my first peach. Alastair's classmates and mine were alike in that they were drawn from all over the country but were from entirely different demographics. Trent was bigger and more affluent; whereas Trinity Hall was religious and modest.

Everything about Trinity Hall was modest. It was founded in Victorian times for the daughters of Methodist ministers and missionaries and not well endowed. Methodist clergy were not at all privileged: they lived on 'circuit' going from manse to manse, and all that was thought necessary for them was provided by their successive chapels. But we were to discover that Trinity Hall's brother school of Kingswood at Bath was on a grander scale.

At twelve, I was suddenly plunged into a different world: urban, religious, and war-time. I think that Trinity Hall's mission statement must have been to prepare its girls for a 'calling': that is for a life devoted to the church, or the acceptable female occupations of nursing or teaching, and not unlikely in a far flung part of the Empire. We were to hear a lot about missions in Africa and India; and at least two of the staff had been missionaries. As yet, there was no hint at Trinity Hall that all of that was to change. In the end I think that Trinity Hall succeeded in their aim: the girls did go into the feminine helping professions. For me, Trinity Hall was goodbye to skipping about in Eskdale.

My belongings for the term were packed into mother's tin trunk, and went with me on the train. An A was added to the ML (for Mary Leece) painted on its side; so I became MLA, giving me a possible second name having none of my own. My siblings all had two names. But as Granny pointed out, I was a month old before they could decide on a first name. In the war it was common for civilians to sit on their suitcases in the train corridor, since the compartments were often filled with exhausted servicemen who were asleep, and that is how I remember those early journeys. It was an adventure. I was alone but I managed a train change successfully and got to the right address.

Since Southport was a seaside resort it did not get many bombs, but the Port of Liverpool was not far away and a major target. It was most likely due to the relative safety that Southport's Grand Hotel on the beach, was converted into a hospital for American forces. Our 'crocodile' walks to the beach, two by two, graded by height, were enlivened by the sight of recuperating Americans sprawled about on loungers and beach chairs. Heaven knows what they made of us, walking so formally dressed, hats and gloves, in our crocodile.

Trinity Hall was spartan to an alarming degree, and with very little thought given to the comfort of the girls or to recreation. Of course, the war did not help. There was a great deal of religion and plain living; indeed Jane Eyre's stark Lowood School comes somewhat to mind. Many years later a talented classmate, Eileen Parkes, said at an Old Girls reunion, 'We were dirty, we were hungry, we were cold, we were badly taught and repressed.' Coming from a Methodist Minister's daughter it was harsh judgment indeed, but it seemed to me to be entirely fair. I would gone even further and added boredom and the absence of rationality.

Trinity Hall School was housed in two buildings. The old Trinity Hall building, dated back to 1875, was on Duke Street in Southport, and used as a residence for the senior girls. Wintersdorf, a mile or so away in Birkdale, was the junior residence and also had the classrooms for daytime instruction for the entire school. The seniors walked to and from Wintersdorf six days a week. Wintersdorf was architecturally less impressive than Trinity Hall, but had more space. Whereas the Trinity Hall building had only a small lawn and one piece of asphalt of tennis court size, Winters-dorf had generous grounds that included three grass courts with a sports pavilion and a hard court used for either tennis or netball, it also boasted swings and a see-saw. One side of the property was a wild section with sand hills and trees, we were permitted to play on one half of that, the other half being nominally out of bounds. Not long after I left, in about 1954 I believe, the old Trinity Hall building was found to have some kind of rot, and the senior girls had to move to Heukensfeldt, a neighbouring property to Wintersdorf, where we had earlier climbed a wall to use the outdoor swimming pool.

Since the school was independent, Trinity Hall was not subject to any kind of official inspection. There was an all male Methodist Board of Governors that I once saw at one of their routine meetings. I had been se-lected by the staff on duty to present a courtesy buttonhole to one of them, the chairman I suppose. He said 'May I?' and kissed me, whereupon the entire board fell about laughing. For a long time I blamed the afternoon dress that had led to my selection, the pattern on it is fixed in my mind.

The old Trinity Hall building was side by side with the impressive Trin-ity Church, both were in the same Gothic style. The church could seat 775 persons and had been much admired by John Ruskin who thought it the finest Non-Conformist church in the country. That the two buildings were handsome and historic did not save them. Years later I saw that Trin-ity Hall had been taken down, all that remained was the perimeter wall. I am told that Trinity Church has gone the same way – Ruskin notwith-standing.

It may seem curious to write first about the food situation and war-time rationing, instead of the academic standing of the school, but that is what hit me when I first arrived. The poor food, so badly cooked, was a fearful shock. I had only eaten fresh food, well cooked. To be fair, and to give an idea of the time, it is worth reviewing the weekly war rations. The back-ground to the problem was the country was blockaded by U-boats and the sailors of the Merchant and Royal Navies were risking their lives bringing in essentials. The carnage and loss of ships was frightful. At the outset of the war, I am told, about 70% of Britain's food was imported, and so feeding the nation became a major concern. The government ran a rationing system by coupons, in order to ensure that all received enough food on which to live; a bit of deja vu for most since there had been ra-tioning in the First World War, just over twenty years before.

Food rationing did not affect the Woolpack so much but in the urban areas it was drastic. The official weekly ration, per person, was as follows:

> four ounces bacon or ham
> eight ounces sugar
> four ounces tea
> two ounces cheese
> two ounces butter
> four ounces margarine
> two ounces lard
> one pound preserve
> one egg or one packet of egg powder

Twenty four points were allowed for tinned and dried food, three and a half pints of milk for the under eighteens, and a tin of milk powder every eight weeks. One shilling and two pence worth of meat was allowed. Vegetarians could get other protein in exchange for meat, but unfortunately Trinity Hall showed no interest in that provision as they did not recognize vegetarians. Sausage was rationed for only two years, but it was not at all clear what was in it; we were always dissecting it at table making an uneducated guess. Curiously bread was not rationed until after the war. Nor was fish rationed but it was understandably in short supply, since the fishermen, although not in uniform, faced much the same hazards as the navy. There was little fruit, tropical fruit especially, the few oranges around were reserved for the very young. Vegetables were not rationed but not easily obtainable in the towns either; anyone lucky enough to have access to a bit of earth grew their own.

It is true my two and a half junior years at Wintersdorf were the war years but still the low standards of cleanliness and catering, and the pilfering of food by the part-time kitchen staff, were unforgivable. It was just as well that we were not front line troops, and that no-one was depending on our war-effort. My mother could have cleaned up the kitchen, hired reliable staff, monitored the supplies, and ensured that care went into the cooking without skipping a beat. We might even have grown some vegetables ourselves. Matron, who was in charge of domestic matters at Wintersdorf, hired casual daily help all the way from Liverpool and the train fares must have been costly. Under matron's supervision, they produced dreadful meals in a filthy kitchen. Girls on kitchen duty observed the staff packing carrier bags with school food, a lot of it in the original wrappers, every afternoon as they left. I hope that we were feeding poor and needy families in Liverpool, but the food in original wrappers could easily have been sold. It all sat oddly with the high-minded and religious precepts constantly drummed into the girls. I can only guess what would have happened if a child had stolen from the kitchen. Certainly, the punishment would have been severe and led to a letter home.

Wintersdorf meals were indescribable, a real horror to me. Bread came in 'doorsteps' in baskets on the table. The real excitement was when you banged the basket down and the white mites scurried out. We put it down to the veneer of bacon fat on the cane. Often the bread itself tasted of kerosene; I was later to discover the reason, bread and kerosene were kept in the same cupboard in a kind of outhouse. How lucky we were to have margarine and war time jam. We were assured that jam was made with turnips and wooden pits. Breakfast was tinned beans, bacon, or scrambled dried egg, all served on fried bread. It was, by far, the best meal of the day, in spite of the green patches in the dried egg that it seemed prudent to avoid. We did very occasionally get a real egg but that was worst of all. I don't know why they had lions stamped on them; but even non-farmers could tell that they had been stored for much too long.

The lowest point was the main meal at mid-day. Quite often it was a nominal beef stew – blobs of fat floating around in gravy browning; a complete nightmare for a near vegetarian and absolutely no pleasure for anyone else. The stew was accompanied by nearly transparent under-cooked potatoes pressed into a dish, their black eyes unattractively dotted about, and topped off with watery cabbage. After one of these meals the headteacher stood up and gave an extraordinary speech, the gist of which was that science had shown that it did not matter what food looked like or what it tasted like, it was just chemicals to the stomach. Teachers too, seated at the heads of the tables, listened without expression. I wonder what they were thinking.

My mind goes blank over Wintersdorf desserts. There was nothing like the old English puddings, and there could have been, the ingredients were available. An exception was a sticky syrup pudding that was just edible. There was a milk junket, looking and tasting like nail polish, which had to be forced down if in public. The only fruit we normally saw was dried bananas, though we did once we get a crate of lemons – how I don't know, the hopeless kitchen gave them to us to eat 'as is'. It is hoped that no one died bringing those into the country. We could have used the Vitamin C.

We lucky children did get 'care' packages from Canada. These New World gifts containing protein might well have saved lives. There were soy flakes that were made into a milk pudding and it was not half bad. It was gratefully eaten, even though, somewhere along the line, the soy had been colonized by little black weevils. We could cope with that. The cooking killed the weevils and they floated to the top, so that if you pulled back the pudding skin their little black bodies could be carefully skimmed off. Another thing in the care package was peanut butter, an item with which we were totally unfamiliar and we weren't so keen on that.

The milk that we got at break time bore little resemblance to fresh milk off the farm. Perhaps it was watered down, maybe it was wholly reconstituted powdered milk or a combination of fresh and powdered. The suffocating smell of it is with me still; it permeated the basement where it was dispensed, slopped over onto the benches and the floor, formed near transparent concretions, and it was never cleaned up. It was served with a wedge of bread smeared with an appalling dripping, quite unlike any dripping I had known. Later we saw the groundsman use it to oil the swing. I don't know if I need go on. I was learning how some lived during the war, and it seemed one horror after another.

Was there anything good to eat at Wintersdorf? We had a daily spoonful of cod liver oil and malt, a life saver, and I think a government war time requirement. Tate and Lyle syrup was strangely abundant and welcome; there must have been a pre-war stash somewhere. Sunday morning was a reprieve with a slice of superior delicatessen type ham and a crispy bun. The daily kitchen staff were not there that day, and the assistant matron appeared to be in charge. She was a young person and seemed more efficient, certainly friendlier. Once we uncovered a treasure trove in the air raid shelter. There were tins of dry biscuits with barley sugar sweets. As you can imagine they didn't last long. It was a good job that we were not personally bombed and in a real emergency, or our crime would have been exposed. Like mice we found what we could. I won a daisy eating competition, seventeen in all, in a challenge with the hands behind the back crawling along the ground. Hawthorn berries too disappeared from the grounds.

Interestingly we were to find that the food at the senior Trinity Hall building was better looked after and cooked with care – so we knew it could be done. The atmosphere in that building was much more pleasant, and it was even clean. The reason was a different matron in charge, and two full time maids, Annie and Millie, both decent and sympathetic ladies. Since we had chores in both Trinity Hall and Wintersdorf kitchens, we became quite familiar with the secrets of both. Trinity Hall's kitchen was friendly and clean, including the maids room, Wintersdorf's was a nightmare, with a suffocating foul air and the lingering odour of gas, the maids room too awful to enter. Sadly, since the whole school had the mid-day main meal at Wintersdorf, there was no way that we could escape its kitchen.

What of our bedrooms at Wintersdorf? The dormitories ('abodes' to us) took six or so girls each. I close my eyes and try to think if I saw anyone ever cleaning at Wintersdorf, and I come up with nothing. We had a bed, a dresser, and a small locker each, and a complicated system of dark cubicle curtains. The curtains a drab olive colour, very Victorian, out of the ark even, like a hospital but more funereal, and most curiously they were never drawn, just collected dust in the corners. The framework for the curtains was substantial and even strong enough to be climbed and some of us did that for entertainment. Our labelled laundry was collected once a week, 'in 'eaps', as demanded by Maddy, the matron in charge. We had baths twice a week, in four inches of water, two girls to one tub. The four inches was a war time restriction; the two girls at a time an add-on economy. For some reason washing one's own hair was an absolute no-no. Rimmers, who had enjoyed the salon contract since 1930, came in to do that, with a coal-tar shampoo – afraid, I think, of livestock. Nothing could have survived the shampoo, it reeked like sheep dip. It was a real extravagance in the school's straightened circumstances.

As with everything else at the time we tended to make the best of it. I developed a clandestine business of drawing cartoons of the staff and sold them to the girls. A goodly number ended up behind the two permitted photographs on the dressers – they were later recalled in a school magazine, as a class member had made a collection. The cartoons were part of the feeble, ongoing, underground protest. Another manifestation was after lights when one of us read the others to sleep with the aid of a torch. Each night's reader was selected for suitability to the particular piece of literature. And Speck (Jill), still a close friend, once entertained us by going down the fire escape in pyjamas, climbing up a nearby tree on the sand hills and chirping like a bird into our window. We could laugh at anything.

Occasionally we managed some kind of midnight feast in the dormitory. The most memorable occasion was in the Fourth Form on the eve of our departure for the senior school, an event of grandeur and held in the sports pavilion, with its lockers of hockey sticks and netballs. The midnight route took us through the studio, past the portrait of Lawrence of Arabia, out of a back window, down a fire escape, and over the tennis courts. The food, whatever it was, had been secreted during the day in the Ivy Hole; regrettably it had first been discovered by the slugs. We hung our blankets over the windows, since we had to disguise the night-lights and torches.

Later I heard that the assistant matron and a music teacher had observed the activity, but wisely turned a blind eye. Not Maddy, she was waiting for us in the dorm when we got back. She stood heavily and squarely in the middle of the floor and gave the usual inexplicable lecture on the lives of her daily kitchen help. On this occasion it was something about their 'sticks of furniture'. Speck later said that she thought that the phrase referred to the ministers way of life – and it just could have been. That was the thing with Maddy, to her the girls were always in the wrong, either too middle class and so privileged, or too pitiably poor and easy to take advantage of. It was not easy to make a logical connection between furniture and our midnight celebration. Our guffaws under the blankets were difficult to stifle. In fact our hilarity was more or less continuous, it didn't need much to set it off. About the same time as our major midnight episode, some girls got right away from school, ran away that is, and got all the way home.

What happened when we were ill at Wintersdorf? We had a sanatorium and a resident nurse and in a dire emergency a doctor could be called upon. In theory it sounds workable; in reality it was just another mess. Unbelievably the food there was worse; it was cold often smelling and tasting of gas, since the nurse carried it up to the 'san' after the dining room had eaten. The good thing was that she did not stand over us, so that the worst of it could be quietly flushed away. One term we had a huge mumps epidemic. Those in the 'san', and in a co-opted dormitory or two, were diagnosed with mumps, the rest of the school walked around on a normal schedule, being described as having only swollen glands. I did spend some time alone in the 'san' with a serious case of measles. The nurse went into town without notifying anyone and left me with a high fever. Fortunately, the assistant matron thought to come along to check and finding me delirious set about bringing my temperature down; I lost some hearing.

It doesn't seem surprising to me that some girls didn't do very well psychologically, and were left with issues to be treated after leaving. Years later, Eileen reported that an old girl she knew consulted a psychiatrist at the University of London, and he had moaned, 'Oh no, not Trinity Hall again'. Somehow I became responsible for looking after a girl in the year below me, who had breakdowns that culminated in distressing screaming fits. I made an arrangement with her that when she could not cope, she was to meet me at a default location, and in prep time it was the library. Hearing a scream I just stood up and excused myself to 'gov on vig' (staff on duty) who did not question me at all, and I went to calm her down. I don't understand even now why the child was ignored by the staff; it was an astounding lack of care – shades of Lowood – and she wasn't the only one.

How much religion did we get? Well, the maximum. So much so, I would say, that it did regrettably lead to a certain cynicism amongst the girls from the Manse. Grace was sung before and after meals and the morning assembly was mostly a sung religious service. Actually, I do confess, I miss the constant singing. (Thinking of Julian Barnes – who didn't believe in God, but who, nevertheless, missed him.) We had Scripture classes in the course of which the head pounced delightedly on my King James Bible (1611), the others had the Methodist Revised version in everyday language. She seemed genuinely partial to the older, grander, version. There was no doubt of her faith; it must have been why she got the job of headmistress.

Sundays were sober indeed. There were the morning and evening church services. There was also a religious class in the afternoon, sometimes addressed by a lay preacher. I regret to say some girls teased them mercilessly. Not me, I had Auntie Gladys looking over my shoulder. In addition there were two completely silent hours. The first being silent reading of some worthy book, checked first for suitability, followed by an hour of letter writing home, and it is possible that the letters were censored as well, I don't think we sealed them.

We did not complain about anything, we just adapted. However by lights-out on Sunday night there might be a wild reaction, a spontaneous break out of noise and manic behaviour that was difficult for the staff on duty to control. On one of those nights, when we had all settled down after such an upheaval, Tibby came back to the 'abode', having been to the 'across' (bathroom), to find a figure standing before her in the gloaming. She tapped the figure imperiously on the shoulder, at the same time gave an imitation lecture as from the headmistress. Lo and behold, it was the head, interrupted in full flow! 'What larks!' Dickens could have said.

We walked to Sunday services obediently in crocodile fashion again. Services were long, maybe a bit Church of England really, but with the long Methodist sermon added, in place of a short address. It seemed that we got the long parts of both worlds. The church was a public one, with some of the public sharing the choir stalls with our girls choir. We had a resident Minister and visiting lay preachers. For us, the church was not without its entertainment value. In fact you could see, as the crocodiles entered the church, that spontaneous broad smiles broke out all down the line. There was a giddy and expectant air. We were ready for anything that might translate into fits of stifled giggles and merriment. The pews each had little doors on them that gave a certain amount of privacy. Our challenge was not to be discovered howling uncontrollably on the floor, to be able to keep a modicum of control, this being a holy place. The staff-on-duty, and the headmistress, must have been in an anxious state: the school in public, daughters of the church, etc. This was an age, after all, of ubiquitous school uniform, and standards of public behaviour referring directly to the uniform. Uniform was a give-away in public; we once had to cram ice creams into our pockets when staff were spotted: eating on the street was just not done in those days, and besides we weren't supposed to have any money.

Hypnotism was big in church. We might have a prior agreement to hypnotize, say a member of the public in the choir, at a certain juncture, perhaps to feel nauseous and to throw up. Pairs of eyes and moving lips had an immediate effect on the luckless singer, who was discomforted and reddened, but sadly there was nothing more. The most dangerous times for our ability to control ourselves were non-school solo vocalists, a certain elderly lady's rendering of 'Wa-a-a-ving corn' most certainly won. Many of us lost control that day. Lay preachers were treated shamefully in church too: perhaps it was due to their lack of polish or practice, maybe a certain accent, their earnest posture or their palpable sincerity. (One could almost see Maddy's point of view on the girls.) The regular minister in the pulpit might be treated to pepper bombs, brown paper bags containing pepper were popped right under him as he spoke from the pulpit above. We watched expectantly, but he never sneezed, indeed he appeared disappointingly immune. More likely he saw it all – the Trinity Circuit cannot have been much desired as an appointment.

One particular joke of ours in the junior school was to go to church minus a skirt. Under our navy coats, the hats with the blue and gold ribbon and crest, were the white blouses and school tie, the navy blue school knickers, and the suspenders from our liberty bodices holding up the black stockings. Properly we also had our gloves. We walked like this through the town in crocodile. The dare was that should it be hot in church, we might be ordered to take off our coats. Naturally this would have been a newspaper-worthy event, but regrettably it never happened. Later on, when we discovered the cartoonist Ronald Searle's 'St Trinians' it seemed to have been written just for us. The name, and the uniform were a fit, most especially the iconic black stockings with their suspenders. The St Trinian's girls overarching 'bolshiness' was pretty much our mindset. We were a world apart. I believe that Searle was drawing, and writing in a prison camp in the Far East; another war-time incarceration, but one of more consequence.

So how did I fare when I first went from Eskdale into this almost Dickensian situation? Again we are right into food, since there was a very particular trial waiting just for me. At my first lunch, at a table with the house mistress at the head, I refused red meat. Innocently I said 'Oh, no thank you, I don't eat meat'. She eyed me severely and insisted 'Oh yes you do Margaret'. Foolishly, I took that for the state of things. We were not permitted to refuse any food – only to ask for 'a less' twice a week. As a consequence, and on my very first day, my life became a thing of horror and I lived fearfully from lunch to lunch. The way that I coped was to wait until the teacher at the table was looking elsewhere, then I quickly flipped the meat into a linen napkin, and buried it after, on the sand hills.

Unfortunately I was spotted by staff, seen to be by myself daily on the sand hills, and they reached a wrong conclusion. Later, I was told that since I had arrived a term late, after the rest of the class had settled in, that I was diagnosed as having difficulty adapting. Apparently the class was addressed, somehow in my absence, and told that they should help me to settle in – they must have been mystified. No staff member thought to ask me, or any of the class, what I was doing on the sand hills. In this, as in countless other things, the staff were not attuned to real problems. For me the meat business went on for all the years that I was at Trinity

Hall, it coloured my entire school experience.

On my arrival at school in the third form, I got the name Legweak, a humorous play on Armstrong. The name didn't last long, since the class found, to their dismay, that I was intent on being a model student, I was an enthusiastic answerer of teachers' questions, an instant obeyer of Hep, the gym teacher, and her hopelessly delivered orders, was an opinionated artist and a reliable performer in organized games. I was valuable on a team. I had arrived fit. Thank you, Auntie Gladys, and for the physical effort required to live in Eskdale. I became the catcher in the gym, and so the name died. You could hardly entrust yourself vaulting over the 'horse' or the 'box', and be caught by a Legweak. I got elected, and stayed, games captain, all through my school career. It gave me an identity, helped me cope with it all. My nickname became Bug, which was shortened school slang for bright.

I might have been named too soon as I proved not to be in the front rank of brightness, but the name stuck. In the severe system of ranking for academics in which the school indulged, I averaged sixth overall out of the 30 plus in my class. Griff and Nina later opined that I might normally have looked brighter, but that in our year, we had an unusual concentration of the brilliant and talented, girls that stood out in their entire teaching careers.

We certainly had three or four very smart and original girls, particularly gifted in language, drama, music and maths. Trinity Hall was not so enthusiastic about any kind of science or even art. I managed to slack off at chemistry, which didn't immediately appeal, and we were not offered physics. I found the art class uninspiring, but it was graded. Physical education was not graded. Now and then we had some sewing and domestic science which we treated frivolously, but they did count in grades. No-one was allowed to take the scripture exam in School Certificate since if anyone did poorly, it would not reflect well on the school. While I started out as a model student, later I became bored and did just enough to get by. For some reason I felt little pressure to do really well. Latterly, in 5A, the School Certificate year, I regret to say that I was so relaxed as a student that I spent a lot of 'prep' time just drawing.

We were innocent of any formal counseling; but Nina had observed me drawing, so frittering away valuable revision time for the Cambridge School Certificate, and she took me aside to observe, 'You know Margaret, you could fail'. I pulled myself together in time to get seven decent

'O' levels. It was true that I was without direction or a goal, and it would catch up with me.

We did produce a well known actress. I think that drama was so prominent with us was because we were forced to find our own entertainment, so we put on elaborate plays. I sometimes painted scenery that I pinned to drapery, and now and then got the part as some male, or a villain; Sir Guy of Gisbourne in Sherwood Forest comes to mind, slowing down Robin Hood and his Merry Men, with a 'Not so fast gentlemen, not so fast'. Our range was ambitious – we once presented *Macbeth*. We played to the school and any interested staff, and occasionally to the children from the local St. Barnardo's Orphanage.

We had a team identity as the school was locked into a system of randomly assigned Houses. The Houses were in constant competition, divide and conquer if you like, but it did create team players. A strip of the appropriate colour, red, blue or green was sewn onto our school tunic, and we wore a sash of the same colour. After some sports achievement, a special yellow sash was given. For instance, I got my sash as captain of the First Eleven hockey team which I truly enjoyed. At house meetings we had to announce the number of credits won for approved behaviour, and the minuses lost over infractions and shortcomings. The whole house attended these and it was a grisly business.

We played grass hockey with other private schools enthusiastically, even taking on a boys team from the King George V High School. The latter was notable for not following rules. They would 'accidentally' knock girls over, hold hockey sticks shoulder high, were even suspected of having masters on their team. However, St.Trinian's would have applauded our efforts. These would be the same boys that waited for us behind their school wall, after a snowfall. We had to walk past this wall on the way from Trinity Hall to Wintersdorf, and they were waiting with a barrage of snowballs. It was another St. Trinian's moment. We responded in kind from the pavement, but were hampered by having to keep a look out for staff going past in the bus.

The academic staff were on a rota to accompany us on forays out or to church. We came to know those that lived in school best. They were all single, as professional women were at that time. Griff and Nina stood out as good teachers, and were certainly the most dedicated to their students. Of course the war had a role to play there too. As many teachers were at the front or in vital war jobs I knew of at least one not certified as expected, in this case with a university degree. The fact is that Trinity Hall was simply not as good academically as it thought it was at the time; and for a lot of us it was all more of an endurance test than an education. I do concede, however, that we were not overshadowed by boys either in or out of the classroom. So we were saved from having to take a second place or to be constantly reminded what girls were not allowed to do. I imagine that in Victorian and Edwardian times Trinity Hall had looked like a very progressive place. I do think some of the staff were aware of that and took the long view.

Griff taught history and Nina Latin. Griff was Dublin born, educated at Trinity College, so for us, every period of British history was enlivened with an add-on of the Irish Question. Griff appeared curiously uninterested in religion, agnostic even, but later her obituary revealed her grandfather to have been head of the Methodist Synod in Ireland. She once told me that, incredibly, before her family went on holiday, the religious affiliation of the hostelry had to be checked! One could see how her half-hearted approach to religion came about, but nevertheless she must have been committed in some degree to Methodism since she taught at Trinity Hall. She did communicate a real interest in history and literature: she kept up with new writers, revelled in good drama, loved the BBC. Long after I had left school she sent me reading lists. I knew less about Nina, but she was a real academic, had a classic head that could have been on a classical coin, and I still find her Latin derivatives useful.

Both Griff and Nina were totally committed to their girls and sincerely thought Trinity Hall was an admirable school and they once told me I was wrong when I questioned the quality of instruction, told me that in fact I was lucky to be there. (Whatever could lucky mean? That the school was good or was I being saved from a peasant life?) They were forever good friends to me, and inoculated me with their left wing politics. Nina, characteristically, wrote me a last letter when she was dying in hospital, with a diagram as to where the tubes were. There was a certain kind of artlessness and unworldliness in both of them, and they lived like students; but they had an insistent morality and purpose. They were feminists but never spoke of it. They once told me that I was not going back to live in Eskdale, that I would go to university and thereafter be a visitor at home. There it is again, the element of rescue on their side. Or it is possible that they saw some 'writing on the wall' as yet invisible to me.

We did not know what was going on in the war, and thankfully, we were not personally bombed, consequently the bomb that landed on the Sunshine Babies Home, round the corner from Wintersdorf, was a complete shock. By intent, or default, we were protected from the realities of the day. A better war than for many – we can be grateful for that. Our complaints might look like whinging: there were indeed terrible war stories, and likely even worse school experiences. It was the shortcomings at school that bothered us, not to mention the awful, endless, boredom. We could have been kept more informed of the situation, grave though it often was.

May the 8th of 1945 was Victory in Europe Day, and staff took us out in the evening to see the jollification. It seemed that Lord Street was mobbed; absolutely everyone must have come out to celebrate, both civilian and military. It was a reckless scene of laughter, firecrackers, shouting, singing, and drunkenness – an astounding sight. We insulated girls had never seen anything like it. I expect that we were still in crocodile formation as it would be the only way that the harassed staff could keep us in sight. The war in the Far East ended in August during the school holidays, but that would hardly be remarked on in Eskdale as it was then the busy time of harvest.

Life after the war, at the age of fifteen, in the senior Trinity Hall building was pleasanter than Wintersdorf with Maddy. The sandstone Victorian building itself was quite grand. It boasted an impressive curved wooden staircase, Jacob's Ladder to us, leading up from the middle of the main hall and set off by a large stained glass window. The girls didn't use that staircase but I have a memory of Mademoiselle, the Swiss French *assistante*, posing on it. We had a huge basement for recreation, but it contained practically nothing in the way of equipment; a solitary ping pong table arrived from somewhere in our time and that was a life saver. The air in the basement was full of the sound of tinkling pianos from the practice rooms, and we became familiar with everyone's assignments. *Fur Elise* comes back. Most of us took music lessons; there wasn't much else to do. There was a gas fire, though possibly just for the sixth form, used to toast crumpets. There was a huge empty gym, just an open space, no equipment at all, sometimes used for dancing.

Upstairs from the basement, there were three levels: first the classrooms and the staff rooms, the dining room and kitchen, above that the dormitories and staff quarters, and then an attic with more dorm and staff space. There was the elegant girls drawing room where we once heard

George VI speak on the radio, painful for him because of his stammer and not easy for the listeners. That wold be the only time we heard the radio. There were the occasional excruciating invitations to tea with the headmistress, in twos or threes, where the little tea table rattled the cups as we nervously stifled giggles.

Griff and Nina had modest rooms at Trinity Hall for all of their working years. The staff rooms were almost as monastic as ours, but with the addition of a gas fireplace and a couple of easy chairs, a small table, a bookshelf. Griff and Nina were perennially courteous and kind to all. I recall a particular incident that illustrates this. One evening a strange young man was found wandering around the dormitory floor, Griff found him and asked him if she could help. He replied that he was feeling faint, so Griff gave him a chair and went to get him a drink of water. After that it is not clear what happened, presumably she assisted him to the door. Nina was once very thoughtful after the war when I was anaemic, she quietly left egg-nogs for me, at a certain 'drop'.

In the senior school we had a certain limited contact with Southport, which was a handsome town with many amenities, but pretty well restricted for us. We were allowed out briefly on Saturday afternoons onto the elegant Lord Street in twos and threes, any purchases and the amount of money that we possessed were supposed to be monitored. In spite of that we somehow managed to get a few treats in the Lord Street cafes; of course we admitted to little at the debriefing when we got in. Dramatically, an older girl got into trouble for accepting a ride in an open landau through the town, and an ice-cream, from an American serviceman in uniform. Unfortunately it was observed by someone in authority. As usual the head over-reacted and the girl got the ultimate punishment: she was expelled. Years later she was still very bitter about it. For my group, a visit to the city pool to practice for our bronze life saving certificates resulted in conduct marks, which was minus ten for the House, and letters home from the Headmistress.

There were very rare organized outings. There was the film of the wedding of Elizabeth and Philip, the only time we went to the cinema in our entire school career. There were a couple of visits to the ballet. At that time all performances of any kind ended with singing the National Anthem, which raised their profile. We were allowed to go to a boring university extension history course; we only enrolled in order to get fish and chips on the way back, which we ate victoriously as we walked, out of the usual newspaper. We took part in Girl Guide marches around the town, followed by addresses at City Hall. There were the perennial crocodile walks on the beach. On one of those, the St. Trinian's mind-set took over, and our smallest two, at the front of the crocodile, led us straight into the Irish sea, until we were all up to our waists, and then out again. Since we were wearing our uniform summer dresses, we then had a dark blue lower half and a light blue upper half. We walked back to school like this, still in crocodile. The discomfort of wet clothing was apparently worth the hoped-for shock value to the citizenry. The crocodile seemed to be the best place to act up, the luckless staff person at the back of it often ignorant of what went on up front, or even what was facing forward. One frequent ploy was to pull down the day hats over the eyebrows and make demented grimaces. We were constant in our desire to entertain the public.

After the war an astonishing thing happened – a school trip was planned to Paris, the war being well and truly over. Somehow I managed to get on it. People at home were astonished as well; a maid we had mar-velled at the distance involved, was agog about the possibilities open to the new generation. People from home did not normally venture that far. We took the ferry from Folkestone to Dieppe and then the train to Paris, where we stayed in La Cité Universitaire. Other groups were visiting as well, including a party of constantly singing German schoolboys. Sadly the food was on a par with Trinity Hall. In terror, I had to scream, over and over, from the line-up, '*Pas de la viande*' the smell of it was suffo-cating. Parisian students, we understood, had not been doing well either. We were cautioned not to speak to, or to even look at, a 'flic' (a slang word for a French policeman), certainly never to ask for a direction: they were not British Bobbies. Apart from that restriction the trip seemed to be rather lightly supervised.

We saw the many delights of Paris. We explored the Louvre, Versailles, the Madeleine, we climbed Montmartre, giggled helplessly around Napoleon's tomb (amazed, we thought he was a megalomanic), and we must have gone up the Eiffel Tower. We did, somehow, get locked in a shed on top of Notre Dame and were graciously let out by paying a tip. The Louvre was an eye opener. *Pas mal!* The only other gallery I had been inside was that at Southport with Griff and Nina. The only artists I knew were two who stayed at Woolpack. I was not familiar with art books – there were none at Trinity Hall. I had not yet seen the London Galleries. My interest and my drawing seemed to be spontaneous.

The Louvre was the ultimate, miles of art from all over and from many points in time. There were no huge crowds then; the vast empty wooden floor echoes back. The Mona Lisa, for example, was just another small picture discovery that could be viewed close up; there were no barriers at all. As you can imagine the Rubens Gallery was a surprise.

Our ferry trip back home was a different kind of adventure. The sea was suspiciously rough in the harbour, and once out into the Channel the waves towered memorably above the little ferry. At the bottom of the wave, all one could see was water hanging up. Absolutely everyone on board was seasick, and when the buckets were broken out they went quickly from hand to hand. Only one person was not ill. It was the head-mistress. She sat solidly in her mac, with a scarf tied around her hair bun, a few grey wisps blowing about, and laughed with evident enjoyment. I have to say she looked very well and was enjoying a thrill. You might also say that she was the picture of remoteness from her charges. She did-n't help anyone, she showed no concern or empathy, not even apprehen-sion. I have to assume that had the journey got worse and become truly life threatening, she would have accompanied us out in the same style.

Looking over what I have written about my school career, it is aston-ishing that I have devoted so much space to bad food and plain living. A large part of that was being forced to eat meat. Griff and Nina would have been horrified; they were single-mindedly committed to our education.

I left Trinity Hall with a confusing set of subsidiary 'A' levels and no clear idea of what I wanted to do. I had little idea of choosing a subject or a profession in the urban and modern way. I had some chops and changes to come. It was almost rule of thumb that if I dropped a subject, I expected that I would pick it up later. It was always a problem of mine: being interested in far too much, afraid I might be missing something I can only suppose.

8

Inn Work

There came the day when I was mixing dog food when Tyson Cowman, our farm man, took the mixing stick from me saying 'You can't do that'. I stared at him in total amazement and inquired why not – I'd been doing that kind of thing since I could walk – apparently it was because I was a girl. I could not have been more taken aback, and very likely did quite a bit more staring: wild cogitations on the possible implications of this. Tyson had a strong sense of fitness, and this was his way of alerting me to the fact that I should be working inside, that I had reached an age when I would no longer be expected to do farm jobs.

Tyson was always concerned to do the right thing; no-one could argue with that. As it turned out he proved to be quite correct, his timing accurate, it could have been a plot. Tyson was also remarkable in his sense of family history. He once told me where he was when I was born – 'guttering' in the Big Meadow at Paddockwray. He also claimed that, as a child, and just before the First World War, the entire Armstrong family had asked him the way to Woolpack. I have no reason to doubt it.

Girls and women worked in the house, in our case it was an inn, and I had crossed a line from a child to fractionally older. I was now more useful inside. What the sexes did was prescribed, and doubtless there were very good historical and cultural reasons for it. We might only expect to work outside at times when a lot of hands were required in the summer. The rest of the year we worked indoors.

Mother hired local girls to work in the Woolpack Inn, she explained that they were already trained in housework and familiar with our kind of farming, and finally that the relative isolation did not bother them. I am sure she found the locals easier to manage since she knew their families, and the girls time off would be less of a worry. There was, of course, plenty of work to do. At the beginning of the war we were still doing everything possible in the old and traditional way, and it was the same during the war and after it. The problem was that, in the war, only one member of staff was permitted in the inn.

The family on an ordinary working day.

Having only one official help was an obvious difficulty. In the season, there was work for women from seven thirty in the morning to as late as nine at night, seven days a week. After nine the bar was still open but Father was in charge of that. Every evening he was transformed from hands-on farmer to landlord. One nice story has him carrying a guest's cases to his room in the day-time, while attired as some kind of dressed down hand, and being rewarded with a shilling; and then after his transformation, in the evening being introduced as the landlord to the suddenly disconcerted visitor. (A key part of the change of role was aggressive flattening of the hair.)

Fortunately for us serving in the bar at night was not considered woman's work; and just as well as the day was already long enough. Not that our clientele were rowdy – our drinkers were mostly students from the Youth Hostel, with just a sprinkling of locals and passers by. Still we had the license, and so we were stuck with the official hours.

Since we had no formal reception room during the war, or indeed after it, the kitchen was again the headquarters. There was Mother and Granny, Irene Dawson, our one allowed uniformed help for a long time, and us children, and maybe some other occasional and casual help. Father was in and out, wearing his many hats. It was a skeleton staff in view of all that had to be done. The earlier banks of bells on the kitchen walls had already been ripped out: quite gone were the spacious days when there were staff to answer them. Woolpack's style was much changed from its pre-war standards.

Still, there seemed to be a lot of us around, never fewer than a dozen sitting down to eat at the kitchen table. And we could take sixteen or seventeen full time guests in the season, which went from just before Easter to early October, and there were many people droping in during the day. In the absence of a formal reception room, we all had to be alert to someone new walking in, and there were many conversations held at the kitchen door. Callers might come in for lunch or afternoon tea or for a drink in the bar or with just a question. When I waited tables after the war, and the road over Hardknott had been repaired, the number of cars about greatly increased. There might be as many as twenty extra people for lunch and 60 extra for tea. It was important to process them all and to get them out of the dining room before the all important residents dinner. For this reason Mother discouraged the idea of high tea (a later tea and with a protein dish) sometimes asked for, as the dining room had to be set for dinner promptly at seven.

Woolpack could be a very busy place indeed for a waitress: flying up and down the tiled passage all day between the kitchen and the public rooms. And numbers varied a lot from day to day so that it was difficult to plan ahead; and it was not considered reasonable to prepare much food ahead in case it was not wanted. The local culture and the war-time situation, and the 'austerity' after it, simply did not encourage waste. Just occasionally we might be about to sit down, in anticipation of a meal, and an influx would change everything: such an event might take the dish we had just been contemplating for ourselves.

Mother actually preferred to work in the kitchen; she did not really care to be out front, but she was the one who decided whether, or not, we could meet requests. We could usually manage a meal, but we might be full of residents, and so have to re-direct overflow trade to a neighbouring farm. We discouraged one night stays as just too much laundry. Mother was in charge of the bookings for the resident guests. She operated out of a small untidy attaché case with a calendar and a blunt stub of a pencil and an eraser. The case contained the booking letters; if a booking was made by phone we requested a confirmatory letter. The booking calendar was the only planning ahead that was obvious, otherwise Mother carried it all in her head. She normally preferred to do all the cooking herself, but where possible delegated the daily baking, the daily cleaning and all of the serving out front. She was an excellent regional cook. I do remember her once trying out a hired cook, but it didn't work. It would all have fallen apart if Mother had taken a sick day, but I do not recall one – we were all pretty healthy.

The GP occasionally came in, but for a social drink to have a chat with Father in the bar. Once Mother complained about her back, and he joked 'You women and your backs!' Sometimes the doctor had a meal in the dining room, observing that the Woolpack was one place that he felt confident of the food handling, since he often came through the kitchen, he had seen us all at our tasks – even ventured a few suggestions. Mother too, was cautious about eating out.

Granny manned the sink, working on the dishes, the milk buckets and separator equipment, and the vegetables. Then there was the bread both brown (Beacon brown flour) and white. Any fresh game that came in had to be 'dressed', and she might also do that. We were all familiar with the gut. Granny tut-tutted if she found half formed eggs in a hen, and they were a memorable sight: yolks of all sizes. A mistake had been made, the hen should not have been killed as it was not a pullet or gone off laying. Our cooked chicken was very different from a lot of modern chicken, it was more flavourful and made very good soup. Father and Granda also brought in available vegetables and fruit, fresh in season, and out of the storage heaps if not. There were weekly visits of the meat and fish vans. Mother put it all together from what came in daily and what she had on hand: she did not write menus. Different parties might well get different set meals.

We did not gather much that was wild. The berries around were not plentiful enough and at too great a distance. We had plenty of wild hazel, but I only remember raiding that crop as children – along with the red squirrels. In spring Granny sent us out for nettles and Easter Ledges (young dock), they conveniently grew together in an unfrequented corner of the cow field. These, with barley, were the basis of nettle pudding. The ingredients were put into a muslin bag and lowered into boiling water to cook – it was considered to be a spring tonic.

As children we helped where we could. The washing up was endless and at any time we could get co-opted for that. Hughie, as a small boy, sentenced to the kitchen sink at tea time, once humourlessly commented that he had '...seen that jam dish before'. There was a lot of picking fruit or salad ingredients in the garden. I do remember serving draft beer when reaching up as far as the high counter from the barrel tap near the floor was a stretch. Nobody worried much those days about what minors could or could not do. Nowadays I suppose one would see a problem in being served alcohol by a child who had difficulty reaching the counter. To be fair there were a lot of children involved in the 'war effort'; we were fortunate to be making our contribution in Eskdale.

The kitchen was a ceaseless hive of activity. In dizzying sequence, the tables saw cooking and baking preparation, bread making, sandwich making, kitchen meals, trays for the dining room, piles of dirty dishes, piles of clean dishes, laundry to fold or to iron, flowers to arrange, silver or brass to clean. And the tables were all at eating level, not one was at a comfortable working level. And of course there were no labour saving devices of any kind. A sharp knife, a fork, hand whisks, a hand cranked mincer, mixing bowls, pots and pans and wooden boards and a rolling pin was about it. The kitchen ceiling was covered with hooks that held sides of drying bacon and the hams. Sausage too might be on the ceiling, or al-

Steps down to back kitchen.

134

ternatively in the dairy. Meat was kept in a wire cage on the outside north wall of the kitchen at ambient temperature, but perpetually in the shade.

The Esse range was the most important item in the kitchen, it was always hot and working on the next meal. Over the Esse there was a long rack that was used to air ironed laundry. That was old farm kitchen style and a bit of a nuisance in a catering situation. The range had two fires that had to be watched and fed with anthracite as required. One of the fires heated water for the inn, the other the large hot plate with its lid and the three ovens. Enough heat had to be maintained for the demands made at different times of the day, and at some point, we did get an additional smaller range to help with the load. Stacks of dishes were warmed on the top of the range. We used aluminium pans for a lot of the cooking as they were light to lift; but that was possibly our most glaring mistake. The problem was that our water off the fell was acidic from the bogs, and so over time it gradually dissolved the bottoms of the pans. Unbeknown to us at the time we were all getting a daily dose of aluminium.

The dairy was our cold room and held the food supplies and any prepared dishes, also bread, butter pounds, jams and bottled fruit. It was large and cool with a slate floor and slate sconces. It was much later that refrigeration arrived. Everything had to be well managed, and with respect to food safety it was. I do not recall a single case of food poisoning. The vegetables intended for kitchen were partly prepared on a sconce at the back door, before going inside. The incongruously named boot house held the milk and cream; it was also a cool room with the customary slate floor and sconces. It was called the boot house as it also had remnants of supplies for cleaning boots and shoes, a service that largely went out with the war.

Cleaning the guests boots was a hold-over from an earlier time, but some guests still did expect it. They left their boots and shoes at the bedroom doors at night in the hope that they would be cleaned by breakfast. It must have been a big item in the past when there was generous staffing. Father was the only one with a cultural memory of boot cleaning, and the only one who obliged guests in this regard. He cleaned them outside on a sconce in the early morning. I suspect that he had cleaned a lot of boots in his childhood. Cleaning leather boots was important; they had to be dubbined to cope with the wet ground on the fells.

The cream separator was housed in the boot house as was the butter churn. The separator was an Alph-Laval model – a bowl on top held the whole milk, the machine was hand cranked and the cream and 'blue milk' were separated by centrifugal force: they emerged from two different spouts. The cream bowls were set in a line and when enough cream had accumulated it was churned into butter. The 'blue milk' went into the feed for young stock. Enough whole milk was reserved for cooking and for the table, along with a generous quantity of separated cream. The washing of equipment for separating and churning, along with the milk buckets from the byre, had to be done correctly, using hot water.

Another item kept in the boot house were the surplus eggs preserved in water-glass (sodium silicate). They could last months this way; it was a good way to store eggs at the height of the summer laying season.

Serving tables in the dining room was a heavy job as everything was carried on trays up and down the uneven tiled hallway between the kitchen and the dining room. I should know, I did that a lot, and I am sure it was the reason that the transverse arches in my feet dramatically 'fell'. The dining style was traditional in that people ate together at two large dining tables; as a nod to modernity, we also had two small tables. If yet more space was needed, the dining tables in the sitting rooms could be pulled out. We kept any bar only custom in the snug, and later on in an extension that was built between the house and the annexe.

Serving was a complicated business. It was necessary to keep track of where you were with all the parties: greeting, taking orders, seating, checking what was available with the kitchen, serving orders from the bar, remembering which course the diners were on, moving them out of the dining room and into a sitting room for coffee in order to free up space, and then taking the money before they left. We did not write bills; somehow it was all carried in the head. With all the coming and going one had to make sure that diners did not leave without paying. On more than one occasion I had to rush outside to catch a party getting ready to depart; someone having forgotten to pay or thought that someone else had paid. Being the waitress was a hectic job; my sister Helen too, recalls being on the go all the time.

To further compound the job, the old currency of pounds, shillings, and pence was not as simple as the decimalized system. There were twelve pennies in a shilling, twenty shillings in a pound, and a guinea was a pound plus a shilling. We still talked about guineas; and at one time a guinea was our tariff for the day – for a room and all meals. Coins came in the following denominations: farthings, half-pennies, pennies, threepenny bits, sixpences, shillings, florins (two shillings), half-crowns (two shillings and six pence – mercifully full crowns had gone out), and then there were the notes, ten shillings and one pound, and the larger denominations of five or ten. Addition was done in the head: the till did not do any calculating, and I have no recollection of using pen and paper.

The inn had to be punctilious about bar opening times: it was the one thing that police were known to check on – not that we saw much of our policeman as he lived over three miles away in Eskdale Green. We had barrels of both bitter and mild beer and also cider, various other bottled beers, and non-alcoholic cordials. A few spirits were be dispensed in optics that were calibrated to serve the correct quantity. Otherwise, spirits and sweet wines were measured in the old pewter quarter or half-gill tankards, and then tipped into the appropriate glass. Half pint and pint glasses in the bar had to have a government stamp stating the measure. Glasses were hand washed in the bar sink. Table wines, mostly French, were available by the bottle only and stored in the cellar, so they had to be looked for and got to the right temperature before serving. Since we were independent of any brewery, we had freedom in what we sold. Our supplier companies were all local, except for some Scottish beer, and the cider was from somewhere down south, possibly Herefordshire. One story about Father was of him serving a different beer from the one requested. After the customer had left I asked him about it. Father responded sadly: 'They don't know what they want'!

Importantly the bar contained one of the few telephones at the time in the upper valley, and a few locals came in to use it. We were Eskdale 230 and there was an operator – no direct dialing. We might even be asked to make phone calls for a local who came in just for that. Not everyone one was familiar with the phone. There was a lovely story about Granda Armstrong and the phone – he was reported as holding up a stray umbrella and asking the caller at the other end if it was the one she had lost – I am laughing again.

Cleaning was a serious business. Everyday the guest bedrooms had to be tidied up and beds made. Bathrooms were scrupulously cleaned. All the tiled and flagged floors in the public areas and in the kitchen had to be scrubbed on the knees. The sitting rooms and dining rooms had rugs, there was a carpet runner on the stairs, and the bedrooms had rugs. We did not have an electric sweeper early on, but a less powerful rotary one. Our back up was that in the winter one of the jobs was that all the rugs were taken outside and hand beaten on a line, using special carpet beaters or a walking stick grasping the non handle end. That was a long job, and an amazing amount of dust was released.

There was endless furniture and brass to be polished. Fresh flowers from the garden were everywhere and needed constant refurbishment. The furniture was mostly antique, and in those days antique meant more than a hundred years old. Since we were in the country, there was not a lot of dirt around, so windows did not need much cleaning and when they did it was a chamois leather and plain water. Mother sometimes employed our postman to do that since he was at Woolpack for a few hours each day; after he delivered the mail in the morning, he stayed till three in the afternoon when he left to pick up the mail on the way back.

Those in authority could walk into a room and see at a glance what was needed. I would say that the inn was very, very clean but was not in any way fashionable or noticeably had a lot of money spent on anything new. I was once privileged to listen to a young male guest who advanced the opinion that the inn looked a bit worn. I expect it did look worn – a few hundred years worn. Mother's bottom line was cleanliness. To an observer, the outside of the inn was seen to sit well in the landscape, it had an antique look itself. No attempt was made to look like a pub in any modern or aggressive way; we had more than enough work and custom.

The fact is that the Woolpack was a piece of history itself, run on traditional lines. My father did sometimes, in a somewhat professional manner, speak about 'value for money'. His emphasis related to the fact that his family had been in hotel-keeping for some time, and so had a certain assurance about what was important. 'Flash' was certainly nowhere to be seen, there was absolutely no display at all, not even of style; no-one felt a need to impress. However having said that the standards did run to damask tablecloths and napkins, silver cutlery, silver coffee and teapots, and glass and china of solid hotel quality; at the time those things were seen as necessary in the trade – and the quality and design were appreciated. An often quoted line of Keats by the wider Armstrong family comes back 'A thing of beauty is a joy forever'.

In those days it was possible to leave valuable items around in the rooms since callers did not appear to steal until, maybe, in the late 1950s. It seemed to start out innocently enough with beer mats but went on to small antiques from the tables, then a small framed carving disappeared off the wall. Still our young critic had a good point: he did not see anything up-to-date, there was no self-conscious attempt at interior decoration, and there was no attempt at any exaggerated kind of service. Wartime and the austerity after it were not a time of display, and it could be that a certain emphasis on the basics and making do lingered on. Mother's hobby was antiques and she had an entertaining dealer. She laughed about inspecting a likely piece with him. He had licked his finger and drawn it through the dust on the surface and, in awe, wondered: 'Is it hoak?'

Laundry was a huge commitment in time and energy. The wash house had a large boiler with a fireplace under it. On wash day work started early since the fire had to be lit, and the water in the boiler heated. The sheets and towels were brought to boiling then they were hauled out on a long pole, so it was dangerous and heavy work. After the hot water there were two rinses in zinc baths, the last one with added Reckitt's Dolly Blue to whiten the linen. (Dolly Blue was either ultramarine or indigo added to baking soda.) The linen was the fed into the hand-turned mangle which pressed out most of the water. After mangling, everything was flat and folded, then it was taken outside to be pegged on the lines in the Show Field, strung near an impressive oak tree. Hopefully there would be enough sun and wind to dry it all, but this was the Lake District and a shower was always a hazard. If it started to seriously rain you had to run out and get the laundry in, but if the rainfall were judged to be slight then it could stay. When dry enough the laundry was brought in carefully in the traditional local baskets called 'swills' – nothing could be marked by touching the grass with its daisies and buttercups. The swills were made by Billy Hartley of Eskdale Green and composed of thin strips of wood woven over a framework of bent wood in a coracle shape.

Once back in the kitchen, the sheets were folded between two people and put into the airing cupboard, as were the rough towels. The airing cupboard was next to a large horizontal hot-water cylinder in the bathroom. Smooth hand towels, pillow cases and table linen were ironed on a kitchen table using the old flat-irons that were heated on the range top. We could not spend a lot of time ironing personal clothing, that might get what Granny referred to as 'a rough straight-out'. The damask tablecloths required more than one person. Ironing consumed a lot of time, and one had to be careful not to take too much heat from the range, since that was needed for dinner: the hot plate lid could not be up for too long. I think that at some point in the war laundering linen became too much for the hands available and we started sending the hotel linen to the steam laundry in Whitehaven. Packing and unpacking hampers was a lot less time consuming, and there was still plenty of the personal stuff to attend to.

What did we eat in the kitchen? We ate in the traditional country way, not as was presented in the dining room. Kitchen food was porridge oats, eggs and bacon for breakfast, and traditional dishes like mutton stew, maybe chicken, shepherd's pie, or steak and kidney or other pies, at midday. There were always potatoes as farm men required a lot of carbohydrate. Vegetables were according to season. Pease pudding – that was an old one. The dessert was often a milk or bread pudding, or it could be a fruit tart, and it might be served with cream. There was the important afternoon tea at about 3.30pm – bread, butter and jam, scones, biscuits and cakes. All of that was home made. Supper was a lighter meal and eaten promptly at six, it tended to be dinner left-overs, of which there were plenty, or an egg dish, and a lot of salads in the summer. Unlike many city people we ate plainly, but the quality of our food was good.

What did the guests eat? Well not exactly the local stews and pies of the locals, but still very traditional and entirely regional. First there was soup, and then roasts of beef, legs of lamb, ham, with fish on Friday. Steak and kidney was one pie that was customary in the dining room. All entrées were served with potatoes and two vegetables, and with the correct accompaniments. Sunday night was exceptional as the dinner was more relaxed: the main dish was a salad and served with fragrant pots of café au lait – guests often said how much they enjoyed that. A specialty in our area was Cumberland ham and Cumberland sausage and the guests would occasionally be given that, but Mother never made a big thing about it; she tried not to create a demand for it. There was formerly a special breed of Cumberland pig, but it had disappeared I think at about our time.

Guests' desserts were the old fashioned English puddings, bread or cake based, sometimes a milk pudding, perhaps a tart, and fresh fruit in season. Desserts were always accompanied by fresh cream. Then dinner ended with a water biscuit and cheese course, followed by a demi-tasse café au lait. Lunches for the dining room were still fairly formal but had fewer courses than at dinner: there might be casseroles or salads followed by dessert and coffee. It was our dream to be a guest at Woolpack.

Since dishes were traditional, we had no need of a stack of recipe books. Recipes had been learned early; if I ever dared to ask Granny for precise quantities of an ingredient she would look slightly exasperated and say: 'Well, just enough'. There was an antique Mrs. Beeton's recipe

Alastair and Tyson on the Ferguson leading hay, near the postbox.

and household management book, a left-over from Victorian times, that was consulted from time to time. Father joked that its recipes started with 'Take a dozen eggs and a pint of cream.' We still used a lot of eggs and cream, but by our time, Mrs. Beeton's recipes were thought to be excessively rich.

On the rare occasions that Mother was away for the day and Granny was in charge of kitchen meals, we were in for a special treat that we looked forward to. Granny's best meal for the kitchen staff was traditional and authentic; it was our own Cumberland ham and eggs with vegetables, plenty of dripping on the potatoes, followed by our own apple tart and cream. I would just love a meal like that again – real flavours of home grown items. There was nothing low-fat about Granny's cooking: she would have been incredulous with disbelief if she had ever heard of the fashion. She even liked cream in her tea. In a sense the culture thought that fat, and especially cream, was highly nutritious. Father referred to fat as '… the finest food.' The lifestyle was very different then, people rarely had time to sit about.

Quite honestly, to war-weary guests, it must all have looked pretty good: fresh food – the provenance of which was known. The cuisine was of the area. The style of catering continued like this for some time after the war. At some point the trade did change as customers became more numerous and more broadly socially based. At this time the expectation of complete traditional meals at lunchtime disappeared and soup and sandwiches and Cornish pasties appeared in the bar. Such meals were easier to produce and to serve and were less expensive for everyone.

And was there any waste? Absolutely not. There was always an animal to eat the few left over scraps and the scrapings off the dinner plates before they were washed. With all of the home production there was, happily, not much packaging to handle. Bones were about the only thing that persisted as they took time to decay, but even they were helped towards this end by being well simmered for soup stock, and after that gnawed by the sheepdogs.

There were some jobs that were done as required when the ingredients were available, such as butter making, jam making and bottling of fruit. Butter was churned by Granny, given a break occasionally by a child. The cream from the standing bowls were emptied into the churn, the lid screwed down, and then turned by hand. Since the churn was wooden with metal parts, it was heavy and hard work. As the churn turned, you could hear the cream sloshing about, and then as the fat started to separate from the whey, the sound changed. The change could be monitored through a small window in the lid. Near the end, turning became more of an effort, and the butter mass clunked. The buttermilk was then drained off into a bucket, and since it was said to be very good for the complexion, we might drink a bit, and the remainder went into animal food.

The heavy mass of butter was taken out onto slates and fashioned into roughly guessed pounds using ridged wooden paddles called Scotch hands. These took out the remaining buttermilk and worked in the salt. When the rectangular shapes were assembled, they were decorated on top with a slotted pattern. The pounds were loaded onto the butter slates and stored uncovered in the dairy on the sconce where it was cool enough. Amazingly there was an enormous difference in spring and winter butter: in spring it was primrose to buttercup in colour and tasted wonderfully of the spring growth, spreading easily, while in winter it was whiter and more solid, very slightly translucent, and recalled the winter feed.

Jam was made according to season and exclusively from our own fruit, except of course for the Seville oranges that were bought for marmalade.

Our own fruit was bottled for the winter. In winter, cooking apples were taken as required from their cool storage place. We did not can any fruit. We were familiar with commercial tins of food but very rarely used one for anything. In fact, Mother had grave reservations about bought tinned food on grounds of both nutrition and cost, so it was difficult for her to contemplate using any. She trusted neither the metal nor the seal. Father laughed about that as he had all kinds of faith in technology and progress.

Winters in the hotel were given over to the usual farm concerns and to a more normal family life. It was also a time for spring cleaning of all public and family rooms, done slowly and methodically. A few rooms a year might be painted or papered, and we normally did this decorating ourselves. Still, overall, winter was a time of much less activity. We had time to hook rag rugs from strips cut from discarded woollen clothing. A wooden frame was set up and left on one of the kitchen tables since it was an ongoing project. Hooking was our default winter activity, what you did when all else was done or you had just come in, out of the cold, and needed a breather. It was a warm, communal effort that we enjoyed and a relief from the weather outside.

And so it was that in the middle of the war and all of this activity that I went away to school, into a town and got the shock of my life. From the age of twelve I came home for the holidays, first from school and later from university, and I would drop into the work and do my share as if I had never been gone, back into my distinctly female yet familiar role.

– 9 –

My day at the Woolpack Inn

At the end of school term we had a certain special song, from the Sunday School Hymnbook, that we sang loudly and with great relish. 'The happy days have come again, that bring us sweetest pleasure, a time to rest, a time to play and hours of quiet l-e-i-s-u-r-e.' We were ecstatic at being let out, and that was good. The train home was a real pleasure especially when the fells came into view. Sadly, I was not going back to a great deal of leisure – maybe some at Christmas. Mine was not a middle class holiday. For many years Woolpack had to be an immediate family concern on account of the war and the following years of 'austerity'. It wasn't really until after my heyday that things returned to the pre-war situation of reasonable staffing. My Easter and summer holidays were busy indeed, and mostly indoors.

One of the head teacher's rare insights was to announce to all my peers that 'Margaret was worked too hard.' To the family I was just doing what we all did – spending time away at school was the oddity. I was older and finally truly useful, and I have to say that I did not question the situation, in fact I enjoyed both the work and the guests. The busy farm kitchen and the leisured guests were two very different worlds. I laughed my way around the Woolpack Inn, very likely too much, as there have been one or two past guests who recalled it.

The drill was pretty much the same every day and for all of my school and university holidays and for a gap year in between them: I was waitress, bar maid, chamber maid, cleaner, general kitchen help, greeter, cashier, and for a while, baker. Every day was hectic in our farm and inn combination kitchen. The steady stream of people came even though no-one would have dreamed of advertising. We were, of course, on the Ordnance Survey maps – marked as an inn. During the war it was obvious to the guests that they should help out, and even after – well into the 'austerity' period – some of those so trained continued to clear tables, dry dishes or do small jobs. The guests liked the informality.

Luckily, the day didn't begin so early in the inn. I got up about 7.30am and washed the tiled floor in the hallways; we were super clean. In order to dry the floor all the downstairs doors had to be opened to get a breeze going through. Since we had no central heating there was no heat to lose. There might be fires to lay in the sitting rooms: paper, thin sticks and small pieces of coal and then wood. There were a few mats to be shaken outside – quietly so as not to disturb the guests. The staircase had to be hand swept quietly, there was no question of noisy equipment, or of any banging about. After that I might take a breather outside, especially if it was a sunny morning, even get down to the river for a few minutes. Taking a pause in the fresh air and a look around. Get lost in a bit of countryside for a few minutes – and in spring it was spectacular with the sunshine and the new growth.

Then it was a hasty dish of oatmeal porridge with the family and staff, and for me it was off to finish laying the tables in the dining room. I had to fill the milk and cream jugs and the marmalade dishes, put the toast into racks, and generally get everything into the right place. Father was on toast duty: he made it flat on the hot plate, then it was cut diagonally. Obviously, by the time the guests got the toast it was cold, dry and hard, but that's how we liked it. It had a quite distinctive character – especially with the homemade butter and homemade marmalade. The idea of warm soggy toast would have got nowhere, except under scrambled eggs. Mother would be down by 8am to start on the guests' proper English breakfasts. At exactly 9am I sounded the gong in the old building and also outside, so that guests in the annexe could hear, as well as those strolling about on the shillies at the front. People would drift into the dining room, not quite as prompt as they were for dinner. The kitchen door was dramatically propped open for me to rush in and out with the trays or with the plates ranged up my arms.

There was no choice in any course, except for the very few who advised us of known health problems. It was old inn style in that guests ate the same meal and together on the large tables. Indeed I was a bit unnerved by those who wanted to know about alternative dishes – like a certain demanding Guggenheim (he was Gug to us). I had to discover how many wanted tea, and how many coffee. At that time it was café au lait served in coffee pots, and the teapots came with extra hot water pots. I used the mahogany sideboard as a temporary place to lodge the dishes in transit.

The first course was oatmeal porridge with cream or milk, and the main course was bacon, or ham, eggs in some form, accompanied with some addition like tomato, mushroom or batter fritters or possibly black pudding or sausage. After that there was toast and marmalade. All the time I had to keep an eye out for any required coffee or tea refills. It was all organized and efficient and there was quite a bit of conversation back and forth. I enjoyed serving; I got to meet a lot of people. I did not find it stressful at all – with the exception of my feet.

When it seemed that everyone at the breakfast tables were served then there were other urgent tasks waiting. I had to rush upstairs and start on the bed making. After a bit of this I had to be back downstairs to check first how the guests were getting on in the dining room and then on into the kitchen, as by now the sandwich making would have started in earnest and I had to help with that. The sandwiches had to be ready as soon as possible as it was expected that nearly everyone would be fell-walking for the day, and our aim was not to keep anyone waiting.

Sandwiches were two slices of brown and two of white bread with a meat, egg or cheese filling. Sometimes there were slices of tomato or cucumber, but not so much that the sandwiches would become too soggy before they were eaten. They could be life-saving on the fell, especially valued in a rainstorm crouched under a rock. There was also a slice of a fortifying homemade fruit cake. The whole meal was wrapped in a certain way in a piece of grease proof paper, cunningly leaving a paper separation between the sandwiches and the cake. It was secured without benefit of string or elastic – only by tucking in the folded edges of the paper. Guests supplied their own flasks for their preferred drinks. The packages and flasks were put out on the hall table ready for pick up and monitored until all requests were met. That was it then; most of the residents left quickly for the day. Some would come back for tea about four and some not until dinner at seven. Sometimes, the guests could come back wet if it had rained, and we would have to cope with their dripping clothing and soggy boots in the kitchen at the stove amidst the dinner preparation.

After the rush of breakfast and sandwiches we reverted to a less frenetic pace. It was at this time that the farm men came in from milking and we all finished breakfast together. We had the proper breakfast course and toast. It was at Woolpack that I learned to eat a meal in ten minutes flat: if you couldn't do that then there was just a chance that a meal might be missed altogether.

After our breakfast the dining room was to be fully cleared and made ready for lunch. There were bedrooms to finish, and those where guests were leaving had to be thoroughly cleaned, along with the bathrooms. Then it was a bit of sweeping and general attention to the public rooms downstairs. One learned to go around with a critical eye on the look out for dust or disorder. For a while I baked the daily brown and white scones, biscuits, and cakes. I cheerfully gave up the baking when Helen came back from Atholl Crescent in Edinburgh. There she was formally trained in catering and I took delight in pointing out that she was now an expert. That would possibly be the first indication to Mother and Granny that I was not fully committed to domestic skills. Indeed, in this regard, I was ultimately going to be a disappointment to them.

My training spoiled me for hotels, since it became automatic to check for shortcomings, and they are not hard to find. One easily comes to question the number of stars. We were patterned before stars became universal, but we knew about them, and perhaps even felt them to be concerned with less important features. Father preferred to be outside any official rating system, but for a while we had an RAC (Royal Automobile Association) sign. The sign was given up over a disputed technicality. Over the years I have often found myself amazed at the enthusiasm, innocence even, of those raised in private homes, at the prospect of staying in an hotel. For that matter, a training in table-waiting doesn't do one any favours in a restaurant either. I am often dismayed by the lack of training, inattentive staff blind even to the needs of the customers, interrupting conversations, picking up dishes too soon and most particularly before all the party are finished. And then, like our GP and Mother, I worry most about the kitchen I can't see.

By noon the bulk of cleaning and some preparation had been done, and we had our main meal of the day along with the outside staff. And then the callers came; some for the bar and some asking for lunch, along with one or two of our own residents who had opted not to walk far on that day. There were different groups of people to deal with all at the same time and at different stages of service. Lunches were still proper meals at that time, that is at least two courses, if not three, followed by coffee. With every meal request, it was necessary to check with Mother on what was available or possible. Lunchtime was actually the most unpredictable and challenging time of day; the usual set meals for residents were simpler for the waitress and the kitchen. After lunch we cleaned up and aimed to get an hour break. I would go outside, Mother and Granny not so much, they must have rested, although Mother might do some gardening.

Promptly at three in the afternoon it was staff tea, and after that the callers started again. In those days, afternoon tea was popular, a big starch and sugar binge, of course. But ours was very much improved by the fact that it was all home made and fresh. We served our own bread and scones with our own butter and jam, followed by biscuits and cakes with the tea. This could be a very busy time but was more straightforward to produce. We might serve tea in the sitting rooms as well as the dining room. Tea trays were large with starched and ironed linen tray cloths. With all of the dishes, and teapots (often silver) the trays were quite heavy and awkward to carry up and down the hall. Tea-trays incurred yet more laundry and yet more polishing of silver.

At six o'clock it was kitchen supper; seven o'clock it was dining room dinner. There was a kind of adrenalin rush about dinner that was addictive. There was a moment when we were all set, all the food was at the correct stage: the soup, the roast or other protein dish, the vegetables, the sauces, the desserts, the cheese and biscuits, the drinks. Mother was poised at the range, Granny already at the sink with the pans, and I would ring the gong and prop open the kitchen door, and we would wait expectantly for the guests. The guests filed into the dining room very promptly. I served, easy to say, but it involved many speedy trips in and out of the kitchen – four courses followed by coffee. After that it was time for me to clear. We were at the same time coping with the aftermath in the kitchen. Breakfast tables were set and the dining room door closed, so we had a head start in the morning. We could be kept going until close to nine o'clock. Once I delivered something to a guest at nine and he asked me if I did everything. In Helen's day, she recalled being asked exactly the same thing. It was a long day and one went to bed tired. The boys had a rather more normal life as they expected to be off duty after their supper, although there was always a chance that they may be required to serve in the bar until closing time, making a really late night.

Father once told me I was worth two staff; regrettably he regarded me as family and didn't pay me at all until very late on, and then not very much. So I collected and lived off my share of the tips. Possibly Father felt that my schooling was costing him a fortune, and he was not completely sure about it anyway. It was often said quite openly at the time that educating girls was of questionable value as 'They would just get married'. It was food for thought. But to be fair, there was the historical angle, a lot of work on the farms had in the past been unpaid, or underpaid, and our house work was largely done by family. A lot of it simply wasn't in a money economy. The modern welfare state too was just getting off the ground. I have to say that the city jobs that I have held since my Woolpack days have all seemed easy with their defined hours, coffee and lunch breaks – not to mention the salaries, the benefits and the holidays.

Did Father run the farm and the inn as a business in the modern sense? Not really. The till, located in the bar, was just a place for putting money in or taking it out; it left no paper trail itself. At the same time, however, the farm and the inn were working as a unit, producing a lot of food. Since most of the labour at this time was family both on the farm and in the inn, quite honestly catering to the guests felt like an extension of our own family productivity. And the war and the 'austerity' after did put everything on an emergency, make-do basis. Mother maintained, with some resignation, that the farm was experimental in nature and was supported by the inn; and it is possible that accounting might have supported that idea.

We just did what was required without a lot of thought. Indeed we were so busy that we didn't have much time for thought. One Sunday I moaned to a sympathetic guest about carrying tea trays and at the same time negotiating a safe path around the out-stretched legs of our resting males in the kitchen. They had time to read the Sunday papers as it was customary to restrict farm work on that day to the minimum. For us in the kitchen, the inn on Sunday was a day like any other: there were just as many people to feed. My guest admonished me; he explained that the men needed time to think. My point was that we all needed time to think.

I did not see much planning, no careful costing out of anything. Indeed it would have been extremely complicated to put a value on all that home production. I do not recall either of my parents ever going over columns of figures. They had a relaxed discussion late at night at the bar closing time over a drink and a cigarette. As children, we were a bit shocked by the sight of that, it seemed out of character. At income tax time, we had an accountant who came to stay for a week in order to make sense of it all. Once a government official turned up asking questions about who worked and where. I thought he sounded like he was the Inland Revenue. I did not even try to help him; he would have had a tough time and ran a real risk 'going native', that is start to look at the situation from our unsophisticated point of view.

Mother and Granny had very little time off, but their winter was a lot easier. Since the inn was closed for residents about October we reverted to a more normal farm situation. There was only the family and the farm men to cook for. Still it wasn't a holiday either. The bar was still open at the prescribed hours, but there were few people about and we did not make meals for people who dropped in. It was a time of the prolonged and thorough spring-cleaning of all of the rooms and of our own.

Granny and Granda never took formal holidays, Mother very occasionally went on a short trip with Father, mostly it seemed to sporting events. Granny and Mother didn't even attend what was socially available for women in the country, like the Womens' Institute. The WI was very popular with farmer's wives. Father on the other hand was the landlord and a special case. From the kitchen window I would sometimes observe him at the top of the back steps in a one-sided discussion with Alastair about what was to be done on the farm, dwelling particularly on what was in a parlous state. Then he would change tack and say that as there was nothing urgent he was going off for the day – perhaps to some agricultural event. We laughed – it was his management style.

Father thought it was in the nature of women (and maybe children) to be doing two things at once, and most importantly, all of the time. He once took me to account for sitting in front of a fire in the winter, staring at the flames, apparently unemployed: not knitting, not sewing, not darning. He was incredulous and explained to me, with quiet desperation, that my mother was always doing something. She was, and more than two things, actually several things at once. Possibly he was afraid that I had a different agenda, maybe he saw some sign. As children or as young adults, we did not reason, did not remonstrate, and certainly never ever talked back. I once saw how this kind of thing looked to others.

Our dear John Pedder, one of our vicars, was in the kitchen one day on a social call, and listened in while Father gave me a lecture on handling fruit. We had learned to handle fruit gently early on by watching Granda and others handle fruit – we knew all about the easy bruising. After Father had gone Pedder observed that if he had done that to any one of his three girls they would have taken him seriously to account and made the most tremendous fuss. He observed that I had just brushed it off and got on with it, that I had not seemed annoyed. As children we were stoic and did not bother about that kind of thing.

How did I find Mother in our workplace? She was the most hard working and capable person I have ever met, and I must have been a great dis-

Eskdale showing Boot and the Ghyll Bank road.

appointment to her and to Granny when it became obvious that, in the end, I wasn't going to help them in their work. The goalposts had somehow moved, and it must have been hard for them to understand. Mother once laughed that I was a model child until the age of twelve, then things changed and thereafter I did what I liked. What changed at twelve was that I went away to school and into a different world.

In my defence I was unknowingly having to make decisions about options that had not been given to Mother or Granny. Whilst I was not helped at home with the decisions that I had to make, at the same time it is true I felt very free; I did not feel in any way constrained. Once Mother had accepted that I did not appear to be very interested in housework as a full-time career, she could laugh about it. It went further than that; my domestic skills had to become a joke, and finally metamorphosed into a lifetime label. I was happy to collude. But I could always make her laugh, which was often helpful. At the frenetic busy times in the dining room, for instance, I came to the range headquarters and delivered the order in the regional accent of the customer. She found that outrageously funny, chortled as she filled plates.

If we could be said to have a corporate personality, it would be that we worked hard, had a lot to learn, were undemanding, asked for little, were unsentimental, reserved, and had a developed sense of the ridiculous.

Mother liked to be in the background. She saw the funny side of things easily, but it went a little further than that. One sometimes felt that she saw the world as full of mad people with mad requests, and she was the one trying to hang onto sanity and reason – the one keeping an even keel. The eyebrows would often go up in wonderment, sometimes it ended in subversive laughter and a confidential aside. It has often helped me since in tough times in the workplace.

Apart from the fun we made for ourselves in the goings on in the Woolpack, when were we happiest in our work? If I have to pick one thing, then it would be hay time. For the girls in the kitchen it was a reprieve to get outside, and since it was hay time, the day would of necessity have to be sunny and hot. There was always a slight chance that we might get roped in to rake the hay and that would be most welcome; it could mean hours of fresh air and sunshine, valley sounds. One absolute certainty was that we could take the picnic tea to the hay field where the men had been working from early in the day. We carried heavy baskets of jam sandwiches and scones, cakes, and milk cans commandeered for tea. Then we had the rare privilege of a picnic sitting in the hay stubble (corn stubble was a little too sharp to be comfortable) with the sweating horses and the sweating men – that is horses before the age of the tractor, but the tractor was fine too. Now that seems like a shaft into the past, paradoxically into a more leisurely and spacious age: the smell of the drying hay, the grass hoppers jumping around and into your cup, the prickle of the stubble, the general and totally unaccustomed torpor.

The Visitors

Those who came to stay in the valley were always referred to as visitors. We made an important distinction between them and us, between incomer and local; the incomers were almost uniformly urban and we were very much country. The distance that we saw between visitor and local was a reflection of our relative isolation and the stability of families on the farms. And it was not only us who felt it, I have heard that some visitors found the locals a little distant, maybe even unfriendly.

While the natives in general stayed close to home and were much focused on local matters, at Woolpack we were exposed to a constant stream of visitors. As children we grew up used to sharing the house and our parents' time. When young we had to have the appropriate behaviour for this – hardly seen and not heard. Still, we managed to meet far more people socially than the usual nuclear family, either country or urban, might expect. We had the advantage, too, that the visitors were on our own turf: we were the host and not beholden to anyone.

In those days everything was on a personal level. Eskdale had not yet developed strategies for attracting tourists: promoting historic sites, prehistoric remains, the watermill, the waterfalls, any specific farming activity or any specific local food items. Similarly, we ourselves did not push hiking routes or specific climbs. If there was any of that kind of thing it was done by outsiders. Farming and local matters were still the main concern of the locals; tourists were just an incidental way of increasing revenue. The fell was our grazing. Of course we answered questions about what there was to see and were helpful about where to go, but it was always on a one to one basis.

At Woolpack we had resident guests, and even in the 1940s and early 1950s there was a substantial drop-in trade. In the evening the invasions from the Youth Hostel could be so big that they took over the allotted bar rooms and then over-ran the kitchen. The drinkers were delighted with that since the kitchen was the warmest place, but we had to beat a hasty retreat to the annexe and join our grandparents. In the winter, we had the place to ourselves: we could spread out into the guest bedrooms use all the sitting rooms in the inn, as well as all of the annexe. We even had Christmas dinner in the dining room, sometimes with extended family – and if Uncle Tony was present, there was a celebratory climb up onto the fell afterwards.

Our resident guests tended to come back for return visits; and the trade was by word of mouth, so most people came somewhat introduced. The people who came to stay were not those looking for the smart, the up-market or the glamorous. Around this time our charge was modest, a pound a day for full board, then put up to guinea a day. This was at a time when a new secondary school teacher might earn about £40 a month. Overwhelmingly our guests came for the fell walking and the fresh food. They were serious hikers and properly prepared, with boots, rainproof gear and walking sticks. They were the kind of people who would sport Wainwright walking guides after they were published. I would say we all got on well.

Although most locals were not interested in other lives, as children at Woolpack we did learn a lot. We could hardly help it, since the guests were in and out of the kitchen and the bar, and we were in and out of the public rooms. All our encounters had a degree of the personal; in no sense did we aspire to the, perhaps, snappier impersonal service expected today. We didn't actually feel like a public service; we were some kind of hybrid. I recall my shock as a young person when, after advising a casual caller that we were completely full for dinner and so could not fit in her party, she observed that she thought '…that was what we were there for'. To be fair it's possible that she thought we were an isolated inn and might be called upon to save lives now and then, and it is true there was always that possibility of someone lost or wet and cold. There was perhaps some residual obligation hanging on from the past. Our stance was always to be helpful. We well knew that the fells could be dangerous.

What did our visitors of the 1940s and 1950s do for a living? A lot of them were teachers, elementary, secondary, college and university. Mother liked teachers and sometimes worked out special arrangements for the one or two she thought especially needy. We had a few general practitioners and specialist doctors, and nurses. Our lady archaeologist was a frequent guest, with a penchant for a certain back room, when she was excavating at the Roman Camp. She expressed disappointment that she hadn't got an overseas job: she said that the men had the advantage there.

We had a writer, journalists, two artists, a photographer, and even some of the diplomatic corps. One family from the embassy in Baghdad was memorable for completely stripping their beds every morning and leaving things in a pile in the middle of the floor. We picked up the linen and re-made the beds. Still we enjoyed them: they told a story of being in a light plane over Baghdad and described the suffocating hot city air up there. We did enjoy our visitors.

Certainly there were some business people as well. A chief executive of a major textile company who was sympathetic spent time talking to us. We had an engineer who, with his theodolite, checked out the fall of the river as it made its way through the Holm Bottom to see whether it could make electricity. It couldn't. The engineer was called Mr. Melton. He gave us children expensive presents, the like of which we had not seen before – books and cameras. He was just a giving man. One guest taught us to shoot a rifle. Another guest gave us a stack of drawing paper and later bought a painting from me: he wanted one and wouldn't take it as a gift. My first real sale.

We had a lovely family from London, the father was the youngest member of the Athenaeum – London clubs were very far from life in Es-kdale. We had visitors from all over the UK, but mostly from the nearest towns and cities of Lancashire or from London. A few aristocrats were visitors and we enjoyed their company. An exception for me was an ec-centric relative of a world famous architect. He questioned the measure of a sherry that I had I dispensed with the old fractional gill measure. I grandly gave it to him without charge. After he had checked out and left I had the pleasure of writing to him, care of some castle, as he had omitted to pay a bar tab that I discovered he had run up with Father – bar tabs were something we normally did not do.

We did have people from overseas now and then, but not so many from the Continent. Soon after the war we had an American family with a Ger-man name who were careful to tell us in their booking letter how many generations they had been in America. An Armenian family who had set-tled in Manchester in the cotton trade, came to visit many times. They gave a chilling first hand account of the genocide in Turkey as they de-scribed the light emitting phosphorus dancing over the mass graves. They taught me how to make breakfast yogurt. There was a single American girl student who really impressed us children by her open and emanci-pated outlook and her friendliness. She was quite noticeably different in manner to us, and we picked up the signs of the New World. She was genuinely interested in learning all about our farming methods and the different animal breeds and actually took notes from us young people – instead of from those in authority.

All the while we plied her with her favourite biscuits (cookies to her), surreptitiously taken from Mother's tins for the tea-time trade. She must have been doing some research. We had a Scandinavian family whose girls wore glamorous athletic clothing such as we had not seen before. (Trinity Hall should have seen it. We had to do gym in the school's navy blue knickers, even in public!) Their father did some forking in the hay field, just for fun. We had an amusing, we believed ex-British spy, who had been in Germany before the war in order to monitor Hitler. He entertained us hay makers by standing on top of a hay-cock and giving Hitler speeches in German, into which he incorporated the salute. We got the pomposity, if not the actual words, and were wildly appreciative.

We knew less about the drop-in trade, those who called for just a drink or a meal. Local business people, we might know of or be able to place. Very often day visitors were from city walking clubs, staying in the area. A group of 22 ordered afternoon tea from me one day, a huge order, and we got it ready, but before they arrived for it another group of 22, from the same Christian Holiday Association came in. I seated them immediately, unaware that there were two different groups of them – then the original group came in and we had to do it all over again. What a day! The Christian Holiday Association was at Beckfoot near the school and used to give city dwellers healthy holidays in the country.

The Youth Hostel had a similar mandate, in their case concentrating on the young. It was among the university students at the hostel that we met our first Africans and Indians, exotics to us then in our area, as our local population was notably homogenous. Our idea of diversity at that time was an Italian family as far away as Whitehaven who owned an ice cream parlour. An Australian arrived one day especially looking for the draft cider. Imagine his disappointment when told that we were out of it. The cider at the Woolpack was on his 'to-do' list in England. We simply had no notion then of tourist expectations in that sense, we were just not that worldly or sophisticated, but were genuinely sorry.

Sometimes I have been asked whether we had any famous people at Woolpack, and we had a few. Josefina de Vasconcelles, the well-known sculptor, and her seemingly eccentric painter husband Delmar Banner, stayed many times. Delmar was once seen going up to the fell in Father's bedroom slippers that he had previously borrowed, after he had amazed us children by swallowing a raw egg in the kitchen. He was the first painter I knew, and we had several of his very good watercolours on the walls. Unfortunately the damp and cold in some rooms, not adequately heated in the winter, caused a mould to grow in places. It could be seen as yellow dots. Josefina had scupture in the church of St. Martin-in-the-Fields in Trafalgar Square, London, and later, on the Continent after the war, she produced some iconic work. She was also much involved in social work with young children, bringing them out of the city for breaks. Josefina herself seemed exotic since her father was Brazilian, sent originally to Britain by his government.

We had Reg Harris, the once celebrated English cyclist, I expect he brought his wheels. We had Professor Joad of the BBC Radio Brains Trust. Joad had a fierce beard and once frightened me badly: he collared me when I was quite young and threatened what he would do to me if I didn't get him some item – promptly. I gave him a wide berth thereafter. We had a government cabinet minister who took a walk up Harter after having drink in the bar. He said he had to ponder and decide on a weighty political matter. I served a drink to a very well known army officer in the Snug while he examined a map. I was impressed by his quasi-military dress and the military arms handling the map. A leader of the British Communist Party was a regular in the bar. He was a quiet, unassuming and friendly man, considering his position we had expected somebody more frightening. I picked strawberries for Eric Shipton, the famous Himalayan explorer. He had led the reconnaissance of the South Slope of Everest in 1951, which was said to have been pivotal to the successful ascent to the summit by Hillary and Tenzing in 1953. Father later met Sir Edmund Hillary himself at the Outward Bound Mountain School after the Everest climb.

Our most famous visitor at Woolpack was, without a doubt, Neil Armstrong, but I'm cheating, that was a quite bit later in about 1969. Sometime after his walk on the moon, he visited the 'debatable lands', which were an historic Armstrong stronghold just north of Carlisle. He had been invited by Langholm Council as a celebration of his walk, and he himself was interested in learning something about his Armstrong antecedents. Aunt Sallie met him while he was given 'the freedom of the city' in Langholm and gave him Woolpack's address. Neil walked unannounced into the Woolpack bar, in a low key manner which we understood to be entirely characteristic of him. Alastair was serving at the bar, and he whispered to Father 'That's Neil Armstong!' 'Oh aye' replied Father with his usual phlegm. The ultimate celebrity and an Armstrong: it could hardly get better. Unfortunately it happened to be a busy night and Armstrongs present did not manage to have a good conversation.

All in all we had a great deal of fun with our visitors. One of them was speeding up some meals and slowing down others while we attempted to correct anomalies in our booking situations. In one case, while serving at table I had to slow down a meal since flies in great numbers had bizarrely got into the diner's booked room and lodged themselves in the curtains. Between courses I had to go up to the room and help shovel and shoo the flies out. After the meal I showed the guests to their room, quite oblivious to the preceding drama.

There was another kind of fun that we had with Griff – at least I hope it was fun. I have the suspicion that it was a bit on the cruel side. Griff had a certain innocence, gullibility even, and we played a few practical jokes on her. I recall a couple of the milder ones. While on holiday, Griff often got parcels of books through the post from a librarian friend in Southport. Naturally they were special orders, either serious history or serious literature, and an important part of her holiday. We opened one of her book parcels and substituted any trashy low-brow item that we could find, left behind by previous guests. Later we helpfully assisted Griff to open the package – those were the days of elaborately knotted string with dabs of sealing wax – and so observed the amazement and wonder that spread over her features as she picked up each book, read the title, and registered the garish decoration on the cover. She clued in pretty fast on this one, and everybody including Griff had a good laugh while we produced her real tomes. So much for 'interfering' with the Royal Mail: a serious offense of course.

Then there was the time Father put his own cracked reading glasses in Griff's glasses case and we waited expectantly for her to take them out. She was, as we anticipated, surprised to find her glasses cracked and was unsure of what to do next, a holiday without reading looming before her. Father came to the rescue, explaining that he was off to Whitehaven for the day and could get her prescription refilled, meanwhile would she care to borrow his? He took her own glasses out of his pocket, which Griff failed to recognize, but was delighted to find that they were really very good indeed, and she was happy about the solution. I wasn't present for the ending on that one but I can imagine that they would both have a hearty and relieved laugh.

Finally there was our *piece de resistance* with Griff, our ultimate hoax. The background to this one was that everyone involved in this deception had become somewhat familiar with Miss Lobb's personality and authoritative figure, through my stories of Trinity Hall in the kitchen. It was generally suspected that a person like Griff might possibly have some difficulties in her position as deputy to the headmistress, Miss Lobb. Griff, of course, had not ever once given any hint of any difficulty, and in any case, we knew her to be always entirely correct. It was all in our imagination.

The plan was masterminded by a resident writer, Dudley Hoys, and we had no idea how far it would go, or indeed if it would work at all. He drew all the resident guests into the plot – apart from Griff and Nina. Supposing that Griff and the headmistress saw eye to eye on all matters educational and social, there could be nothing to laugh at, at all. The plot was to write a letter, as from Miss Lobb, to say that she was interviewing domestic staff in the area and was coming to stay at Woolpack overnight – that very night in fact. Dudley typed the letter and I forged the signature: it was one of my talents. We contrived to be present when Griff got her letter, and as she opened it, as we expected, became apprehensive and questioning, really at her most unsure and innocent, as she read it and acquainted us with its contents. She thought to check with Mother, the only one by now that she really trusted. She walked over to the sink and queried mother who did not actually tell a lie it is true; she simply confirmed that we had a vacancy – and so it began. Miss Lobb, of course, had shown no interest in Cumbria before, or, as far as we knew, any interest in the domestic arrangements at Trinity Hall – but the world is ever full of surprises.

We had quite a few hours of feeling guilty since Griff and Nina went out all day walking and came back unusually late, missing their usual and much enjoyed tea-tray. They announced themselves shortly before dinner and inquired about Miss Lobb. The information relayed was that Miss Lobb had been delayed and was coming by taxi; she had said that, regretfully, she might be a few minutes late for dinner so would come straight into the dining room on arrival.

While getting the dinner ready we had got up a volunteer guest as Miss

Lobb. The volunteer and her Harley Street psychiatrist husband were friends and good sports. I was the dresser since I was the only one with the right knowledge. Our actress did not in any way resemble Miss Lobb; she was tiny and half her age for a start but I upholstered her generously with pillows and encased her in a belted mac, gave her sun glasses for disguise, and a mannish hat pulled down over the brows. Nobody in their wildest dreams would have thought our creation looked anything but a freak. The whole dining room were in on the plot, as well as everyone in the kitchen, and we all waited with bated breath. The guests were all seated for dinner as we escorted Miss Lobb formally into the dining room and to the place set for her.

Griff immediately got to her feet, courteously came over and greeted her effusively, shaking Miss Lobb's hand in welcome. Then the dam broke. Griff finally registered the apparition before her and howled with laughter, everyone else howled, the Harley Street psychiatrist I saw was first doubled over and finally entirely on the floor. The whole place erupted, including the kitchen and the bar. The laughter must have got into the granite walls. It was the funniest, most prolonged hoax, involving the most people, that I had known. It was so long it was more like a play. But it was our last hoax, altogether we had gone too far, and we could never repeat it.

Our tricks all ended well because Griff had a fantastic sense of humour, she was a wonderful sport. Her Irish brogue was irresistible. Nina always laughed along but I had the feeling that privately she might not wholly like the jokes, and it was one of the reasons we gave them up, but they were marvellous fun while they lasted.

Looking back I can see that our final drama was something akin to a seventeenth century comedy or Oliver Goldsmith, in which the exaggerated characteristic of one becomes a comedy for others, an observation of contemporary manners, and the action taking place in an isolated country inn no less. It wasn't quite respectable. It seems to be illustrative of our time warp – our lifestyle, family and inn were in some ways hardly yet into the twentieth century.

– 11 –

King's College

My university career does not directly further the Eskdale narrative, however it is included since this is a personal work with personal observations; and because there were some interesting aspects of King's in the early 1950s.

While still maid-of-all-work at the Woolpack, I transferred from Trinity Hall to university and managed to fit in a degree; it brought me firmly into the twentieth century. There are a few things about my time at King's that seem peripherally relevant. I will concentrate on the course work challenge that I set myself and the situation of female students. It is interesting to look back at university education for girls in the late 1940s and early 1950s as some aspects of it were quite different from today. Although the post-war government was committed to the education of young people of all social classes and circumstances, I was to discover that in practice girls at university were still a minority.

I did not think that the idea of my going to university had ever been discussed at home, but somehow a neighbouring farmer had heard of it. It must have been in 1949 that an elderly Hartley took me to task. I ran into him on the road just outside Woolpack, and we had a curious conversation; he sought to give me guidance. He thought going to university was unnecessary (and after all, the locals had just a few years previously had to get used to the secondary school idea). I quote him, 'There is all you could possibly need right here.' Well, I didn't realize it at the time but there was a voice speaking from out of the past. Hartleys had been in Eskdale for hundreds of years; somewhere it is even possible we were distantly related. He had the weight of history and custom behind him; and he most certainly wasn't trying to be restrictive. At least he talked to me, he was the only person at home that I remember who did.

Most likely Henry Hartley saw the threat to 'our lot' more clearly than I did; it was to him, perhaps, a sign that things were starting to go seriously awry with our centuries old way of life. Possibly it was a plea to keep us all together – not to have me looking like an incomer. I listened politely as all young people did; I didn't even attempt an adequate discussion, and just as well. The truth is that I know now he was right in some respect: things were changing fast. I was just the first to be offered the possibility of further education, perhaps particularly distressing, and thought to be pointless, because I was a girl. The locals had got somewhat used to having male scientific advisers visit the farm, so that the relevance of further education for a boy might just have been conceivable. Later the idea of university was readily accepted.

Trinity Hall had done only a partial job in preparing me for university. I had achieved four subsidiary A-levels. I left school before the final sixth year. Had I stayed that last year I would have got two full A-levels and two subsidiaries. Griff did allow that four subsidiaries in one year was a good effort; and we had other required subjects at the time that were not exam status like Miss Lobb's English. The English class was the occasion of the '...milkweed ballerinas floating to the ground' incident. My prosaic writing style was a trial to Miss Lobb. Once, my classmate Eileen, thought to help me out by writing a section for me – the kind of thing that worked well for her. It was an imaginative passage containing the milkweed phrase. Thoughtlessly I handed it in. Miss Lobb was delighted, thought I had finally got it, and insisted on reading it out to the class to mark my progress – there was just no point in owning up since Eileen would have been in trouble too.

Career counselling was entirely absent at Trinity Hall, otherwise someone might have pointed out that my odd collection of A-level subjects, botany, zoology, history and art, was really not equipping me for very much – straddling the arts and sciences as they did: they were neither one thing nor the other. This was at a time and a place where you had to make directional decisions early: definitely into one or the other, and immediately after School Certificate. A-levels were a serious investment since they were the equivalent to the first year of university in North America.

I took the entrance exam at King's College Fine Art Department in Newcastle, part of the University of Durham, and was offered a place. I also got accepted at the Edinburgh College of Art but selected King's simply because it was part of a university, and later on that proved to be fortuitous. The county council in Carlisle informed that I had been given an award but when I went to collect it they said that they had done a means test on Father and decided his income was too high for me to get any funding. Money was going to be a problem.

At university, I found that my fellow students were fairly well funded by their local councils. Fortunately, King's fees were heavily subsidized by the nation. There was an idea abroad then that those so educated were an investment for the country, that they were expected to make significant contributions to society; the emphasis was not put on getting a well paid job. My living expenses would be the challenge. Working to put oneself through college was not so common then, since it was generally accepted that such an education should be a full time affair; so my working at the Woolpack whenever I could was not as usual as it might be today.

I spent a year in Fine Art at King's and completed all the basic courses. I swam for the college and played grass hockey. Unfortunately I had to travel out to approved digs in Whitley Bay and share with three or four other students. It was in sight of a wild beach on the east coast and there were a lot of walks beside tremendous waves. During the daily bus ride in to King's, we saw the open cast coal mining and the miners coming and going. Tyneside was post-war and gritty. On the plus side, people were working, in the shipyards as well as the mines. I did have a difficult time adjusting to city life and was quite homesick. It was very hard to adjust to the dirt and the ugliness, the impersonality of city living; it took me years not to let it bother me so acutely. I was privately distressed by pollution well before it became fashionable or was even given a name. It is a sad fact that urban life pretty well separates people from nature and that was difficult for me.

I had no problem with my art courses, found them easy enough, but by the end of the year I had decided to give it up. I simply could not restrict my interests so severely. With the benefit of hindsight I can see I could have made it work, it would certainly have been an easier option – I could have taught art, had summers off, and painted at the same time. I have often thought about that. Lawrence Gowing, the Head of Fine Art, when he bid me goodbye, was handsome enough to say that I was a promising painter. Gowing himself was to become well known for both his painting and his writing. My painting instructors were Chris Cornford and Roger de Grey; the latter went on to become a President of the Royal Academy. A marvellous recent follow up of King's painting instructors is Lee Hall's play 'The Pitmen Painters', in which one such instructor is a major character. While the play is set in the 1930s, it nevertheless brings my instructors strongly to mind – I had not met that kind of artistic privilege before.

My problem of being interested in far too much and of not being adequately focused, was coming home to roost. What next? I took a gap year working at the Woolpack to think about it and to make applications. I was quizzed about my change of direction by at least one of our visitors, a kindly middle-aged business man. I expect that a country waitress with educational aspirations must have looked interesting. It was a distinct oddity then – entirely commonplace now. Notably, no woman expressed the slightest interest about changing fields or in what I planned to do. In fact, about this time an aunt asked me what I was doing. Actually she meant what kind of needlework did I like; a permissible female interest in the past. I had needlework to do of course, we all had – but of necessity. We made a lot of our own clothes since they were expensive to buy. Even so, my needlework would probably not have met the high standards to which most aspired.

Looking back it seems odd that in this year at home I didn't seek out Auntie Gladys to discuss my future. After all I had been imprinted early with her ideas on the importance of education and in some respects our lives were similar. We were both the eldest of large families; we both worked at Woolpack when not elsewhere, as a kind of default occupation. I was going to end up as a teacher; she was always a teacher. Auntie Gladys had taught at elementary schools in Patterdale and Watermillock while living with the family at both places. While she had received some earlier teacher training in Penrith she was a mature student by the time she attended teacher training college in Darlington, County Durham; it is likely it was there that she became familiar with the Montessori Method.

Eventually King's offered me a place in their three year Pure Science programme; it was a real gamble on their part. I would not ever have got direct entry into Pure Science without the right array of A-levels. Fortunately for me, there was an option to transfer between departments at King's – once having gained entry somewhere. There had been cases of students from other departments transferring into Fine Art, but leaving Fine Art to go to Pure Science was generally considered an eye opener. I was notably deficient in chemistry and physics; I didn't even have them at school certificate level. I appeared in front of the same county educational board in Carlisle and they managed a token £40 a year.

Since I was ill prepared for the course work to come, I had to make choices for the first year that would not overwhelm me. I had to survive at all costs. Therefore in my first year I opted for botany, zoology, geography and geology. I did not have geography or geology in school certificate either, but they seemed to be more achievable than chemistry or physics. The geography department was small and friendly, and I was very fortunate to be helped by other students there; two of them later went to Africa, one at least to became a District Commissioner – an anachronism today. Geology was also a small department but not a friendly place, as I will explain later, but I had good exam results. Botany and zoology were large departments and I had no problem. Overall I did alright in the first year exams. The university exam results were pinned in a public place, the names in order of mark, any failure was obvious to all. I went to view them disguised under an umbrella; as it was to be a moment of terrible truth.

I was very much helped by living in the new Ethel Williams Hall of Residence: it was modern and purpose built, most conducive to study, and set in attractive surroundings of an old country house that housed some of the lecturers. There were about 65 students, girls from all university departments; the small number shed light on our minority status. My wing had four student rooms with a shared bathroom and kitchen; at the time it was total luxury – a room of one's own. I was accustomed to communal living, but this was a world away from Trinity Hall. The dining hall was formal, we wore gowns and there was a high table, sometimes with guests. Breakfast and dinner were provided on weekdays, and all meals at weekends. It was not so important then that some of the time I could not afford a weekday lunch on campus.

We had quite a few overseas students in hall, some seemed exotic to us. There was an aristocratic Portuguese who ordered male students to carry her bags, which, so surprised them, they did. A wealthy Indian girl – with elephants at home – floated around in silk (silk was only known to us as war-time parachute material); she had once shaved her head on a bet at home. An Egyptian who had been obliged to leave her country because she had turned down an offer of marriage from a cousin she didn't know, it was considered to be such a serious insult to his branch of the family that it wasn't clear if she could ever go home. We also had a girl from Thailand who expressed a great deal of fear of communism.

In the second year, basic chemistry and plant biochemistry was added, and life became very real and earnest. Chemistry was all the shock I had imagined; I started out hardly familiar even with the symbols. It was possibly my sharpest learning curve, ever. My ploy was to bring myself to staff attention by any means possible, to get noticed and get some help. I continually tested the degree of help on offer. Nevertheless, at the Christmas basic chemistry exam, in a class of over a hundred, I was fourth from the bottom and was profoundly shocked. I had never before experienced being bottom of anything. However the professor discussing results pointed out, comfortingly, that it was to be expected if one was starting out more or less from scratch. Incredibly, by the end of the year I had pulled myself up and in the final I was fourth from top. How that happened is not at all clear; to be sure I had been extraordinarily lucky in the theory questions. Still it was hardly believable and I kept quiet and held my breath in case there had been an error.

My lab instructor in practical chemistry was on to me. He was one person from whom I had failed to get much help; he was simply appalled by my ignorance. After the amazing year end final results came out matters came to a head; he was quite beside himself with outrage. With real suffering, he told me that he could name dozens of students who knew more chemistry than I did. Of course he was right; but I am happy to say that the basic chemistry practical experience fell off my back 'like a duck shakes water.' Fortunately, a patient woman chemistry lecturer had been open to helping me, and that could have been critical. Later I had the pleasure of serving her something at Woolpack when she called in on holiday; she must have registered my background as I was flinging myself about. It did sometimes happen that someone I had met outside of Eskdale would come into Woolpack for a meal, and I wasn't sure how I felt about it. Sometimes it was a pleasure, and sometimes not, to find myself serving someone I knew in another context.

My third year was a time of serious work, but it was possible. Pretty well all of my study time had to be done at King's. I often slacked off a bit in the first week back at King's, to make a necessary break from hotel work, to change gear; and then I had to work harder to catch up. All my vacations were spent working at Woolpack so that I neither had a holiday nor came back with quite enough money. Without my knowledge my bank manager wrote a letter to Father at one point: I had zero bank balance, what was he to do? In the early 1950s, I doubt that he could have made a loan to a girl student.

It wasn't possible to do much preparation for finals at home. Mother was always desperately busy, and to her, studying looked like not doing anything much at all. I must have looked harangued as my assigned medical doctor at King's once wrote a letter home, that I did know about, asking for some rest and fresh air for me in the vacations. It fell on deaf ears, was never mentioned, and made no difference to our work load. By the end of my final year I was grossly anaemic, tired by it and fainted easily, but I had made it.

While I was exhausted with finals it was necessary to make a quick turnaround, in order to fit in two or three weeks of school-practice for teacher training. I was able to go back to Trinity Hall for that which was convenient. Trinity Hall had changed; there was a new head and a more modern regime and, thankfully, the food was vastly improved.

Worth commenting on, was the purveyance of overt sexism directed towards the few female students in science at the university. We took the sexism for granted, we didn't even talk about it, we thought it was normal. It was still true that there was a tradition of women in important academic positions, but they had to be very bright and very dedicated, and most likely had to have the right families, and overwhelmingly they were not married. One such successful lady at King's, a genetics instructor with Cambridge connections, came to lecture one day with the story about current work on the double helix in the Cavendish laboratory. She was a wonderful corrective and helped enormously in ignoring the prejudice.

There was the feeling abroad that women in traditionally male bastions were some kind of biological anomaly, in order to explain their presence at all. A fall back position being that they must be somehow unattractive for a more traditional role. I remember it being said at the time that university girls in general looked different; one informant opined that we sported a no nonsense air. It's true we did not wear so much make-up and our wardrobes were limited. At this time at King's girls were most likely to be in an arts programme; which was often and quite openly said to be more educationally acceptable.

Since there were so few girls studying science, we were looked on as curiosities. We had to get used to queries as to why we were there at all. On occasion there might even be an outright objection to our presence; but mostly it came from the less successful male students. There were direct questions such as, 'What are you doing here?' or more seriously, 'Do you realize that you are taking the place of a man?' Well we did, it was constantly brought to our attention; and it's not so easy to explain that you want to know stuff. It was true, there was a lot of competition to get in, there were few universities then; and ex-service men from the war were still going through, adding to the pressure.

I was smart enough not to let it be known that I was a transfer in from Fine Art: hardly legitimate at all, 'grandfathered' in by an old benefit, entirely without the right background. Still I remember nervously laughing about my prospects while waiting outside an exam hall, and being sobered up by a male student who said with some bitterness that I would do alright '…your kind always do.' The sexism had something to do with competition. That particular exam was genetics, and our lady instructor, Dr. Blackburn of the Cambridge connections, wouldn't give me my question paper until I had first looked up at her and managed some kind of smile. It did reduce the tension.

In a lot of first year science classes there were about six girls and maybe over a hundred men. In biology four of us sat on the front row for protection. With me was Heidi from Hamburg, the daughter of a German diplomatic family posted to Tyneside, Sonia from Nigeria, a friend that I got to know well, and Grace from Ghana. The other two girls were local, and tellingly they sat somewhere at the back. The girls at the back confided to me that they were acutely conflicted as to why they were present at all, they were bothered by the problem of how much time they should spend studying, and how much time they should spend looking for a husband. I don't know how it finally went for them. It was simple for me, I only looked forward and hung in. We were in similar tiny groups, huddled on the front row, in all my Science classes large or small. The other notable minority were the 'colonial' students, and we gravitated to each other, or were pushed together by the staff. My assigned lab partner was Nick Otieno, a lovely boy, a Luo from Kenya, and a graduate of the famous Makarere College. He was traumatized by having gone fishing at home with a friend who had been caught by a crocodile. Come to think of it we had about as many students from overseas as we did girls.

Much the worst sexist episodes occurred in geology, and there an instructor was entirely responsible, and thankfully the only instructor who was like that. It was not a large class, and as usual the few girls were isolated in our perceived relative safety of the front row. He found endless clever ways of ridiculing the female presence in geological subjects under discussion. There were certain words he could ingeniously make into some kind of innuendo – permalift was one. We sat on our front row with stony faces and waited him out. Meanwhile his gallery of male students behind us stamped their feet and hammered on the wooden desks in front of them – ribald laughter and shouting all around – wild appreciation. It was all very puerile. I do not believe that our security was seriously being threatened, what we were subjected to was supposed to be wit, but one certainly got some insight into how it might be if security had truly been an issue. We never thought to complain; and who to? We were not about to 'rock the boat': we had to pass the exam.

In the late 1940s and early 1950s, female students could still be singled out as unusual and special cases, but the writing must have been 'on the wall'. Extraordinary to know that now, 60 or more years later, in the UK, for every two men that achieve a degree, in either arts or science, there are three women, biological oddities no longer. I was there on the post-war cutting edge in mass female university education, but we were not conscious in any way of being revolutionary and quite unaware of any implications for the future.

In the Bun Room (coffee shop) we mixed with more worldly and re-laxed groups such as the Fine Arts students. Their questions were a bit more sophisticated, more friendly, more academic. One male artist posed the question as to whether women were the equal of men – as in some ranking exercise. Hazel, a friend from my Fine Arts year, appeared to go along with the ranking idea by exclaiming 'Of course not!' A dramatic pause followed, and then she went on, 'They are much better!' It seemed to be quite adventurous at the time; we were a long way from being con-sciously feminist. I didn't know anyone then who could be described as an activist; but we did hear of a project at another university in which some women whistled at particular men and followed them home. We ac-knowledged that took real guts. Being whistled at was so common it was not even remarked on, building sites were a notable hazard, being fol-lowed was less common but was known.

When the time came to leave King's, I found I was not ready to go and tried to get accepted for a Joint Honours year, but it didn't work. It was the only time I remember seeing my assigned tutor. She was German and possibly a refugee, and it was her job to turn me down. She could not give me the reason but it seemed to upset her greatly, reduced her to tears. So I opted for a real change, the other plan, and got accepted for a year at the Institute of Education in the University of London which was the rea-son for the school practice. By this time Father was firmly beyond speech on my education: there was obviously not going to be an end to it.

12

Country to get lost in

What did we do for entertainment at home in our rare bits of down time? If you were a girl, that is – the boys had more freedom of movement. The familiar urban excitements and diversions that could have been afforded by public transport, shopping, movies, plays, libraries and the like, were so far away that they were not even thought about – ever.

We had to walk or find one's own transport. I did raise the subject of learning to drive with Father, after all I'd had a bit of early experience in the hay field. That ambition proved to be a step too far; it was not going to happen. He eyed me directly and said, very deliberately, 'If you want to go somewhere, I will drive you' – and that was generally accepted as going to the train station to go back to school or college. I could have been a bit more insistent, after all I had won on wearing trousers. I had appeared in trousers not thinking that there would be too much of a problem, but he was shocked and demanded that I go and change – just as he had with shorts. Unexpectedly, I was rescued by Granny Leece. She volunteered the thought that I looked very nice in trousers. Unaccountably, Father caved in. It was a seismic shift. Granny had done farm work in long skirts with petticoats in her time, she had not ever worn slacks herself, but was striking out for some kind of progress, I must suppose. Mother could have helped me on the driving or the trousers, but didn't; she herself never drove, or wore trousers – maybe not permitted either.

Alastair privately volunteered some lessons; since he was allowed to own a little old van. There were a couple of sessions in the Front Field and all went well until he asked me to intentionally stall the motor, which I did, to find the gears stripped and a disaster on our hands. The mechanic in Eskdale Green assured me that the gear box was an accident waiting to happen, nothing much to do with me. But it was the end of my driving career for many years. I waited until I could buy my own car.

For entertainment we walked, out of any door, front, side or back, into the countryside, tailoring the length of the roam to the time on hand. You could walk out of Woolpack, or Paddockwray, or any of our farms in upper Eskdale, in any direction, and you could anticipate having a worth-while time, since it was all beautiful; it all held possibility. Our farms were well spaced for walking, they were all historic and 'sat well', and there were the many paths between them through the fields and also on up the fells. As you went, there were the constantly changing valley and fell views, rocky outcrops, tree patterns, and the meandering waterways. One appreciated the air, the smells, the sounds, and the constantly chang-ing weather effects, the moving clouds and splashes of sunlight. It was watercolour country.

In short, it was 'the morning of the world.' I have not since lived in such a place, right in the middle of so easily accessible and unspoilt coun-tryside, and free of human detritus. It wasn't wild, of course, it was pas-toral: it had a history, had been lived over, and was on a human scale. It was a picture postcard; I grew up thinking that was the natural state of things and it became a reference point. Over time I have got used to the city and its uniformity, the asphalt, the alien imported plants. I have then to imagine how it was there, before the onslaught. How did the landscape lie, how did the rivers go, and what were the native plants?

In our time when you walked, there were not many people about. There was the odd local or hiker, an occasional car, a bit of farming activity, an

Eskdale from the Roman camp.

odd barking dog guarding its farm. Today in Eskdale, the cars whiz by, people you meet might be from anywhere; there is such mobility. Everyone has become a bit more citified. In our youth Eskdale was still ours, especially in winter, where we were familiar with every corner, identified with it, felt part of it, worked in it, talked about it, celebrated it. We owned the geography, not in the narrow legal sense but collectively: we were committed to it and responsible for it, and there were absolutely no distractions. There was a sense of freedom and space; it was a place made for walking. The maze of footpaths meant you could avoid the main road if you wanted, not that that was much of a hazard in my time. You weren't afraid of anyone you might meet. You checked a field for what animals were there before you opened a gate or climbed a stile – bulls were to be avoided and growing crops. Up the valley was the pass, and down the valley, past Paddockwray, was the village, north, east and south there was fell. It all held promise, we were spoiled for choice. There was a spaciousness. I wonder did they feel that space in the Middle Ages, or was it obscured by poverty and possible violence?

We felt that the landscape was our private property and were always uncovering new facts about it – a specific place, a plant perhaps or an animal. A lot of the time one would be alone and wander off to one's

Upper Eskdale – Slight Side and the Scafell range.

favourite spots. Up the road was fine, past Wha house and on to Hard-knott, up to the Roman fort perhaps, and gaze north upon Slight Side and Scafell, or follow the river up past Butterilket or Taw House to the uninhabited bit towards Esk Hause. You could go south to the river, a big draw, and go on past Low Birker and perhaps up the fell to the tarn on top and look at Harter from there and backwards over the valley. You could follow the river either up or down.

Possibly the most private and personal walk was to go up the rake behind the inn onto the fell, because of the heaf I suppose and the legal connection. One might go as far as Eel Tarn with its waterlilies; looking back down were the marvellous views of the green valley, with the soft rounded trees hugging the lower slopes. It felt like home ground. At Eel Tarn there were views of Scafell with Black Apron (pronounced Appron) in front of it, both rock faced and bald. Further on was Burnmoor Tarn in its sea of heather; turn east of the tarn and you could look down into depths of Wasdale, or turn west and you come upon the Whillan beck and follow it down to Ghyll Bank, or branch off to Paddockwray at the solitary Monkey Puzzle tree. How had it got there? Or you could go north east from the top of the rake, up the drift road, past Blea Beck and try to find bleak and lonely Stoney Tarn. You might climb up little Hodge Howe, the rise in the middle of Woolpack fields and in the middle of the valley with its all around prospect. Just below the top I found a complete fox skeleton. You might sit by some running water somewhere, and there was plenty of it, listen to the rush and examine some freshwater life. I have never again lived anywhere like this: clean, fresh, immediate, easily available. These were places that felt transformative.

When I was a schoolgirl, I might get off duty for the day and go walking with Griff and Nina when they were staying. We had a few day-long wanders. Once we went to the top of the Screes above Wasdale and then got lost trapped in a thick mist by Burnmoor Tarn at the Ghyll Bank end. I thought I knew the geography like the back of my hand, but mist is surprisingly, and completely, disorienting. I only realized we were heading into the water by noticing a sudden straight line on the bottom of the vague stone shapes. Absolutely everything becomes a light silvery grey – land, water and sky. It feels close and damp. The mists were not uncommon and a bit of a hazard, eerie as well as disorienting, sound was muffled, and visibility could be cut down to two or three feet. A lot of hikers got into trouble in such situations on the high fells – by keeping on walking and falling down something. Unless you were certain of your path and direction it was advisable to stay put until the mist had started to lift

In our case two ghostly figures emerged from out of the mist with a lantern, its light only a slight yellow glow. They had heard faint voices from near the tarn and thought we might need help. Cheerful boys – they were on an adventure camping rough in the old gamekeeper's lodge. As soon as the mist started to lift, and I felt sure of the direction, then I led Griff and Nina out of it. On occasion, we wandered around the Wasdale valley. Griff and Nina sometimes stayed at the Strands Hotel (built by a Tyson and most likely an ancestor), and I would walk from Woolpack over Burnmoor to see them. On one of our wanders I was ahead of our line and going through high bracken when I spotted an adder reared up in front of me, looking not much different to a bracken stem. We backed out cautiously before it could strike.

On one occasion Griff, Nina, Mother and I were unusually ambitious, we walked from Woolpack, over Hardknot and Wrynose Passes and down to Fell Foot, then on to Elterwater, where we had a meal and dried out from a rain shower. Then we managed to find a bus to Coniston, to the south of Eskdale and two valleys over. We hiked back on the old pack-horse trail over Walna Scar, with the peak of Coniston Old Man on our

Scafell from Birker Moor.

The Screes and Wastwater.

right, and then down into the Seathwaite Valley to the Newfield Hotel. That was a serious day's undertaking. Alastair was waiting for us with the car at the Newfield, anxiously scanning the fell, doubtless relieved not to have to go to look for us. It was as well that Mother was along as it was a bit misty and cold over Walna Scar and I was flagging; she gave me an apple to eat and it kept me going. At the Newfield we were greeted by Mother's great friend, Mrs. Longmire, the owner, which was probably why Mother had been persuaded to go along in the first place. The last leg was in style by car. How great it was to come into Woolpack's warm kitchen to a dining room dinner on the kitchen table. We were exhausted, footsore, hungry but happy. I could have eaten two dinners before sleeping the sleep of the dead.

Most of our walks were not so heroic, indeed such heroism was rather a marker of an incomer: something to talk about, perhaps even brag about, most definitely an endurance test. It was characteristic that our normal walks would have some purpose: farm business, visiting neighbours, delivering something or collecting something, seeing a bit of history somewhere. We did not much admire endurance tests for themselves – very ambitious undertakings could look more like foolhardiness. A search party of farmers might have to go out; so we didn't ourselves take unnecessary risks. There was also an idea of an appropriate use of energy. We were like animals that put out just enough effort to get the food, but not so much energy that might seriously deplete the bodily reserves. An exception to that kind of economy, and much later in time when endurance feats became widely popular, was our own local farmer, Joss Naylor of Wasdale, a serious fell-runner.

I got well acquainted with Bentham and Hooker's *Handbook of British Flora*. I had the good fortune of seeing our common wild flowers in their natural environments: primroses, violets, wood anemones, bluebells, celandines, pig-nuts, cow parsley, meadowsweet (that one was seriously attractive – in the hay, feathery, fragrant), vetches, clovers, harebells, bedstraw, campion, cinquefoil, cranesbill, toadflax, valerian, yarrow, speedwell, the nettles, eyebright, the daisies, buttercups, cowslip, plantains, thistles, ling, bell heather – to name a few. Then there were the grasses: sedges, quaking grass, fescue, timothy, and the rushes. Then there were the tree species, and the fungi, the algae, and the ferns.

We learned where the rarer plants grew: orchids in Christcliff field, marsh marigolds near an old iron ore mine behind Low Birker, royal ferns in Bleabeck Ghyll, the waterlily surprise on Eel Tarn with cotton grass and tiny bleaberries in the sphagnum moss. Sundew and butterwort grew by the streams and water. Then there was the variety of invertebrate life – vertebrate life – and so on, and so on. And for a while we had a school microscope, probably it was Michael's. This uncovered previously unknown features, like the nature of the brown spots on the under surface of fern fronds – my favourite.

Of course for myself, there was the possibility of a painting or drawing session outdoors. I didn't have too much to go on artistically, but very early on I was impressed by a Chinese artist who had visited the Lakes, and turned out work on local landscapes with stylized symbols for trees. It was an article in a magazine. It was fascinating, not much observation, no attempted accuracy with the subject, but it worked artistically. Not my style or understanding at all, but attractive nonetheless, and it did pick up some of the pastoral quality.

Then one had very particular places close and nearby that one liked to go for a few minutes, that seemed to be especially private and personal, chosen for the prospect, the angle, the sound, the feel. Almost too personal to say where they were or why they were so satisfactory – one had to be there. The top of Hodge How was one, the top of the easterly intack be-

Penny Hill Bridge.

hind Woolpack another, or I might favour a small stream into the Blea Beck, completely overhung in a bit of neglected deciduous woodland. The word neglected comes to mind because a few of the trees had impressive fungi growing through the bark and standing out from the sides of their trunks. In my day the locals did not draw and paint, my odd habit was unremarked, the results not displayed at home. But I gave Auntie Gladys a few drawings and she framed them.

The night and the dark were another dimension. Obviously there was no such thing as outdoor lighting so that the night became an inviting place. The sky became dominant in the dark, and starlight and moonlight had their own qualities. Other-worldly ghostly shadows appeared on the grass. We were not experts on identifying stars, but we made a wild attempt. It felt safe in the dark, even if it was pitch black it was still comfortable, an enveloping velvet. If one did sense something questionable, there was total freedom to change direction, we were not hemmed in. We all know how city lights change the night: detract from the night sky, how the physical confines and the artificial light make one vulnerable, how the dark, for many, becomes a place to avoid.

Apart from walking and natural history what else did girls do for entertainment? Girls could go freely into pubs in the daytime but in the evening they became male haunts. I have already described the constant

Penny Hill Corner with lane end on left.

sewing and knitting at home: some embroidered, I tatted. We had our piano practice. A few books came our way. Did we have some social life, you ask? Well yes, the locals and the visitors. There were births, deaths and marriages. Aunt Nellie, at the New Dungeon in Langdale, once held one of our family get-togethers. The down side of these events for us was that we had to display some talent, but cousin Marjorie saved us that day with wholly professional singing, as she often did. They loved that. I struggled through something on the piano. There were quizzes, again children were in the spotlight, for what we knew. There was no imported entertainment. There was church now and then, and Easter, Christmas, Harvest Festival and the agricultural shows. There were occasional dances in the schoolhouse with Auntie Gladys on the piano; the dances a mixture of country and modern. I had a twenty-first birthday party complete with fiddler and dancing – Auntie Gladys screaming 'No John No!' as cousin John carried her bodily around the floor. Looking back we seemed to be self contained, cut off from any concern of city life, but did not feel deprived. No local confided in me about their disaffection, or of a hankering for the bright lights.

13

The Archaeology and the History

The upper valley was tidy, unspoiled, a pleasure to look upon, even though it had been lived in for a long time. There are some historic records of the last 2,000 years and some evidence from prehistory. The archaeological sites, like our farms, blended well with the landscape. The sites were not always easy to find. In our day none of them were signposted in any way or much studied; we heard about them casually in conversation. Maybe it was because we were not distracted by city attractions so that these sites loomed large in our imagination, and had a presence in our time. The sites were somewhere to visit, check on, in a bit of free time. We just discovered these curiosities in our midst.

Our buildings and fields, our accents, our words and names, were centuries old, and we had a dim idea about that, and of the continuity – people 'knew who they were'. One would have liked to have known more, to have had more to go on. One date that we had at Woolpack was that inscribed on an old black oak cupboard door set into a passage wall, something like 1607. Butterilket Farm we knew had been a place where monks from Furness Abbey once farmed in the 1200s. This was occasionally acknowledged in an outdoor church service, memorably surrounded by grazing sheep and marked by valley sounds – occasional sheep blares and bird calls. Not much of the history of individual farms was written down. The kinds of records that survive are of sales or rents, farming rules and there were the church and voting registers.

We identified with all upper Eskdale farmsteads, some with Norse names, Butterilket (Brotherelkeld), Taw House, Bird How, Wha House, Bleabeck, Low Birker, Christcliff, Paddockwray, Arment House, Hollins, the Howes, Ghyll Bank, to name those nearest us. Each had its own charm. They looked to be of comparable age, maybe not built later than the sixteenth and seventeenth century, but possibly in existence in some form before that, nearer to the Norse invasion of about 900AD.

The farm names are all there in the document known as the 'Eskdale 24 Book of 1587'. The 24 refers to the jury of 24 farmers of the Manor

Court who met to regulate the common pasture: the boundaries, the rules about numbers of sheep, cattle and horses permitted, at what time of year and exactly where they might graze, exact details of each 'drift' and heaf on the Eskdale Common. The 24 jurors had local names, the same names as those occurring on the documents relating to the farms and spanning the generations up and into our own time. Two of the 24 were named Tyson – Granny Leece's name, and in the revision of 1659 four of the 24 jurors were Tysons.

Reference has already been made to the interesting old words in the documents referring to legal matters, of levancy and couchancy. A direct translation of these, originally French terms, refer to the time an animal lies down and rises up, taken to be a day and a night, and this might be applied to legitimate or to strayed stock. There are references to turbary rights: the right to cut peat and where, a reference to estover: what is allowed to be taken by custom, for instance, wood from the landlord, or the right to cut bracken, by a particular farm. To assist the Manor Court in its enforcement of its rules there were certain medieval professions whose titles have their charm. Those of 'hedge looker' and 'peat moss looker' seem self explanatory. A 'pounder' was responsible for counting the number of permitted kinds of stock on the farms and for impounding strayed animals.

In medieval times, the numbers of stock were so regulated so that they could be entirely fed off the farm and its allotted common grazing – importing fodder was not acceptable. There is a record of father questioning the rules in 1945, asking if he could take stock in from the outside and feed them for the summer. I cannot imagine he was in any way anxious to do that; it was just a theoretical idea. We were wintering hogs by the sea, and that was commonly done, and presumably it was a transgression. By the Second World War the Manor rules were thought to be somewhat in the past and practice was loosening up. Then it went out of the window during the war, when the government encouraged farmers to import fertilizer and to increase production. However the Eskdale 24 Book is still an important document and a reference point for today.

Interestingly, the 24 Book recognized three height levels of fell for the stock: the lower fellside behind the farms was designated for milk cows, the median height area, and notably that around Burnmoor Tarn in the Eskdale Common, was for geld goods, heifers and bullocks; the high fells were the heafs for sheep. We kept the heaf for the sheep and in father's youth we had used the intermediate level for horses if not cattle.

Our Norse inheritance takes us back to the early 900s. There is a famous Viking cross at Gosforth Church, where the Eskdale and Wasdale roads meet on the way to the coast, that is dated about 925AD. It is a tall, slender, and much weathered stone that has both Viking gods and Christian themes incised into it. It is assumed that this date must be about the time of the actual Norse invasion from the Irish Sea in the west and the subsequent settlement. Also at the church there is a hog-back stone coffin of approximately the same period. It is said said, by some, to commemorate a battle on the top of Hardknott Pass where the Saxon King Ethelred (The Unready) with a 10,000 strong army was defeated in 1000AD. He was ambushed by his Norse enemies. It is true, he did harass Cumbria about this time. Even so 10,000 on the top of Hardknott seems an astonishing number – try feeding that number on the fell.

Our dialect was 'broad' which is a way of saying it was slow and deliberate, deep to guttural, and in my opinion, somewhat theatrical. There were significant pauses for the imagination. It contained many Norse words; grandparents particularly used them, not so much our parents. Sometimes our dialect was exaggerated to entertain but mostly it was on

Boot village, the mill on left at the packhorse bridge.

the level. Our generation were starting to drop a lot of the old words and expressions, no doubt in the interests of being intelligible to the wider world, but to be honest there was a bit of prejudice against dialects in general. The intonation in our dialect was very different from modern standard speech: the latter is faster, clipped, on a higher key, the speakers seem to exchange more information – less is left to the imagination and it is less dramatic.

To give a flavour of the dialect I will list some of our words, a lot of them are Norse; those that persisted were certainly descriptive of life on the farms. Fell, dale, tarn, ghyll and beck have been used throughout this account, and the meanings must now be clear: hill or mountain, valley, small or large lake, ravine, stream or river. A few more of our words might give an idea of how our speech sounded:

Aboot: about	garth: enclosure near	muck: manure
ars: I am	the farmhouse	reckon: consider
bait: carried food	gey: very	rive: rip
bairn: child	happen: perhaps	seaves or seives:
blaeberry: bilberry	hey up: look out	rushes
brigg: bridge	howe: hill	slape: slippery
clap: slap down	keld: water well	strang: strong
forcefully	kytel: milking coat	teem: pour
dee: die	laik: play	thrang: busy
dollop: lump	la'al: small	thwaite: clearing
flag: paving stone	lig: lie down	yacker: acre
foss: waterfall	lug: carry	
frae: from	moss: bog	

And a few phrases to give a flavour:
    'Werster gaan?' Where are you going?
    'Werst thew off te'? Where are you off too?
    'Gaan yam.' Going home.
    'Hasta.' Have you.
    'Shut-t-yat.' Shut the gate.

It was common for a 't' to be used in place of 'the', as in t'road, and sometimes it was more like a click, as in t'doer (door). I can still hear the elders and the natives. One of Father's favourites was 'Gaan tak it' meaning go on take it.

Then there was the curious way of counting sheep that the farm men might employ for our general entertainment as children, but that was Celtic from the Iron Age we were later to learn. Sheep were counted in twenties. There were local variations of the counting, it was supposed to differ according to the valley, and so some might disagree with this recital of the supposed Eskdale version of one through ten: yaena, taena, teddera, meddera, pimp, hofa, lofa, seckera, leckera, dec. (There was a dramatic pause of emphasis after each five.) Eleven to twenty went yaena-dec, taena-dec, teddera-dec, meddera-dec, bumfit, yaena-bumfit, taena-bumfit, teddera-bumfit, meddera-bumfit, giggot. However, what I think I heard was yan, tan, tithera, mithera (and I can't remember five, six and seven), and then it went on to hovera, dovera, dic. At the count of twenty you moved a stone and started over. It was dynamic recitation, one in step with the sheep trotting by as they were being numbered off. That style of counting seemed scarcely credible to us as children; we were always on the look out for being teased.

Apart from the old farmsteads, what notable or communally used buildings did we have? Boot Village (from Botel or Botl, Anglo-Saxon for dwelling or fold) was tiny, with the church and the school a little removed from it. It was all clustered on one short stretch of road, and could be taken in with a glance. The granite buildings were all old and looked of pretty much the same vintage, including the watermill, on the Whillan Beck. The church and the school were still used of course, but the mill became a relic of the past.

The watermill in Boot does not have a certain date, but it must have been a going concern very early on, since it provided vital functions for the valley. For the same reason, it was likely to have been continually worked and improved. It is said to have a Roman design, similar to mills found along Hadrian's Wall; however is much later, the earliest recorded date being 1294. The mill was used to grind oats (called corn by us) and presumably to process wool. It can still work, the ancient wooden cog wheels creak characteristically as they turn, powered by the turning waterwheel that scoops water from the beck as it rushes past. The grindstones are still there. Ground oats were used for haverbread (oat cake), oatmeal porridge and chowdy (a meat soup thickened with oats).

The mill closed in 1937 and farmers had then to go to Muncaster Mill a few miles away. Boot Mill's last owner was Ned Bibby, he was still operating the mill in my lifetime. I recall his name being used. Boot Mill is now a place for tourists. I expect that the Ghyll Bank Mill, also on the

Whillan Beck, may once have had the same functions as Boot Mill. In our childhood the mill belonged to a carpenter named Bailiff, who made small items of furniture from local wood. He particularly liked bog-oak. Regrettably, the saw-dust ignited one night and the mill burned down. We walked up to see the ruins; he gave me a bit of the melted glass. We knew the Bailiffs well. We used to go for tea in their cottage, which was across the yard from the farmhouse at Ghyll Bank; they had a pet bird in a cage, the only caged bird we had ever seen.

A possible date for St. Catherine's Church is about 1445, one of the bells is of that date; but there was said to be a place of worship there much earlier – as long ago as the sixth century. There is a record from 1445 of the people of Eskdale, it was a larger population then, petitioning the Pope, via Calder Abbey, for permission to construct a church for themselves, the reason being given that they had to go ten miles to St. Bees on the coast for baptisms, burials and the sacraments. The church was restored in the late 1800s, and the present stained glass put in. At the time of Henry VIII's dissolution of the monasteries (Calder Abbey was dissolved in 1536), the right to appoint clerics passed to the Stanley family of Dalegarth. We were all baptised at St Catherine's Church, including my children DeeDee and Catherine.

It is said that there was a sixth century hermit living a short distance east of the present church on Arment Hill, and that was the site of the Holy Well. Our local amateur antiquarian, Miss Fair, described the well as being lined with tile. I would suspect that most people do not know where to go to find it; it is just a short distance along the path from the church to Doctor's Bridge, just past Birker Dub. One has to scramble up the fellside called Arment Hill and look amongst the bracken. Auntie Gladys, of course, took us there on a school field trip, and told us that we were all supposed to be baptized with water from the well; I have no idea if that was actually the case, it was quite a scramble and a hunt, and the Esk was handy.

The ancient octagonal font in the church is incised with St. Catherine's wheel and has a marigold design commonly found on Roman altars and on early Christian tombstones. Widely differing dates are given for it, all the way from 1330 to the mid-1600s. An interesting bit of history was that the font had once had to be rescued from nearby Kirk House farmyard, in 1876; presumably it had spent a time feeding stock during a more secular period.

St Catherine's Church.

The large board on the inside church wall and above the font records money given by locals for education in 1798; the interest from which was for the school and its pupils. I had been one lucky recipient as a local child. The school was endowed in 1723. Poor children were taught free. The school had therefore been around over two centuries before I was taught there. The schoolmaster in the 1700s was paid a basic salary with extra sums of money added according to what subjects he taught – Greek and Latin were mentioned. Auntie Gladys would have been very surprised by a request for the classics.

Generally, parish registers did not start until about 1538; that was supposed to be when surnames were first commonly used. St. Catherine's earliest entry is about 1626. A first recorded birth was in 1627, and was a Hartley, the first marriage was a Hartley and a Wilson, and the first death a Nycholsonne. The names occur in many historic documents, and are still common today. For instance, one of the original jurors named in the Eskdale Book of 24 was a Hartley.

The graveyard at St. Catherine's served all of Eskdale, and at one time Wasdale Head as well, since prior to 1900 the tiny church in Wasdale Head did not have a graveyard. Coffins were historically brought from Wasdale over Burnmoor on horse back or cart down through Ghyll Bank to the village and then on to the church. It was even called the Coffin Road. The graveyard is always a big draw for local people since a lot of their deceased relatives are there – ours too naturally. It is not uncommon when visiting to find people going around from one stone to another looking for a familiar name. On a visit home, many years later, I found an old Eskdale High School friend doing just that; as children we had walked to school together when she lived at Penny Hill. The church could be approached from all four directions. There is the beckside path from Doctor's Bridge in the east, and another from the south on the opposite side of the river with a stepping stone crossing over the river at the church. From the west there is a proper 'lonnin' from Trofuss, and from the north a wider and gravel road, but still with hair-raising tight spots, for vehicles from the village and the main road.

Our Post Office in the village was one of the few amenities. In our early days, it was run by Mrs. Martin, a very frail old lady in long black Victorian type dress, ending comically in bedroom slippers. Customers rang a bell and she shuffled down the hallway from her kitchen. Fortunately for her, there was not a lot of custom. Mrs. Martin took the official nature of her job seriously and looked at 'incomers' in a questioning manner: she was given to reading lists of the 'wanted' that she received from the postal service and was generally on the look out. Thus strangers, or any incomer, might be kept waiting for their packages while she perused the list.

As a child I was present one day when she dressed down an impatient Lord Lindsay who was making a mild objection at being kept standing. 'I've seen the likes of you before' she intoned, fixing him with a corrective glare over her glasses. He did have quite an unkempt appearance, as a child I could acknowledge that. He was dressed down, as for life in the country: wrapped in an old mac, and was that binder twine around the waist? It is true that the classic dress of our farmers could be very smart: the tweed jacket, the riding pants, the hand knitted wool knee socks, sometimes leather gaiters, and leather boots. Our farmers were work and fell ready – and that dress did give one real confidence that all was in hand, that all was being taken care of.

Later I discovered that Lord Lindsay had a very interesting background. He was a Cambridge don – and we did have quite a few academics about then. The family had bought the Bailiff's Ghyll Bank cottage for a holiday home, beautifully situated half way up the fell to Burnmoor Tarn, the very place of our early tea parties. Before that the Lindsay family had spent holidays at a farm on Birker Moor; so Lindsay had been around for years; he even took the name of Birker, as in Lord Lindsay of Birker. He was a Labour Peer, the title given in recognition of his contribution to the educational policies of the post-war Labour government. Their free secondary schooling affected all of my generation – perhaps more than anything else. He was therefore not a historic landowning aristocrat who would have been well known to Mrs. Martin; and the social engineering of the post-war era may have meant little to her.

To the locals she was tolerant but serious. I think I only saw her smile once and that was when I took my very small sister Barbara into the Post Office. (We were forever miles from home and on foot. Not that Barbara was an enthusiastic walker, one of her memorable sayings as a five year old was 'Me legs is aching already.') Then Mrs. Martin's pale, lined, face melted as she peered down over the counter. She was charmed, the 'likes' of a small child eminently to be preferred to those for whom she had to consult the 'wanted' list.

Did we have an actual manor house, then, from medieval times? Where did the great historic landowning aristocrats live? What evidence was there of the social structure from the past? The nearest manor would be Dalegarth Hall, the farm near the school over Trofuss Bridge. It had Elizabethan features, an enormous fireplace one could walk into, and the characteristic rounded chimneys. It belonged to the prominent Old English Stanley family. I believe that Aunt Gladys told us that a Stanley had gone on Crusades, (crusading times were between 1096 and 1272). Stanleys had a long and influential history in Eskdale: they managed land on the south side of the Esk in the jurisdiction called Austhwaite and Birker. Theirs was a separate jurisdiction from our Eskdale Manor on the north side of the Esk. (The word manor in that sense refers not to a mansion but to an area under a jurisdiction.) In medieval times the Eskdale Manor was owned from a more distant place and that was Egremont Castle.

On the north side of the Esk you would have to go four miles down the valley to Eskdale Green before there is a manor house, that would be the Gate House, but that wasn't at all old. It dates from 1896. It was built as a large country house for the Rea family, attractively set with its own spectacular lake and boathouse. The original Rea was a coal and shipping magnate, and the estate comprised significant property in Eskdale Green and in Miterdale. In fact our Armstrong family had bought Woolpack from a Rea. The knighthood had been given in 1937 in recognition of Parliamentary service. We saw a bit of the Reas as they sometimes came to dinner at the inn, and the Gatehouse was the setting for the annual garden fete that was much enjoyed by the entire valley. When the family finally sold, it became an Outward Bound Mountain School, first for city boys, and later girls; we are told they abseiled down the tower, and greeted daybreak by a dive into the cold lake.

Further away, near the mouth of the Esk, is Muncaster Castle. It is a real and impressive castle of obvious age; well set amongst the trees on Muncaster Fell. Its famous long terrace has fabulous views: up the Esk valley to the central fells, across the valley in the Barnscar direction, and down to the estuary. It dates most certainly from about 1208 but possibly was there well before that and thought to have been built on the site of Roman remains. The Norman Conquest was 1066 and the original owner was there before, and during, the conquest, and was granted land around this time. Amazingly, the original Pennington family still live there. This area of Muncaster was my mother's home ground. She loved the grounds, and on a walk around, might suddenly appear out of the bushes with a cutting from something hidden behind her back. Recently my nieces' girls have enjoyed working on the estate.

In Medieval times, our north side of upper Eskdale and its farms were included in the southern part of the Barony of Copeland (Copeland is derived from the Norse word for bought). Copeland Forest once covered the western valleys of Cumbria. My understanding is that the headquarters was Egremont Castle; the title of the owner being Lord Egremont. A record in 1338 puts this in the Lucy family. Egremont itself is a market town on the road to Whitehaven, a good few miles away from Eskdale, and the castle is now a ruin at its centre. About 1539, the Percy family of Northumbria acquired our bit of Copeland, that is Wasdale Head, Miterdale and Eskdale, the whole then being called the Eskdale Manor, and later surrendered it to a Whyndham.

The Manor of Eskdale, the jurisdiction, was talked about in ancient documents, and this is where the Eskdale 24 Book comes in. There the Eskdale Common is named, the 7,590 unenclosed acres of common grazing on the fell, sectioned into individual heafs, and to which our farms in upper Eskdale had rights. By my time, we were a freehold property with grazing rights on the Common. Previously things may have been very different for the locals and they paid rent. Still we get the idea that the

Eskdale Common farmers finally did rather well in political terms; in making their own rules and finally getting ownership of their farms. In 1979 the Common was transferred to the National Trust and so now belongs to the nation and the National Trust have now bought up most of upper Eskdale, certainly that above Woolpack.

There is an arresting fact in the ancient agreements on the boundaries of the heafs in our Common; a central portion, that centred on Scafell, but including Slight Side, was excluded from the heaf plans. It was retained as the exclusive hunting area of the landowning aristocrat. People had space then. Scafell is not easy to get to from any direction, one would have hours of climbing over the lower fells, and it is not very suitable as horse country. The aristocrats would have to put in a lot of effort getting there and getting back with the game; they must have been just as fit as the farmers. There were deer then on Scafell, but unfortunately not into our time. There were still deer down Birkby and into Waberthwaite. There is a sad account, from 1793, of the last deer off Scafell being driven into Wastwater and taken there. We were left with the Staghorn Moss on Scafell, said to be eaten by deer.

The name Scafell is said to be from the Norse words Scow-fell meaning wooded hill, which is surprising since it is now bare of trees or of shrubs. The tree line is very much on the lower fell, and it follows ravines. It is hard to imagine that Scafell could have been wooded; but one supposes that a thousand years, and more, of cutting and grazing must have had a major impact on the landscape. The summit of Scafell was given to the nation in 1919 by Lord Leconfield, '…subject to any commoner's rights', and possibly about the same time, a bit of the Wasdale side of Scafell was bought by the Fell and Rock Climbing Club. Both were dedicated to the fallen of the First World War.

We had signs of pre-history in stone circles on Burnmoor and in the Bronze Age village of Barnscar on Birker Moor, and there were many cairns dotted about. I don't know what the cairns were originally for but they were a common sight on the fell, just piles of stones amongst the bracken. Perhaps they were a way to clear the land for agriculture, perhaps they marked borders, or maybe they were religious. We felt impelled to add one more stone as we passed – if that could be a clue. We had the Roman Camp on Hardknott, constructed in early historic times. To us these monuments didn't look much different from our own granite walls, the stone itself was of the same age, it looked exactly the same, and it boasted the same covering lichens.

It is now said that there are at least four, possibly five, prehistoric stone circles on the way up the fell to Burnmoor Tarn from Boot Village between the Whillan and Mite becks and north west of Ghyll Bank. There are also cairns there, and it is thought there may have been a settlement, too. I don't know if there is any proof of what these circles were used for, just like more famous stone circles. It is assumed that the purpose was religious, but they could have been a sign of a meeting place or expressed ownership. Burned bones and deer antlers are said to have been found there. In my day the circles were a vague rumour only; we had very little information to go on. I did once did go off on my own to look for them, and that was a longish walk from Woolpack directly over the fell by Eel Tarn and towards Boot Bank. I have a vivid memory of standing still, feeling that I must be close, and uncertain of where to go next when I realized that I was standing in the middle of a circle, and that was eerie. They were medium sized stones, you had to be right upon them before they could be seen as a circle. That was the only circle I found.

We had seen more impressive circles outside of Eskdale, particularly the one on Cold Fell above the ruin of Calder Abbey. The circles are 4,000 years old, dating from about 2,000BC. They are half way up the fell and in pretty exposed places. Why there? Had there been any circles lower down and subsequently cleared out of the way?

Another rumour we children followed up on was a visit to the prehistoric Bronze Age site of Barnscar. We went on that adventure with cousin Michael; first climbing Birker Moor and then walking west past Devoke Water to get to it. Interestingly for us another possible approach is from the west side from the grandparents old farm of Dyke Croft. The cart-track that climbed up behind Dyke led to Barnscar, the same track that we went a short way along to collect the eggs.

We did not have much idea of what there was to see at Barnscar, but we came on what looked like a group of cairns covered in vegetation. I have to confess that we did something that would be much frowned upon today: we did some excavating. We pulled off the sod and a covering layer of smallish stones on one of the mounds to discover, underneath, a very large roundish boulder with quite a peak. An unlikely shaped stone to have been in a hut, we thought, since you couldn't set anything on it, and it would be difficult to sit people around it, the space would have been too narrow, the covering stones too small to support a wall. We thought the central stone very large to mark a grave since moving a stone of that size would have been very difficult. We couldn't make it into anything meaningful; and that was the sum total of our investigation and of our vandalism. Maybe it was a burial mound.

We now hear that Barnscar is a huge site of burial mounds and a stone city. The stone dwellings are connected together by a path running between them. Some urns have been found under cairns indicating burials. We did not get as far as the stone city, we missed it entirely, and perhaps just as well or we might have yet more on our consciences. Whereas atheism is not a threat to the natives, and Republicanism might be considered a personal choice, and both known in Eskdale, vandalism most certainly was not. Destruction of any kind was deplored; so obviously we did not admit to our excavation at home. Dislodging stone was thought to be a tourist trait. Like the Burnmoor circles Barnscar is high up, mid-fell level, and had good views, particularly of the Irish Sea. Anything on the valley floor would have been lost to agriculture one assumes, but a certain height may have been preferred for the good views with regard to defense. The Bronze age ended about 700BC and I don't have an actual date for Barnscar, but it is conjectured that the site might still have been inhabited when the Roman army arrived.

Without a doubt our most celebrated monument was the Roman camp at Hardknott, the Romans called it Mediobogdum. This was again half way up the fell; and just off the pass road on the north side. The situation on Hardknott was logically chosen since the pass, and that of Wrynose, the next one over, took one to the eastern Lake District. It was well situated directly on a road from west to east through the mountains of the central Lakes. Hardknott camp was constructed to link the Roman fort of Ambleside, inland, to the fort of Ravenglass on the coast. Perhaps a Roman scouted for the best crossing to build a road or possibly they used an already existing road. The camp has a magnificent view down the valley to the sea, an obvious advantage for an occupying force. On a good day it is said that you can see the Isle of Man, although I never did. It is also thought that the location might have been chosen for a possible future Roman invasion of Ireland. A few steps from the camp, at a point looking over the valley, there are the stunning views of Scafell to the north.

Apart from linking the forts of Ambleside and Ravenglass, Hardknott was believed to be some kind of military back-up for Hadrian's Wall, which marked the margin of the Roman Empire creating England on one side and Scotland on the other. Presumably the wall was some protection against the Scottish raids, which were a hazard, and one that continued for a very long time after the Romans had left. Agricola the Roman general, had reached Carlisle and the Tyne by about 78AD and established garrisons, and his name did appear on a sandstone at Hardknott. Later, about 122AD Hadrian started his wall which went from the Solway Firth on the west coast to the Northumberland coast in the east, at Wallsend, with forts dotted along its length.

Hardknott camp dates from about that same time and was occupied on and off until about 400AD. The fort is made of the local granite, a square plan with four gates, north, south, east and west, with towers on the corners. The living quarters, granary and commander's headquarters are in the middle. There was some freestone brought from St. Bees, notably for the large supports on which the gates turned. The extensive bath-house with its hot and cold rooms, was curiously outside the fort; it did not then appear that the Romans were much afraid of the local population. Slightly above the fort was the flattened parade ground. A Roman road went down the valley crossing the Esk at Wha House and proceeding on the south side of the river until it got to Forge Bridge where it recrossed and went on to Ravenglass. A bit of the original Roman road west of Wha House became obvious to me on a painting trip, it can be seen in the contours in a field. Farther out of Eskdale there are known bits of Roman road and they are remarkable for being straight; our later roads became less martial and efficient, following the terrain, full of ups and downs and corners.

There were said to be about 400 soldiers at Hardknott, some from the Dalmatian coast, and I have to assume they had horses. A formidable group to feed, one would think; at Woolpack we would have been hard pressed to feed this horde on any continuous basis, although it is a possible number to consider, unlike Ethelred's reputed 10,000 and the opposing Norse. The Romans would have had to deal with the locals, the Celts, presumably a sparse population amazed at the army were perhaps not much of a threat. Once, on a visit to the camp, sitting on the wall, Mother wondered aloud what our ancestors would have looked like to the Romans; the answer, I now presume, would be that the ancestors of most of the locals had not yet arrived in Eskdale. Tacitus, the Roman writer who accompanied Agricola on his campaign did say, in a general way, that the Britons were cheerful about paying the levy and the tribute provided there was no abuse but that they '…were not broken to slavery'.

The Roman camp at Hardknott.

In the Roman period, I envision the valley floor to have been a dense forest with abundant game, the rivers full of fish. After all, the adjacent Harter Fell was so named for its deer. Perhaps they brought in their grain, necessary for their animals as well as themselves; the granary being a prominent feature in the fort. In our tenure at Woolpack, we had one of those sandstone blocks with a hole drilled in the middle which had been used for the hinge of a fort gate. I do not know who was responsible for that vandalism. At Woolpack it had once been used as a mounting block.

Miss Charlesworth, our lone visiting archaeologist, gave us some excitement by digging up a bit of a Roman leather jerkin, and a disconcertingly lightweight Roman sandal; very different footwear from our farmers' boots. The leather had been preserved because the ground is acidic, bog-like, in spite of the height above the valley floor. One fears that the soldiers were basically dressed as for the Mediterranean, a tunic with bare arms and legs, hopefully they were allowed extra clothing for Hardknott. Tacitus was direct about how they found the weather. 'The climate is objectionable, with its frequent rains and mists, but there is no extreme cold.' Tacitus also comments on the agricultural angle. 'Crops are slow to ripen, but quick to grow – both facts due to the same cause, the extreme moistness of the land and sky.' We are told that a long time ago other items had been unearthed at Hardknott: Samian (Roman) pottery shards, glass, nails, lead piping, brooches and coins. I expect they are in the Carlisle museum.

Very soon after the collapse of the Roman Empire, about 400AD, and the subsequent departure of the army, there were the Anglo-Saxon invasions, and those people came to stay. They came from modern Germany and southern Scandinavia, originally to the eastern side of England, and to begin with they stayed in the east. When they filtered into Cumbria they are reputed to have taken the best farming land around the coast, at sea level first, and, one assumes, some reached into the mountainous areas and on into upper Eskdale. While I am not familiar with any specifically Anglo-Saxon remains, we had some Anglo-Saxon family names – Hartley was one. We heard much more about the Norse invasion of 900AD, and understood they favoured the fells.

Apart from the archaeology and the medieval farms, there are few remains of much else, except for some old mines. Mining was widespread in West Cumbria and some of the valleys had iron ore, much used in the Bessemer process of making steel. The seams came to the surface on the lower slopes of the fells. Investors came into Eskdale and Miterdale to mine for a very brief period in Victorian times, from about 1841 to 1885. We had about seven small mines. On the north side of the Esk these were into the fell at Beckfoot near the school, Nab Gill just above Boot, behind Paddockwray and Christcliff, and between Bird How and Taw House. On the south side of the Esk, there was the mine near the church where Auntie Gladys took her school children on an outing, and one behind Penny Hill. I believe that the Nab Gill one was the most productive mine, barely visible now as you look up at Boot Bank from the village, not much of a scar. You could just make out a pile of tailings, pretty well disguised by overgrowth. Right at the Nab Gill site, there is not much to see on the outside, but apparently there are a lot of passages following the seams inside. That mine was briefly reopened in the early 1900s when the price must have been worth it. Our post office was said to have been the mine manager's house.

As children, we idly picked up the kidney ore (haematite). We did not ever think of exploring inside any mine, which is surprising. I suppose it was a real oddity to us, a very foreign thing in fact, not like the serious business of farming. The farmers had innocently used the iron for the smit marks on their sheep. The mining venture did leave the narrow gauge railway, originally used to carry the ore away. Later on it was turned into an open train route plying between Eskdale and Ravenglass, going through the woods on the side of the valley, and on to the main line at the coast. The train (the 'Ratty') ran in summer and was a minor attraction to us on the way to school; the miniature engine turned on its turntable as it prepared to go back. I would guess that the little row of brick cottages, set back from the line at the foot of the fell there, could have been built for the miners and rail workers. Irreverently, the cottages were referred to as the brick huts by local people, the very name may express something about the local attitude to mining. In modern times the cottages with their gardens would be considered attractive housing. We knew them well since we had schoolmates who lived there, but they weren't the ancient monuments in which we lived, and under the present rules, they very probably could not have been built in upper Eskdale, since they were out of character, constructed as they are of brick not the local stone.

The first evidence of mining was from before Victorian times. Our local amateur archaeologist, Miss Fair, documented iron smelting in Eskdale Green at Bankend Farm much earlier, about 1590. There is a record of a Pennington buying the farm and incorporating it into his bloom-smithing activities. That industry demanded a lot of charcoal, and consequently a lot of lumber was taken from the surrounding country. There is a record, for instance, of 1,000 trees being felled in Eskdale, Miterdale and Wasdale for charcoal for the close-by Muncaster Head Forge. That industry folded about 1710 as the more productive, and less expensive in terms of wood, blast furnaces came into being and in a more distant place. The blacksmith's forge of our youth was very close to Muncaster Head at the aptly named Forge Bridge.

In our day there was no mining, no industry; farming was still the major undertaking, and the 'taking of visitors' that presumably came with the Victorian era.

14

Celebrities and the Lakes

Just how did the Lake District get into the national consciousness as such a desirable place to visit, to buy into and to preserve, eventually to become the most visited National Park in England? In short, to be seen as too good to leave to the locals. What happened? There are attractive mountains in Wales. Scotland is altogether on a much bigger scale, is full of scenery, has many more possibilities, and much, much grander and higher peaks. Undoubtedly it had a lot to do with writers, particularly the poets. The other thing is the inescapable fact that the Lakes are not too far away from industrial towns and cities where the urban population has a desperate need for somewhere to go, for some contact with nature.

The Lake District has not always been seen as desirable. In the Middle Ages, the county of Cumbria, of which the Lake District is the mountainous centre, had been a difficult place to live because of the long-standing conflict between Scotland and England who both laid claims to the area. There were 'set' battles between Scotland and England that particularly devastated the north of the county; they established a military style of life that allowed the reiving (robbing) by people on both sides of the border to look like normal behaviour. Even away from the immediate border, there was an alert system of bonfires set in high places throughout Cumbria, such as on Hardknott. Fires were lit when a Scottish raiding party was spotted; and then there were the reserve call-up arrangements to counter those raids. Presumably this unease entered the national consciousness; I imagine that one would have needed a compelling reason to visit Cumbria at this particular time.

It was not until the late seventeenth and the early eighteenth century after the union of England and Scotland, that Cumbria began to be considered as a possible place to visit merely to take in the scenery. And even on scenic grounds, Cumbria was at first questionable. Daniel Defoe (1660-1731), of Robinson Crusoe fame, thought it a fearsome place. About fifty years after the peace had arrived (by way of the shared Crown and subsequently by the government), Defoe journeyed around the island of Great Britain writing his travel advisory. Speaking of the Westmorland part of Cumbria, he wrote '…a country eminent only for being the wildest, most barren and frightful of any that I have passed over in England, or even Wales itself; the west side Cumberland, is indeed bounded by a chain of almost impassable mountains which are called fells.' Somehow, during this visit, our Tyson relatives were already making a living in Wasdale right up against those '…almost impassable mountains.' The hill farms at the heads of the valleys were established and working. Presumably Defoe's severe judgment must have put off casual travellers.

It took a while, but that reputation was to be supremely altered for the better. In 1769 the poet Thomas Gray visited the eastern section of the Lake District, the area of Keswick, Grasmere and Borrowdale and wrote a more positive guide. At the same time he foreshadowed the later Romantic Movement of Wordsworth and the 'Lake poets'. He wrote a poem on his visit entitled *The Jaws of Borodale*. At that date Borrowdale was indeed … 'far it was from the madding crowd' (a line in his famous poem *Elegy*).

Another guide to Lakeland was published in 1778, written by Father Thomas West, a Scot and Jesuit, who had settled in Furness in West Cumbria. He too challenged the view that the Lake District was a wild and savage place. Importantly, he emphasized specific viewpoints. He called them 'viewing stations' and this was to become a mark of the Lake poets. In Cumbria his favourite viewing stations were down by a lake, which he turned his back to and looked at through a mirror rather like an artist might when composing. West was much travelled in Europe. This was a time when the gentry extended their formal education by going on Grand Tours through Europe and beyond to the Orient and had become familiar with the current idea of the 'picturesque'. This was a way of looking at landscape as if it were a painting by Claude Lorraine or Nicolas Poussin, admired French Baroque artists of the sixteenth and seventeenth centuries. These artists were genuinely interested in landscape, but made it into an idealized pastoral one, possibly with the addition of a ruin, perhaps an animal or two, or a few bucolic or mythological figures – not quite the real place.

Father West sought to extend this European idea of the picturesque to the Lake District. He suggested that instead of going around Europe one might try the far North West of England, it was nearer to home. 'They who intend to make the continental tour should begin here; as it will give, in miniature, an idea of what they are to meet with there, in traversing the Alps and the Apennines; to which our northern mountains are not inferior in beauty and line, or variety of summit, number of lakes, and transparency of the water; nor in colouring of rock, or softness of turf; but in height and extent only.' Since West uses the word miniature here, I suppose that he is also warning those to whom the height and extent of mountains are paramount, that the Lake District is on an accessible and human scale, it was part of their charm. Importantly, West comments on the welcoming locals '…mountain virtue and pastoral hospitality are found at every farm.'

A decade later, William Gilpin went around England consciously looking for picturesque landscapes. He was a curate and a schoolteacher, Cumbrian born of an 'educated' class. He thought, very much as a present day painter might, that landscape as created by nature was seldom perfect. He talked about foreground, middle ground, background and the added interests. The idea was to look at a known landscape and take liberties with it: to improve it for aesthetic reasons. This was to enter a different realm. In fact he took the idea of looking for the picturesque to wildly entertaining levels until it became a joke, sometimes mocked in the literature of the day. For instance, the pass of Dunmail Raise that rises up from Thirlmere did not meet with his requirements: it was, for him, a frightful experience. 'The whole view is of the horrid kind. With a view of adorning a scene with figures nothing could suit it better than a group of banditti. Of all the scenes I ever saw this was most adapted to the penetration of some frightful deed.' One does wonder what the local farmers might have made of his wild imaginings on their grazing land; but then they would not be likely to read his guide or be asked for their opinion.

It was William Wordsworth who did most to popularize the Lake District; he personified the Romantic Movement. His guide to the Lakes was published in 1810, and there were many later editions. He echoed the idea of the Grand Tour being extended to the Lakes. This was pertinent at the time since there was political unrest in Europe: the Napoleonic Wars. Those who could have been on a Grand Tour might instead be now in real need of something safer. Wordsworth was also Cumbrian born, at Cockermouth on the fringes of the Lake District (his family were neighbours of the Christians, and so of Fletcher of the *Bounty* fame). Wordsworth's father was employed as a legal agent for Lowther Castle. Wordsworth too had travelled in Europe, but by 1799 he had come north again to live at

Dove Cottage, in Grasmere. He was very much on the positive side concerning his birthplace, going as far as to express his preference for the Lake District over Wales and Scotland.

Wordsworth saw 'no barren and frightful place' or 'horrid view'. Far from it. 'I do not know of any tract of country in which, in so narrow a compass, may be found an equal variety in the influences of light and shadow upon the sublime and beautiful features of the landscape.' He wrote, 'Such clouds cleaving to their station, or lifting up suddenly their glittering heads from behind rocky barriers, or hurrying out of sight with speed over the sharpest edge – will often tempt an inhabitant to congratulate himself on belonging to a country of mists and clouds and storms, and make him think of the blank sky of Egypt, and the cerulean vacancy of Italy, as an unanimated, and even a sad spectacle.' Then about the geography, the way the valleys radiate out from Scafell, '…from Scawfell, a shepherd would not require more than an hour to descend into any one of eight of the principal vales by which he would be surrounded; and all the others lie (with the exception of Haweswater) at but a small distance. Yet clustered together, every valley has its own distinct and separate character…'

Wordsworth is correct about the valleys having their own character. Wasdale and Eskdale for example. Wasdale is dominated by screes, the spectacular rockfalls going down into the lake, Eskdale, by comparison, is a lush green garden.

Wordsworth is also correct that from the central fells one can drop down easily into the valleys that radiate out from Scafell. David, my niece's shepherd husband, and his dog, started out from Butterilket farm at the head of Eskdale and became disoriented by thick mist on the central fells. They followed a sheep trod out of the mist to find themselves in Langdale by mistake. They then went back up onto the fell again to come down into Eskdale at Butterilket. Similarly, on another occasion, David left Ennerdale with an Ennerdale shepherd and they got into a thick disorienting mist on the high fells. The Ennerdale shepherd dropped down into Wasdale by mistake but David came down correctly into Ennerdale and so was able to drive around to Wasdale to pick up his companion.

Wordsworth's guide book and his poems were the beginning of the serious popularity of the Lake District. One cannot over-estimate Wordsworth's influence on the national consciousness: the English sensibility. Since his time he has most likely been represented in most Secondary School curricula, so reaching the young early, but that was not all. Not only was the Lake District lovable for itself, there was the important question of to whom it belonged. Wordsworth went on to describe the Lakes as '… a sort of national property, in which every man has a right and interest, who has an eye to perceive and a heart to enjoy.' This was advancing from the poetic into something quite different: a national treasure, a right of ownership, a right of access. Wordsworth was prescient, even clairvoyant. Two centuries later that is what the Lake District has become, a National Park, a public place. His ideas on the landscape not only inform the visitors and new residents, they also inform the institutions of the National Park and the National Trust.

It was more than just looking and admiring. Wordsworth himself, perhaps with his sister Dorothy or with his guests or other Lake poets, seriously walked the valleys and the fells, miles a day, commenting, writing and composing wherever he went. He chose itineraries with the finest views, in line with the custom of looking for the picturesque. He wrote the following on the view down Eskdale: '… the green vale of Esk – deep and green, with its glittering serpent stream, lay before us; and on we looked to the Mountains near the sea, – Black Comb pre-eminent, and, still beyond, to the Sea itself, in dazzling brightness.' He was notably fond of the Duddon Valley, next door to Eskdale, and he also composed at Cockley Beck, the other side of Hardknott from upper Eskdale.

Not only did Wordsworth walk, but he promoted public footpaths with a contemporary enthusiasm, readily going through farms and grazing. He was showing his public how to do it: how to take ownership. He was able to do this because of the existing ancient customary paths between farms and over the fells. To the farming community he was perhaps an entertaining diversion, one of the gentry muttering to himself as he strode about. It seems that he did not talk much to the locals, but did sometimes use them as guides. According to Canon Rawnsley's research, while local people did not read Wordsworth's poetry, they curiously imagined it to have been written by his sister Dorothy or perhaps by Coleridge's son Hartley.

One supposes that no-one commonly asked for the opinions of the residents at the time; and obviously their interests were quite different from the poets. Local people were always getting on with making the area as agriculturally productive as they could; they certainly were not looking through a Romantic prism. They identified with their geography and were part of it, and that is pretty much how Wordsworth saw it. He talked about the farmers working with nature to produce the specific landscape of the Lake District. This was seen as a new aesthetic idea: the residents and the landscape working together towards a specific outcome. Still there is a gap there, the lives and interests of local people were generally not paid as much attention as was their landscape, and that was to become a mark of incomers. But, most importantly, Wordsworth did see the vulnerabilities of the landscape with too many visitors. He did not, however, remark on too many sheep.

We have now arrived at a time when the lifestyle and the resultant landscape that Wordsworth so admired and celebrated is very much changed, is on the way to being taken over entirely by tourism, by visitors coming to look, to admire, and to walk. Those that took a part in fashioning the landscape are on the decline; much farming activity has been arrested. The Lake District now has some aspects of a museum: nevertheless, we, the native born, are grateful for this conservation effort, from being saved from outright commercialism. Many parts of the Lake District still have an 'unspoilt' look, and for this we are indebted to Wordsworth. When one goes back to Eskdale, it still on the surface looks pretty much the same, and in the fields and on the fell it still feels pretty much the same, but the signs are there. With the reduction in the stock and the crops, the landscape must be changing.

Geoff Brown lists the still existing Herdwick flocks in upper Eskdale in 2009. Woolpack is not on the list but other farms are, for instance, Penny Hill, Wha House, Taw House, Butterilkit, Ghyll Bank, Spout House, Dalegarth. Paddockwray is not listed but does still have a flock, but perhaps not pure Herdwick. The National Trust owns much of upper Eskdale now including Woolpack land and grazing, and, I believe, it is their policy to keep Herdwicks as the indigenous breed of the central fells.

The mass tourism of today was not really on Wordsworth's mind any more than it was on that of the peasantry. He writes in what today reads as a class conscious manner. He wanted his guide '… to be a companion for the minds of persons of taste, and feeling for the landscape.' He is recorded as being appalled at the coming of the railway to the Lake District. There is his famous complaint: 'is there no nook of English ground secure from rash assault?' He was afraid that too many people would come from the newly industrial towns and cities; while he sympathized with the urban residents' plight, he was nevertheless nervous about their needs. He rightly worried about what tourists and their money might do to a small and vulnerable landscape, but, conversely, he was attracting people to the area.

The railways were bringing in people desperately in need of that of which Wordsworth so eloquently wrote. He was afraid '… that the railways are also ready to devise or encourage entertainments tempting humbler classes to leave their homes.' In this regard he also speaks darkly of the 'lower class of inn-keepers' (Armstrong hoteliers might have laughed about that). Wordsworth wrote long letters to the *Morning Post* on the subject of the railway coming to the Lake District and may have been influential in having it stop at Windermere. Wordsworth was not to know of today's stream of cars on the narrow roads and their parking needs.

Wordsworth was not only worried about temporary visitors but also about settlers coming into the Lake District, attracted by the scenery. Again he was prescient: 'The feudal tenure under which the estates are held has indeed done something towards checking this influx of new settlers; but so strong is the inclination that these galling restraints are endured; and it is probable that in a few years the country on the margin of the Lakes will fall entirely into the possession of the gentry, either strangers or natives!' The tide is not now restricted to the gentry settling on the outskirts; now people of all social classes have penetrated the whole, reaching into the heads of the valleys in central Cumbria as well. Wordsworth hoped that '… skill and knowledge would prevent deviations from the path of simplicity and beauty along which, without design and unconsciously, their humble predecessors have moved.' Those strange farmers again, that had fashioned his landscape. Wordsworth's ideas were influential and we have to suppose this played a part in the eventual banning of new building and in favour of the conversion of existing farms and their barns to satisfy the rising demand for housing.

The Armstrong family, by the 1800s, were seeing an opportunity in tourism and establishing a family tradition of hotel keeping. By that time David, John and Benjamin, the sons of Benjamin and Mary were managing the imposing new hotels that Wordsworth was so unsure of, even though built of the local stone, and catering for Wordsworth's 'persons of taste'. This kind of clientele became part of Armstrong experience and mindset; it was where they started off in the business. My great-grandmother is reported to have cooked a meal for Queen Victoria, the latter presumably being on her way to or from Scotland. Victoria liked the bread buns so much she asked to meet the cook. Over time the clientele was to become more broadly socially based, and the catering needs changed.

A century later, cousin John Armstrong Bulman, at the New Dungeon Ghyll Hotel in Langdale, complained when bus loads of tourists first appeared at the hotel for a drink and a snack. He threatened that he would put a slot machine for snacks on the grounds, out in front of the bar. I don't know if he did. We were accustomed to guests being resident in manageable numbers, eating breakfast, lunch and dinner, hiking, seen and talked to long enough to get to know them. But there had been a shift in customers and their needs, they now wanted much less and more quickly. Many were in fact just passing through; some seeing the Lakes pretty much through a window. Eventually cousin John became a Lake District warden, an employee of the Lake District Planning Board, and so completely in tune with the times becoming central to decisions taken in the Lake District and to the enforcement of the rules as they were made. We were fortunate in upper Eskdale in that we did not see bus loads of tourists.

Wordsworth had a constant stream of personal visitors, said to be as many as 500 a year, and notably he attracted other poets. The Poet Laureate Southey (of the Three Bears fame) took up residence at Greta Hall, Keswick, followed by Coleridge and de Quincey. All of them celebrated and popularized the Lake District. There were two poet laureates in residence and at the same time. These poets, too, had streams of famous and other influential visitors: writers, politicians, scientists.

Coleridge proved to be a serious long distance walker. In 1802 he did his nine day walk around the Lake District, starting and finishing at his home (and that of the Southey family) at Greta Hall, in Keswick. He used his own sketchy map. On this walk he went up Wasdale and stayed overnight at the Wasdale Head Hotel and wrote about the proprietor Thomas Tyson. Tyson gave Coleridge suggestions on the difficult route that he had chosen to take over Scafell and down into Upper Eskdale. In one of Coleridge's letters he speaks of descending into Eskdale. 'I must drop down into Eskdale that lies under to my right – the upper part of it the wildest and savagest surely of all the Vales that were ever seen from the Top of an English Mountain and the lower part the loveliest.'

At the head of Eskdale he stayed overnight at Taw House and the next day walked down Eskdale, writing as he went. He would pass by Woolpack, might well have gone in for some refreshment and direction. It was on this walk that he noted the attractive farms that he passed by 'nestling in the trees at the foot of the fell' as previously quoted. Woolpack and Paddockwray must certainly have been two of them. He passed Boot Village and after the Forge Bridge walked south up onto Birker Moor to Devoke Water. There he looked for the Barnscar site but failed to find it and went down into the Duddon Valley, which he described as 'eminently picturesque'.

There were notable visiting artists in Victorian times. John Ruskin, the art historian, took up residence in Coniston, and he had an enormous influence on English minds. He thought about, and wrote about, the relationship between people and nature. Ruskin's ideas, in fact, were to become the foundation of the National Trust. He involved himself with local people and their crafts. Ruskin, too, had visitors: his artist friends included the pre-Raphaelites and Kate Greenaway. Turner and Constable came to the Lake District to paint. John Sell Cotman famously painted Greta Bridge. George Romney was himself from Dalton just to the south of the Lake District.

Canon Hardwicke Rawnsley was another incomer in Victorian times and perhaps the most influential of all since he had practical concerns. He was vicar at Wray, Windermere, and later at Crosthwaite Church in Keswick; but he did not confine himself to spiritual matters. For a time he was on Cumberland County Council – so making political decisions. He was much attracted to Ruskin's ideas of preservation and was a co-founder of the Friends of the Lake District, along with such figures as Robert Browning and Alfred Lord Tennyson. Subsequently, in 1896, Rawnsley co-founded The National Trust for Places of Historic Interest and Natural Beauty, to give the National Trust its full title. Another co-founder was the social reformer Octavia Hill of London; she too was interested in saving open spaces for the public (one of her notable successes was London's Hampstead Heath).

The National Trust was not solely confined to the Lake District: it covered the whole of England, Wales and Scotland. The Trust took Ruskin's idea of buying land and important houses in order to preserve them for the benefit of all. In the Lake District, one of the first gifts to the National Trust was the peak of Great Gable. It was given by the Fell and Rock Climbing Club in memory of those killed in the First World War. But ordinary people gave, and continue to give, to the National Trust; it has always had an army of volunteers and now counts over four million members.

A productive meeting at Wray was that of Canon Rawnsley and Beatrix Potter, another incomer who turned out to be very influential. At the time of their first meeting, she had not yet published her children's books, and Rawnsley encouraged her to do so. After she inherited some money, she bought Hill Top Farm at Sawrey and married her agent, William Heelis. Beatrix was unusual in that she immersed herself in the lives of the local people. She became a well respected, hands-on sheep farmer; taking on the locals at their own game. After her books became a commercial success (and we were reading them too), she gave the income to the National Trust. Her most particular interests were preserving the heads of the valleys in the central Lake District, and so it was that Eskdale got her attention. She also championed the Herdwick breed. She bought up farms and land as she was able, and when she died, in1943, she left the National Trust 4,000 acres in the Lake District, together with sixteen farms (including Penny Hill), and her Herdwicks. I saw her once at the Eskdale Show at Woolpack, in 1942, a lone woman exhibiting Herdwicks. She was a stocky mackintoshed shape not unlike that of Mrs Tiggy Winkle herself – minus the prickles – the cloche hat substituting for the bonnet. It must have been about that time Delmar Banner painted her as at the Eskdale Show, with Harter Fell in the background, and the portrait now hangs in the National Portrait Gallery.

Then there was a rather different visitor, Alfred Wainwright from industrial Blackburn in Lancashire. He came from a background of which Wordsworth may have been most afraid, that is from the streets of an industrial town and with a limited formal education. Wainwright was considered gifted as a child, but he left school at thirteen and started in office work, eventually working for Blackburn City Council. As a young man, in 1930, at about the age of 21, he first visited the Lake District and fell in love with it. He wrote, 'It was the first time I had looked on beauty, or even imagined the idea of beauty.' He focused on walking and the 'look' of the Lake District, was interested in cartography and drew well with pen and ink. He gave himself a project. It was to write about his favourite Lake District walks and to illustrate them, firstly for his own pleasure, and then he started publishing. Between 1955 and 1966 seven of his *Pictorial Guides to the Lakeland* came out. Wainwright's Guides became standard reference works and he himself a television personality.

Wainwright wrote affectionately about Eskdale, '…one of the loveliest of Lakeland's valleys, descends from the highest and wildest mountains in the district to the sands of Ravenglass, in a swift transition from bleak and craggy ridges to verdant woodlands and pastures, watered by a charming river.' This must impress even those who might have missed reading Wordsworth. He portrayed Eskdale as a place from which one can make hikes up Slight Side, Scafell, Scafell Pike, Broad Crag, Ill Crag, Esk Pike, Bowfell, Crinkle Crags, Hardknott or Harter Fell. There is even a Woolpack Walk. He offered a smorgasbord of walks. Wainwright's guide books have been much admired, and there are many who follow his walking maps. I believe there are about 214 walks, and that is how it is today.

From poetic wanderings and thoughts about nature and the fashioning of the landscape, there is a new group abroad, enjoying prescribed walks. Actually it is now more than that, there are now hikers on endurance tests, often in groups, going from peak to peak in a competitive fashion. It is called peak-bagging. In some places the erosion of pathways has become a problem and the Lake District National Park staff or volunteers have to go out to repair them.

We, the locals, also produced one of our very own celebrities: a native shepherd who was born at Wasdale Head in 1936, and then farmed in Wasdale. Joss Naylor had back surgery as a child and it is supposed that his fell-running may have started as part of his rehabilitation. Fell-running was a peculiarly local entertainment, but Joss took it to a new and aston-ishing level. He ran up and down fells for over 40 years, establishing records as he went. Fell-running is not like running on the flat: one runs up and down the fells, going through water and scree, over rocks partially obscured by bracken and heather, and one can expect mist or to be rained upon. Joss's achievements have been spectacular, scarcely credible. He does what now is called successive peak-bagging. In 1972 he ran 72 peaks in 23 hours and twenty minutes; that was a hundred miles and a total of 38,000 feet of ascent. Chris Brasher, the Olympic runner spent time as his pace man. Joss has done Wainwright hikes as runs and also runs out-side of the Lake District. He naturally attracts the endurance athletes and has his own Lakeland Challenge for charity for the over 50s, Wasdale to Pooley Bridge, ending at Ullswater.

All these celebrities have brought fame, fortune and change to the Lake District and to Eskdale. They have described the attractions of the fells and valleys and mapped out hiking routes. There have been successive waves of visitors: beginning with the well-heeled, then the writers, artists and the intelligentsia, the hikers and the drivers, and finally the peak-baggers. It was all about looking and walking; farming and local people did not get much attention with the exception of Beatrix Potter and to some extent Wordsworth. Visitors now come from all social backgrounds, anyone who has the time and can afford holidays and many international visitors besides. Now we are at a point where the Lake District is completely opened up and thriving in the modern age, awash with vacationers. I have seen records showing about 15.8 million annual visitors and 23.1 million daily visitors – but doubtless those figures are now out of date.

15

The Antecedents

All of our ancestors had been in Cumbria for the generations of which records have been found. That is, the families of Tysons, Leeces and Kennedys on Mother's side, and Armstrongs and Munros on Father's side. Some of the information here was provided by my cousin Sara Holliday and my niece Jane Holmes.

Tysons

Granny (Hannah Tyson) Leece is our closest claim to the heads of the Wasdale and Eskdale valleys and their fells: our strongest and most direct family connection to them. For three generations before Granny all her forbears are well documented in Wasdale, Eskdale or Ulpha. There are also records from before that, from the 1600s. Granny was the best informant on what was, by custom, considered important on a hill farm in our exact locale, things that had perhaps been crucial in the past. She was born in 1876 at Rainors Farm in Netherwasdale, and the family later farmed at Stang Ends in Wasdale. She talked about both. I always thought that she was an only child but it turned out she had a sister Margaret who was seven years older, and also an older brother who did not survive childhood. Granny never spoke of Margaret; I have to assume that she was gone by my time but that I could very well have been named for her. She did speak of Margaret's two daughters, Annas and Nellie. We didn't know Annas either, only heard her unusual name. We visited with Nellie and her Skelton family, her four boys and a girl, on their Tallentire farm at Cockermouth.

In the past, the name of Tyson was commonplace in Wasdale. The old church records in Netherwasdale are full of Tysons, in fact every other person seems to have been a Tyson; and, at the time, families were often large. In 1800, for instance, half of the houses in Netherwasdale are listed as occupied by Tysons. The three-legged small oak card table that I have came from just this place. Mother once showed me a headstone in Netherwasdale churchyard of a Tyson who once owned the table. Possibly it was that of Mary who died in 1831, the unmarried sister of my great-great-great-grandmother Hannah Tyson. There are records that Tysons built both the Strands Hotel and the Screes Hotel in Netherwasdale and had lived at the Wasdale Head Hotel. At least three generations of Tysons before Granny lived around Wasdale, and Eskdale, and there are references to ancestors in the area well before that. Granny could have told us a lot about our relatives, but she didn't in any formal way, which was surprising given her abiding interest in genealogy.

Granny spent much of her married life farming at Dyke Croft on the coast, in Muncaster, at the mouth of the Esk. I know very little of my grandparents' life there, apart from our occasional holidays as young children. It all seemed quiet enough then; but there were the deaths of her two boys in their twenties. The year I was born the oldest, Tyson, drowned himself in the river, the Esk I assume, and no one tried to explain that to us; it was said that he was recovering from flu. Mother did say how terrible it was looking for him, and what a relief when they found his body. Uncle John died when I was two, quite suddenly beyond medical help. It was said that he remained up-beat though they desperately took him around doctors. I think I may remember Mary Jane Kennedy, Granda's mother, who lived sometime at Dyke until I was about five. My memory is of a serious, beautifully dressed lady in Victorian black; but then it is always possible that I may be remembering her photograph.

When Granny and Granda moved to Woolpack it was not to an easy retirement. It was a much busier place than Dyke, but then it was one of their maxims that 'Hard work never killed anybody.' Granny lived to 91 and Granda to 90; and that was the second suicide in the family. Granda shot himself at the bottom of the intake, between the two woods behind Woolpack. He left a note to say he was sorry but could not stand the pain any longer, perhaps from his untreated heart condition. No protracted illness, no fuss for Granda. The immediate reason for it, I imagine, was because he was no longer able to do what he thought was 'a day's work'. He was always testing his strength. I remember seeing him from the kitchen window set down two full buckets of milk at the top of the stone steps, to mop his brow. He had carried the buckets all the way from the byre, and there were others who could more easily have done it. When it became obvious that Granda was having difficulties the doctor was asked to make a house call, and not without some trepidation, since it wasn't known how Granda would react: he might consider it an intrusion, since it is possible that he had never consulted a doctor in his life. As it turned out the family doctor was away and the locum was a young girl. Granda was charmed and the consultation went well. Nevertheless the heart was mentioned and that must have set Granda's plan into action.

At the end of her life, Granny had some kind of dementia and so spent a lot of time in her room. Mother took some flowers from Granda's funeral and thought to explain to Granny that he was gone. Granny had clear periods and this was one of them. She volunteered 'I know, he came and asked me if I wanted to go too.' Possibly he had. Granny was usually comfortable, but a lot of the time she was 'living in the past'. For instance, when Alastair visited her she sometimes imagined that he was one of her sons and not the next generation. Once, when he went to see her, she was waiting and ready to leave and exclaimed with some exasperation, 'Thank heavens you've come. Bring the horse and trap around right away, we're going home.' Alastair had to persuade her to sit down and have a chat first.

Leeces

Granda Leece (William) was born at the Golden Fleece in Calderbridge, the village with the Abbey. His father, John Leece, was a professional gardener. The Golden Fleece was, and is, an inn; Granda sometimes recalled it fondly. His mother, Mary Jane Kennedy, was in the catering business. He had three brothers and three sisters; we know that the three sisters surprised everyone by emigrating together to British Columbia, Canada, but his brothers stayed nearer to home. Many of the Leece family were notably long lived. Granda and four of his six siblings lived into their 90s, one of them, Sarah Jane, was 101 when she died in Victoria, British Columbia. Mother was in her late nineties. Looking at the family tree, the long life of Leeces appears to have been handed down from the Kennedy side of the family through Granda's mother, Mary Jane.

We learned very little about the Leeces; but there are still Leeces in the Muncaster area. There are records that show that Granda's grandfather and great-grandfather lived a few miles south of Coniston Lake in the Parish of Colton. Granda's grandfather died young in an explosion at Blackbeck Powder Mill in Furness. Granda did not talk much about his family, about farming or himself, and never, ever, about his sons. It was curious that he did talk enthusiastically about his early days as a rabbit catcher. At Woolpack it became obvious that he was a very good gardener – presumably trained by his father – and we, in turn, learned by example. He once had us graft back a Christmas tree, after the festivities, onto the stock from which we had cut it – to him, destroying a tree for a frivolous reason was an affront to nature. Granda was always serious and self-contained and somewhat reclusive: there were not many flickers of humour; but he identified with us children. If there were guests in the kitchen at suppertime he might choose to have a beer, and a posset (an old comfort food of bread cubes with hot milk, cinnamon and nutmeg) delivered by one of us to the annexe. Foxhunt day mornings he became a different person – uncharacteristically demanding. He was up early and in the kitchen, having arranged the night before for a bacon and egg breakfast and a sandwich to go. Years later, the first time that I left for North America, he walked me around his garden and explained that he would not be there when I came back (he expected the worst – his sisters had not returned). Granny just wept – could not speak at all. As it turned out, on my first return, they were both still there; and leaving again was no easier.

The family name Leece is not a common one. It seems probable that the family were named after the tiny village of Leece which is south of Ulverston and not far from Colton. It looks very much as if the family stayed much in the immediate area for the four generations that are known, and presumably they were there long before that.

A bit of interesting trivia is that the village of Leece is old and is mentioned in the Domesday Book of 1086 – then spelled Lies. Sometime later it became Lees and finally Leece. Leece is in the flat area going down to the sea on the southern fringe of Cumbria. Interestingly, the Domesday Book ended here, at the southern border of what is now the Lake District: it did not go into the valleys. (The book was William the Conqueror's catalogue of individual landowner's property from all over England, put together for the purpose of taxation.) It shows that Lies was calculated to have about six carucates. A carucate was an old Danelaw unit of assessment of land: the area that a team of eight oxen could till in a single season, that is about a 120 acres of ploughed land. Lies was on good agricultural land.

One begins to see at least one reason why the Domesday Book did not get into the Cumbrian valleys and their fells. The upper valleys do not have anything like that amount of arable land, and so may not, at the time, have been thought to have been of much value. The larger reason was that, at the time, most of Cumbria was part of Scotland. While King William did take control of Carlisle, a few years after the Domesday Book was created, the Border warfare went on through the following centuries.

Kennedys

Granda's mother, Mary Jane, was of an interesting Kennedy family, assumed to be originally Irish, and I have a possibly unfounded idea they might have come to Cumbria by way of the Isle of Man (Granda always portrayed the latter as a raffish kind of place). In the 1800s, the family were extremely successful in shipbuilding in Whitehaven, when it was an important port on the Cumbrian coast. At that time the harbour was said to be able to take in a hundred wooden sailing vessels, today called 'tall ships'. Whitehaven had been an important port well before the Kennedys' time. Incredibly, at this time, Whitehaven was the second busiest port in England after London, ahead of Liverpool, Bristol and Newcastle. By our time, the dock was pretty quiet; but the old coal mining business was still going on the coast.

Mary Jane's grandfather was the famous Whitehaven shipwright Lumley Kennedy. He had worked at the Brocklebank shipyard in Whitehaven for twenty years and had been manager there, after which, in 1835, he joined a new venture as managing partner of the Lumley Kennedy and Co. shipyard. The Kennedy company launched their first vessel in 1835, and by 1865 had built 64 others.

Kennedy men became sailors. Mary Jane's father, Captain Thomas Kennedy, was Lumley's eldest son. Captain Thomas took the Kennedy built ship the *British Queen* to the West Indies but he, himself, did not come back. He contracted Yellow Fever and died at St. Thomas at the age of 35. There is a painting of that ship now in the Whitehaven Museum. We heard from Mother that there was once a painting of one of Lumley's ships at Dyke, and that it had disappeared with no record; just possibly it was the same one showing the *British Queen*. The career of the brig the *British Queen* ended in disaster, as was all too common at the time. She sailed from Liverpool with a cargo of salt, commanded by her second captain, struck an iceberg in the Atlantic and sank. Fortunately the crew were rescued and landed at St. John's, Newfoundland. Captain Thomas's son Lumley Kennedy was a sailor, he captained the ship the *Sierra Nevada* and died aged 36 of a heart attack aboard his ship in 1879, at St. Helena in the South Atlantic. Three years before that he had been given a

The British Queen.

gold watch by the New Zealand government for his part in the rescue of a group of immigrants whose ship had foundered on the way to Dunedin.

I seem to remember Granda saying that Lumley's company also had a ship's chandler business, supplying all that a sailing ship might need. There are a lot of historical records published by the Whitehaven Museum of all the ships built by Lumley and of their voyages. There is a checklist by Harry Fancy and there is Daniel Hay's *Whitehaven History*, both contain pertinent information. These publications list Lumley Kennedy's ships and their details: tonnage, number of masts, captains, prow figureheads, specifications, Lloyd's classification and details of their voyages. The ship names were often of local places or personalities. It is striking how many of the ships working lives ended in a fire or a shipwreck.

Kennedy built ships to carry a wide variety of merchandise around the world: to Europe, India, China, Australasia, and North and South America. The following are some of the ports of call listed in the statistics: Hong Kong, Shanghai, Bremen, Bordeaux, the Baltic, Dundee, Liverpool, Ireland (a lot of coal went there), Melbourne, Newfoundland, New York, Pensacola, Honduras, Jamaica, Barbados, Antigua, Rio, Buenos Aires, Patagonia, Lima, Pernambuco and Valparaiso.

One of Lumley's partners was R. and H. Jefferson, the wine company, and they were the owners of the *British Queen*. Jefferson's was still a going concern in our time and it was where we bought the wine for the Woolpack's cellar. I have a memory of being in the Jefferson's office with Father. The room was dark and had truly impressive antique furniture, the clerk gave us its provenance while we waited for our order. It is this office that is is now preserved as the Whitehaven Museum.

Granda was not even remotely interested in the sea; the loss of his maternal grandfather Thomas to Yellow Fever at St. Thomas would resound and later the loss of his uncle Lumley. Nevertheless, Granda did sometimes speak about the excitements of the harbour; he must have had some childhood recollection of it or of hearing about it. He kept odd bits of foreign coral brought back by his sailor ancestors, and buttons of their uniforms. (I still have some of the buttons.) He described the Lascar sailors from India that were widely employed by merchant shipping then, they seemed to him to be truly exotic.

Munros

Not a great deal is known about Granny Armstrong's paternal family, the Munros. It is a Highland name, but the family had been on the Cumbrian coast for at least three generations before Granny's time. Her father and grandfather were ships' carpenters in Whitehaven. We did have one Munro relative who, now and then, dropped in at Woolpack – Martin. He was an emotional man, always delighted to see us: greeted us with tears in his eyes. He worked as a shop steward in a Workington steel factory, a man with a social conscience who spent his time bettering the lot of the workers. Father shook his head, opining that 'He will never get anywhere; his employers will see to that.' Father had the gravest misgivings about industrial life – really about anywhere that wasn't Eskdale and farming.

We got very little direct information on any of these families, Tysons, Leeces, Kennedys or Munros. It was Armstrongs who always appeared to be front and centre, yet we got remarkably little direct information on them either.

Armstrongs

Here comes the shock! The Armstrongs, while still Cumbrian, were incomers into Eskdale. They arrived in Eskdale in 1914 having rented the Woolpack from Lord Walter Rea of the Gate House, Eskdale Green. Rea was so keen for the family to take on the Woolpack that he is believed to have waived the first year's rent; and then they bought it.

There were two locals known to have witnessed the Armstrong arrival by horse and cart into Eskdale. Tyson Cowman and Lizzie Fossey both claimed, as children, that they had been asked directions to Woolpack by the family. Lizzie remarked on the girls 'ropes' of hair, wound around their heads. It was a large family, and if they were all together for this occasion it would have been as follows: Granda (Benjamin), Granny (Sarah), and the children : Gladys, Benjamin (Benny), Eleanor (Nellie), Sarah (Sally), John (Father) and Annie (Nance). It is possible that the oldest two may have been delayed, since Auntie Gladys was teaching in Watermillock and Uncle Benny had a farming job. At this time, Nance and John were still quite young, ten and thirteen respectively. The family were an impressive workforce; one can see the attraction of having them as tenants at Woolpack. They had journeyed from Beauthorn, Watermillock, on Ullswater. Granda's sister too, Eleanor, came with them and lived in a cottage at Nursery End in Eskdale Green next to the Forge.

The Armstrongs were rather a 'riches to rags' story. Granda (Benjamin) was born in 1862 at the well known Lodore Hotel in Borrowdale, near Keswick, where his parents were both hoteliers – Benjamin Armstrong and Mary Forrester. Mary must have been an excellent cook, since she once cooked a meal for Queen Victoria in Carlisle, including the well received bread buns. The Lodore was an impressive hotel; while the family were there it was visited by Edward VII. Two of Granda's uncles were also hoteliers, his uncle David was at the Royal Hotel in nearby Bowness-on-Windermere; and his uncle John at the Royal Oak in Keswick. By 1871, Granda's parents had moved on to the Borrowdale Hotel. Both the Lodore and the Borrowdale hotels were, and still are, substantial, in a different league to the Woolpack. They were also in a more celebrated and more visited part of the Lake District at Derwentwater – even in Victorian times, there were plenty of tourists there. The porch on the front of the Borrowdale Hotel was added by my great-grandfather (also a Benjamin). It has a plaque with his initials, BA. The family could be said to be 'doing well'. Granda had a privileged childhood, incredibly, it included a private tutor. Sadly it all went dreadfully, and suddenly, wrong.

It started in 1875. Granda's father died of epilepsy at the age of 45. His bereft family were then victimized by one Edward Goodfellow who had married Granda's older sister Hannah. He was not a good fellow at all: to begin with he gambled and drank. The next year Granda's mother was put in a Carlisle hospital, having suffered a complete mental breakdown, owing to the general situation and the family disagreements. That was followed the next year by the death of Granda's older brother Joseph of tuberculosis, and he was only 23. Two years later Hannah died, and she was only 26. Goodfellow, however, was persistent and moved on to marry the second sister Polly continuing all the while to squander the family resources. Sister Sarah married and left home, and sister Eleanor left to live with Goodfellow's aunt in Keswick; the latter was said to be appalled at Goodfellow's contribution to the family troubles. In 1881 Granda, at the age of 21, was still at the Borrowdale Hotel with Polly and Goodfellow, and it was then that the hotel was finally lost. Auntie Gladys hinted at a gambling debt, but generally speaking the family were completely silent about it all.

Polly took her children and left Goodfellow, who then took off for America, improving his immediate prospects by becoming a coachman for the Vanderbilt family. I did meet Polly as an old lady; Auntie Gladys took me to see her in Workington. We fed seagulls in the paved backyard of her house; as a child I got the wintry and exposed feeling. We got to know Polly's daughter, Fanny, and her son George well. Fanny's husband, George Purdie Porteous, was an engineer in the Merchant Navy, who had the ill luck to be torpedoed three times by U-boats in the Second World War, and finally went down with his ship when it left a convoy. His name appears on a memorial outside the Tower of London. Son George, of our generation, just a few years older than us, had uncharacteristic swarthy good looks. He was a science teacher, and he often came to visit us at Woolpack.

When Granda left the Borrowdale Hotel, he became a groom for the Wedgewood family, of pottery fame, at Barlaston in the Midlands. By 1887 he was back in the Lake District, still working as a groom, married to Sarah Munro and living in Keswick. Auntie Gladys and the older children were born in Keswick; then the family moved on to Deer How in Patterdale, on Ullswater, where Father and Aunt Nance were born. Granda was then working as a coachman. They subsequently moved a short distance to Beauthorn, Watermillock. One of Father's good memories there was of the 'boys whistling choir' in the local church. By the time of the First World War the three older girls and their brother Benny were grown when the family answered Lord Rea's call for a tenant at the Woolpack Inn. It was the girls who were most enthusiastic and carried Granda along, since at one point he got cold feet about the project.

While Eskdale was on the less touristy part of the Lake District there were still enough visitors for the hotel trade, even before the first World War. The inn was small, but there was also the farm. It is reported that it was Granny Armstrong and son Benny, already a farmer, who were initially key to getting Woolpack going. One can see that the Woolpack was a good move for the family: an opportunity to get back into the hotel business. For 22 years or so the family worked the farm and ran the Woolpack Inn. Then Father formally took over, and by that time Father's siblings were dispersed. Uncle Benny, who was quite a bit older than Father, and should have inherited the property in accordance with custom, was badly wounded by shrapnel in the First World War. He married and went to farm at Cragg, Birkby, a bit further down the Esk.

Nellie and Sally married local boys, Nellie and Albert Black lived at Ghyll Bank, and Sallie and Cyril Bulman at Wha House, after which they all moved into serious hotel business in the easterly part of the Lake District. Nellie and family went back to the old family area near Keswick and ran the Greenbank Hotel in Borrowdale, later moving on to the New Dungeon Ghyll Hotel in Great Langdale. Sally and family were already in Langdale, at the Old Dungeon Ghyll Hotel. And so Langdale became a place for us to visit the cousins. The hotels were near to each other and tucked under the Langdale Pikes. The Old Dungeon had been a farm, the New Dungeon was built in Victorian times, both of them attractive in the local slate. Aunt Nance married Tony Priestman and left for Penrith, where Tony had a pharmacy and an optician's practice. As children we got to know Penrith too. When Father took over Woolpack, Granny and Granda Armstrong went down to Paddockwray, along with Auntie Gladys. Auntie Gladys had taught school since she was young and was a mature student when she graduated from her teacher training college in Darlington. After the teacher training and the Watermillock School, she taught in Eskdale.

When a student, I had a rare holiday and it was with Auntie Gladys. I believe that I met one of Auntie Gladys' college friends, Miss Clarke, on the wild car ride from Eskdale to Paisley. We stayed overnight in Paisley in her tenement flat. It was the first leg of an adventure that Auntie Gladys and I were on to Oban, on the west coast of Scotland, and thence by ferry to the islands of Mull and Iona. Driving to Paisley, Auntie Gladys and her friend had a great time, they recited the whole of *Invictus* (an inspirational poem by William Henley). At the tops of their voices they yelled 'I thank whatever gods may be, For my unconquerable soul' ending with 'I am the master of my fate, I am the captain of my soul.'

The adventurousness of their college days must have been coming out. We called in at a farm where Robbie Burns had worked, and that was no accident, since Robbie was one of our own – a ploughman poet and from close to the Border. Robbie made the Lake Poets look like the gentry that they were, unconsciously drawing attention to their middle class interests and their work innocent hands. After the visit, Auntie Gladys and her friend were off again declaiming, 'A man's a man for a' that, for a' that, an' a' that', and 'Till a' the seas gang dry, my dear, and the rocks melt wi' the sun', and 'Scots Wae Hae wi' Wallace bled'. Even father approved of Robbie Burns, although he was cautious about writers in general and not a reader himself. Even so, he recognized Robbie as the real thing, while dismissing others as writing 'pot boilers'.

On this trip I alone worried about the driving; Auntie Gladys' driving stories were our stock in trade and perceived as our greatest hazard. The quickest way to clear Woolpack kitchen of family was an invitation from her to drive over Hardknott and Wrynose to visit the relatives. Her nearest and dearest left quickly by any door. We all had our driving story contributions; one of mine was her wondering out loud 'You know Margaret, I can't see a thing,' as she stared blankly through the windscreen. Another was of some unexpected profanity as she backed into the stone wall at the Holm Bottom, she had intended to go forward.

It seems that Granda Armstrong had been the same kind of source of affectionate family entertainment for the previous generation. In his case, it was his belief that all the mail coming into the Woolpack was for him alone, as the head of the household; he did not bother to look at names on the envelopes and so was often mystified by their contents. One story was of his indignation over a bill for 'One Pan-NA-ma-hat, one Pan-NA-ma-hat' (he repeated the word in a querulous fashion, the register going up as he dragged out the pronunciation). He had not purchased such a hat and would never purchase such a hat. Finally it was pointed out that the bill was addressed to one of his daughters.

Another story was of a mysterious note that he read out from a local young man asking to meet somewhere down by the river at a latish hour. Again the indignation and the rising note. 'He wants to meet me where?' 'Down by the beck?' 'At what time?' 'What?' Again the envelope was addressed to one of his daughters.

Where were the Armstrong family from originally? Of all our relatives the Armstrongs appeared to be the most self absorbed and possibly the most stressed. Uncle Tony once joked 'I'm glad I have none of that blue blood.' Mother and he had something in common there. One certainly got the impression that there was something interesting about the past, but few details were ever given. There were occasional hints about the family's Scottish origin, like one of the aunts, either Nellie or Sallie, statement 'I was so humiliated I wasn't even proud of my Scottish blood.' Years later, the history of the Armstrong clan on the Scottish Border became public knowledge, and to put the best face on it, it was colourful.

Where the name of Armstrong itself came from is not certainly known. In the far distant past, one story goes that Armstrongs were descended from Scandinavian invaders into Northumberland (and Scandinavians did like nicknames). The name was given when one Siward rescued Malcolm III of Scotland during a battle with the English. For that he was given the name of Armstrong and was granted land on Scottish territory near the border, just north of Carlisle, in the area of Liddesdale, Eskdale (a Scottish one), and Annandale. At some point Armstrongs also moved into a narrow strip of land at the approach to Carlisle called the Debatable Land, debatable because it was contested by both Scotland and England: a kind of no-man's land, officially supposed to be a buffer. An Armstrong fortress, Mangerton Tower, is dated to about 1135.

In any case, our Armstrong branch knew themselves to be Scottish and from just over the border, and from traditional Armstrong territory. It would be from Auntie Gladys that we heard snatches of stories suggestive of a folk memory. There was one about Armstrongs on horseback, picking their way through a bog on their way home from a 'ride' to England, and being pursued by English horsemen bent on revenge. In such circumstances, it was Armstrong practice to lead the English into this bog with the intent of getting their pursuers' horses into difficulty, the sub text being that Armstrongs knew the firmer, safer, bits of ground. The story continues with some of the determined followers appearing in the kitchen of one of the Armstrong riders, and of a stolen sheep wrapped up and disguised in a baby crib. On being accused of stealing sheep the Armstrong rider replied 'I would rather eat the contents of the cradle' – that was the punch line. As it came to us the memory is sparse on detail but is nevertheless telling. The truth is that Armstrongs did steal in England, did lead their pursuers through a bog, called Tarras Moss, on their way back home. It is also true that the kind of wit on the sheep in the cradle was much admired in that time and place.

However, the folk memory aspect is put into question since there is a Border Ballad on this story. The ballad is 'Archie Armstrong's Aith' (oath), by Marriott and dated about 1802, but purporting to be about an event 200 years earlier. It was collected by Sir Walter Scott for his *Minstrelsy of the Scottish Border.* The ballad describes an Archie hot footing it home from England, passing Gilnockie Tower, an Armstrong fortification on the fringes of the Debatable Lands, all the while being followed, getting home hastily and butchering the sheep, dropping the entrails and skin into the river, then wrapping up the carcase and replacing the baby in the cradle with it. All this before the pursuer enters Archie's kitchen to accuse Archie of theft. I include a few abstracted lines of the ballad to give an idea of the art form.

> *The cradle stans by the ingle toom,*
> *The bairn wi' auntie stays;*
> *They clapt the carcase in its room,*
> *And smoor'd it wi' the claes.*

later Archie's reply:

> *If e'er I did sae fause a feat,*
> *As thin my neebor's faulds,*
> *May I be doomed the flesh to eat*
> *This vera cradle halds*

and ending:

> *And Archie didna break his aith,*
> *He ate the cradled sheep.*

This kind of humour was so popular that it got an Archie Armstrong (either the same Archie or another – I don't know) a job as court jester to James VI of Scotland. The jester Archie was brought in front of James who was on a judicial visit from Edinburgh to the Border. James ordered that Archie be hanged for stealing a sheep. Archie asked permission to read the Bible before the sentence was carried out, and the wish was graciously granted. Archie's riposte was that then he would never read the Bible, so it would follow that he could never be hanged. James was amused, pardoned Archie on the spot, gave him the court jester job, and took him along to London – James had just become King of England as well.

The other story that we got from Auntie Gladys that could also have been a folk memory was about a stone in a dungeon in Carlisle Castle that was licked by Armstrongs and other borderers. Water dripped down onto the stone from somewhere up above and so had saved lives. Then there was the information that Armstrong prisoners were liberated from the Castle by the clan. We now know that there is such a stone, the 'Licking Stone' and that one famous Armstrong at least, Kinmont Willie, was spectacularly rescued and celebrated in ballad form.

We got these bits of information in the 1940s, and although light in detail, and maybe not completely a direct folk memory, possibly some of it derived from the ballads, they do nevertheless highlight some of the essentials known at the time. Armstrongs did raid over the Border, they were pursued by parties bent on recovering their stock (called a 'trod'); and they ran the risk of getting caught and of being thrown into Carlisle Castle dungeon. We didn't know any more until 30 years later, in 1971, when George Fraser's *The Steel Bonnets* was published. There we discovered that it was all true, and much, much more besides; and since then there have been other publications. Fraser used routine reports made by the English Border Wardens to the government in London as the framework for his book. These reports are a chronicle of forays from Scotland into England and the chases back north after wards and of raids initiated in the opposite direction, of famous and colourful personalities, and of the trials of caught reivers. What was surprising was the scale of the reiving, the politics, and the prevailing brutality. I thought I might relay a little of this information to the reader, since it must have been formative to the family.

After the Armstrongs got to their land over the Scottish border they flourished. They farmed in the growing season, but after the harvest was taken in the reiving season began: they robbed over the border in England. Reiving was a style of life that went on for centuries and is reported to have involved all social classes. The reivers largely took cattle and sheep, often in enormous numbers, and sometimes household goods. Churches and monasteries were attacked; Armstrongs were credited with destroying 52 churches. To these ends, the Armstrong clan maintained a private army of armoured horsemen, and by the early 1500s the laird could muster 3,000 Armstrongs and their supporters. The reivers also indulged in blackmail (black rent): English farmers could purchase protection. At the same time, border families were quite likely to have relatives on the other side of the border; Armstrongs were said to marry in England. Feuds between individuals and families became commonplace; the politics of the time must have been labyrinthine. Who to reive? It must have been carefully planned.

It was not just Armstrongs who reived, the whole of the Border area was lawless, and largely excluded from both Scottish and English law. The border was split up into districts called Marches each with a warden responsible for order. Border people tended to consider themselves as either Scottish or English as the political situation demanded. While all the clans in the Border Marches had reputations for plundering, bloodshed, and general mayhem, regrettably the Armstrongs were the most feared. Their riders wore a light armour (light for the Middle Ages) and were known as the Steel Bonnets because of their steel helmets. In addition, a rider had steel plates sewn into the doublet, carried a long lance, a sword, a crossbow, a dirk (small hand knife hidden in a scabbard in the knee stocking), and in the later days a pistol. It was an extraordinary outfit for a putative farmer.

Some time, early on, I heard the story, and it could only be from Auntie Gladys that in this Scottish period when a male Armstrong was baptized the child's right arm was held behind its back, since as an adult he might be 'forced to kill' – should someone protest too forcefully about being robbed. The day did come when Armstrongs en masse, all those with the name, were excommunicated by the Church. The Archbishop of Glasgow issued 'A Monition of Cursing' in 1523. It started 'I curse thair heid and all the haris of thair heid; I curse thair face, thair ene, thair mouth ...' and went on at length with menacing detail about their bodies, then onto their families and their possessions. This was required to be read out in border churches. I wonder how that felt?

The worst period of reiving was between 1450 and 1610. 'Derring-do' was an aspect of it, too, and there were many notorious and celebrated individuals, one was Johnnie Armstrong. I am re-telling information about Johnnie since he seemed to be the one who was important to the family and Aunt Sallie connected us to this Gilnockie branch. The story goes that Johnnie was supposed to have been given safe conduct to Caerlanrig where King James V of Scotland and he were to discuss ways of pacifying the Borders. James was angered by the good appearance and turn out of

Johnnie and his riders and petulantly asked. 'What wants yon knave that a King should have?' On the spur of the moment he ordered his army to capture Johnnie and his party and to murder them. Before his death, Johnnie is reputed to have made the speech that began 'I am a fool to seek grace at a graceless face...' It is also possible that these quoted lines were entirely due to the ballad. After the Caerlanrig massacre Armstrongs were even more disaffected and most certainly on their own. In the last official set battle between the nations, at Solway Moss, Armstrongs were on the English side.

Seventy five years after Johnnie Armstrong's murder, Elizabeth I died (1603) and James VI of Scotland became James I of England as well, uniting Britain and creating Great Britain. With this union the Border wars had to end. What followed was a fierce cleansing of the Border clans. Reivers had served the purpose of keeping the border closed and supplying European armies with soldiers, but had become an embarrassment to James, since he now represented the two nations. James had to pacify the region somehow, and his solution was that Armstrongs, and some other 'names', had to leave their land, and all suspected reivers be prosecuted.

James was a cruel and unimaginative man; there were dreadful mass hangings of accused reivers in public places in Edinburgh and Carlisle. Borderers called it Jeddart Justice: hang first, try later. The keeping of riding horses was forbidden. Armstrong land was confiscated. Soldiering was an option for an ex-reiver. 'Bold Buccleuch', the official Keeper of Liddesdale, but at the same time a reiver himself, took 2,000 Scots to the Low Countries as soldiers. The families of the reivers were forcibly dispersed – many were shipped to Fermanagh in Ulster (interestingly many sailed from Workington). Some moved a shorter distance into England.

Armstrongs were now disorganized, dispersed, shamed and excommunicated. Today the Armstrong Clan Trust does not know who is the Laird. The clan motto *Invictus maneo* (I remain unconquered) hangs in the air. One does clearly recognize the redemptive aspect of Neil Armstrong's ultimate foray to the moon, the adventure and the personal bravery. Most of my family gave the impression of being independent in the work they chose to do and not a great deal interested in religion. One has to wonder if this was connected to their history.

We do not know how our Armstrong ancestor fitted into this story of mayhem and derring-do, or just how it ended for him. How he avoided the punishments (presumably he was too young), just how he limped over the Border into England, who was with him and whether there were family to go to. Or, on the other hand, it is just possible the family were already resident on the English side. The earliest documented evidence of our Armstrong branch shows them to be barely south of the border in Cumbria, slightly north of Carlisle at Kirklinton. There were a lot of Armstrongs in Kirklinton. This was also the place from which Neil Armstrong's ancestor emigrated to America, and to where the court jester Archie retired.

My great-great-grandfather Benjamin Armstrong (1789-1851) is recorded as farming in Kirklinton; but there is an earlier recorded Benjamin Armstrong, possibly his grandfather, who was married very close by at Irthington in 1754. The first surely documented Benjamin and his family were not doing so well; he died of tuberculosis along with two sons and a daughter. His wife however lived 30 more years and the three remaining sons, as described above, went into the hotel trade, and did well. Presumably this was the beginning of Armstrongs in hotels. Son Benjamin was our direct ancestor, he was married at the fabled elopement spot of Gretna Green and was the one at the Borrowdale Hotel, the father of my remembered grandfather, also a Benjamin. Grandfather's mother was Mary Forrester and her picture shows the features we always thought were Armstrong and now we see were not; the prominent nose, the long face, maybe even the fine uncontrollable hair – about the infamous 'Armstrong legs' we still do not know.

16

Loved to death

I was about 27 when I finally left Woolpack and Eskdale. I had worked all vacations from school, university and beyond, including longer patches of full time work. In another sense my friend Norma was correct, I have never left: it has been a yardstick for me of what is desirable and attractive, bearable even. It is with me still; it's been a long goodbye.

It took centuries of work to form the landscape of upper Eskdale where I grew up; and in my generation there have been sudden and monumental changes to the traditional way of life. Over the centuries, the farmers struck a balance between their demands on the land and their preservation of it; they had lived cooperatively with their neighbours, had been self-reliant and left this legacy to their children. Eskdale is now full of visitors on a short or longer term stay, but their working life is likely to be elsewhere. They came but once, or time and time again, to appreciate a world apart from their own, a place of great natural beauty where time had travelled more slowly.

Volumes have been written on the Lake District, mostly by outsiders with various interests, not so often by a local, and quite a few locals have left. Farming is not so profitable, its future not so clear, and property prices are high. There has been a frenzy of buying and converting the old granite walls into homes; urban people looking for somewhere authentic to live. I hesitate to use the word quaint – but I fear it may be in some vocabularies: somewhere unspoilt, pleasurable for walking, with clean air, clear water, wild flowers, and history. I do understand the urban and middle class point of view given the opportunity and the income to buy a piece of history in stunning countryside, it is a logical step.

Despite Eskdale being on the quieter side of the Lake District, it now has many more people about than it used to, but it has fewer farmers and agricultural workers, producers of food and wool. The bulk of the work now offered is in the tourist industry; and a lot of workers come into the Lake District just for that.

The main road down the ancient valley of Eskdale was built for the slow, plodding traffic of a more spacious age; it twists and turns, goes up and down, and is narrow. Its stone walls both intimidate and tire drivers; now, in the busy season walking along the main road can be a hazard. Some passing places and lay-bys have been created by carving out sections of fields. Some bits of road have been somewhat straightened with the intent of making the overall situation marginally safer for all. However, one would not now set off a five year old to walk to school – oh I forgot, the school has gone too. The school and its playgrounds are a holiday camp for urban children; there is a sleeping loft above Auntie Gladys' old classroom.

Hardknott Pass is still a challenge but is now an easier prospect to get over than in our childhood. There is now a great deal of coming and going, between the east and west sides of the Lake District. The Roman Camp and the Boot Water Mill are advertised attractions, and so must be on many itineraries. While there are many accommodation options in the valley, the visitors that one might meet down by Doctor's Bridge could well just be there for a an hour or two but actually staying a few valleys away. The majority of visitors are forced to come by car, since there is no regular bus service; in the summer the Ratty train from Ravenglass still functions and delivers day visitors almost into the village. For centuries a remote place of marginal farming and hard won living, to a large degree upper Eskdale has become a kind of playground.

Aside from holiday makers and cars just passing through, there is the more serious demand for housing, for a more permanent presence, and there is a restricted supply of that. Both the National Trust and the Lake District National Park have made great efforts to retain the look of the landscape and the old buildings. The National Trust operates by buying up property, farms and their flocks, so arresting negative change. The Park's planning board has rules over conversions and usage of the area within the park. You cannot easily build a new home in upper Eskdale, but you may buy a stone building that already exists and transform the interior.

In our childhood, there was just a sprinkling of incomers who owned cottages. They were very often academics like the historians Professors Powicke and Pares, and their families, of Christcliffe Cottage. We got to know them over the years; Mrs Powicke gave us children presents. These incomers were small in number and did not much affect the total lifestyle or economy, rather they gave us an interest, a touch of the more exotic

Woolpack from the fell behind.

and some contact with the outside world. Now there is an overwhelming flood of new residents.

The serious demand for housing started in the 1950s when the nuclear plant was built on the coast outside of the Lake District National Park. It brought a surge of incomers desiring to live inside the park and willing to commute to work. To some degree, however, those who came with the plant were involved in the local community, and many became permanent residents. The nuclear plant did raise the price of housing and made it more difficult for local young people either to find, or to afford, cottages. The present wave of city dwellers are looking for a place in the country for holidays and possibly to retire to, some for investment no doubt. The price of property may now be well out of the range of an ordinary farmer or other locals. One would have to be very wealthy today to buy all of Woolpack as we knew it; but then one cannot as it isn't a unit any more. It has been split into parts: valley land, fell grazing, flock and other stock, out-buildings, and the inn.

The influx has changed the entire fabric of life in one generation. What were once working farms in our childhood and early adulthood may now be holiday rentals. The land on such farms has presumably been sold, and as a consequence the farms that are left working may well have a larger land base. Farm buildings have been subject to an epidemic of conversion; it is possible to get multiple dwellings into what were once barns, stables, byres, pig sties, dog houses, calf hulls, haylofts, wood sheds, and storage sheds. Anything in fact with the old granite walls. Whereas the Lake District Planning Board dictates that one must preserve the outward look of a building, keeping its local and historic character, one can have a free hand inside, and bring in light by putting windows into the slate roofs. I have no doubt that the new homes are more comfortable and certainly better heated than our farmhouses were. Meeting the residents still living in Eskdale has indeed become somewhat of an emotional experience. Many are gone, and their centuries old skills with them.

My last visit to Eskdale was not many years ago, in 2006. I stayed at Penny Hill Farm along with Norma, my college friend. Margaret, the lady of the house, knew the Armstrong family well, having once worked at Woolpack herself (she has the Woolpack dinner gong as her remembrance). I ran into her brother Jimmy enjoying a pint at Brook House; for many years he had been a much valued help on the farm at Woolpack. His vigilance once saved my eldest, DeeDee, as a toddler from a bull. Being a city child she didn't have our natural caution about teasing a bull with a stick in the middle of a field – an unthinkable idea to a local child. Jimmy was on the road driving the tractor when he spotted DeeDee in the Cow Field tapping the bull on the nose. He left the tractor running, jumped over the wall, ran over, snatched her up and continued straight on, exiting quickly through a gate into the yard. Jimmy then gave DeeDee a lecture that totally surprised her; she was a little bit annoyed when she appeared in the kitchen as Jimmy was a particular friend of hers.

Staying at Penny Hill, so close to Woolpack, it felt very much like being home again. On the surface most things looked the same, and one can be grateful for that. Very few places can be said to stay the same now, I do understand that and few people can now go home to the place of their birth and find it looking much the same. I had chosen not to stay at the inn itself, it is now out of the family and has changed hands a few times.

With Penny Hill as a base, I had a few days to wander about and see what was left, and what was not. Since the National Trust owns Penny Hill and now Woolpack land there are farming connections between the two. Penny Hill is still working: it has Herdwick sheep and sheepdogs. There was something new, a quad bike is now used to roam the fields and rough ground to check on farming matters. Penny Hill has a small fortune

DeeDee with ducklings at the Woolpack.

of outbuildings if one looks with a developer's eye for possible conversions, but the National Trust will not let that happen. Another new and interesting feature was a herd of a French breed of cattle wandering around the rough ground on the lower fell accompanied by the bull. They came down the intack one evening, as far down as they could get, making a fearful bellowing noise. We realized that one of their cows was calving in the in-bye; presumably they were offering protection even though separated by a stone wall.

My first stop was the inn. On this visit home it was painted white with a black trim to conform to a certain tradition of Cumbrian pubs. The farm buildings were entirely converted into homes – maybe there were four or five of them. The Woolpack itself appeared unchanged on the outside, but the annexe had additions, including a new porch to welcome the trade. To get to the annexe one now walks through some extra parking space taking up the foot of the Show Field and past a grouping of tables with umbrellas. One has to like the look of umbrellas: they make one think of sunshine, holidays on the Continent, sophisticated places, eating out. Nevertheless they were a shock to me: umbrellas put Woolpack in a different light: they speak of a place of leisure where one sits and gazes at Harter Fell. The Show Field that had for centuries seen sheep and cattle cropping about, had now and then grown vegetables or been taken over by the Herdwick Show, was now a place for recreation. It felt a world away from the old hill farming, even from our days at the inn. We were the antithesis of a leisured society.

The coniferous woods behind the hotel had been recently logged, and the lumber was stacked at the far side of the Front Field, so there was a bare look to the intakes. The oak (pronounced yak in Eshdle) tree by the annexe was doing well, it had increased in girth and spread out. The only stock I saw were a few bullocks and heifers in the Hostel Field; they thundered over clumsily – as teenagers might – hoping for some food no doubt.

The main bar in the annexe bottom used to be Granny and Granda Leece's sitting room; with a jolt I recognized one or two of the small antique items on display behind the counter. On this visit the barman was a French student who chain smoked as he attended to customers. I ordered a shandy (half ginger beer or lemonade, half draft beer) but he didn't know what that was, although a traditional drink. Finally, it seemed easier to compromise on a coffee, but then he got my order confused with that of a German family outside under one of the umbrellas. In the old days he would have had to cope with three course lunches, running in and out of the kitchen, to the garden to pick the salad, and at the same time keep the customers occupied, and happy, by serving them drinks. One drinker once asked me how long would it take for his party's lunch to be ready, unaware that his detaining me was lengthening that wait. I was to discover that a lot of the servers in the valley were foreign students, presumably there for work experience and to further language skills, an advantage of the European Union. I even witnessed an international social get-together of a group of them in the village. It might now be difficult to find a local person serving, might even be possible to visit upper Eskdale and not hear the local dialect, or learn any details of a farming life. It has become a very public place firmly in the twenty-first century.

I sneaked into Woolpack kitchen. Sectioned up with stainless steel, nothing was recognizable to me. There was no ghost of Mother at a ceramic range, no back view of Granny at a sink busy with Woolpack produce, no shade of a laundry day, and most certainly no echo of a sheep gather or of farmers' boots on the slate floor. The west window seemed obscured. It had been our connection with the farmyard: children playing in the trough, the comings and goings of animals and the men, and where one could see the hikers collecting at the Rake gate, on their way up to the fell. It was where visiting farm families announced themselves. The locals did not order meals, and rarely a drink; all their business or social calls were conducted via the kitchen door. We locals weren't front door people.

I did not get as far as the dairy, the Boot House or the back steps. I fancy I would have found there the deep freezes that are now ubiquitous, since that is how most of us now live. I don't know if the slate sconces have survived, today that kind of thing has serious antique value.

The old dining room and the sitting room are joined to make a bigger eating area – quite sensible. That work had unearthed a large ancient fireplace in the wall between the two rooms that we had not known about, a photograph had been taken of it. There was a photograph (new to me) in the area that used to be the old snug showing people in long Victorian dress in front of the annexe taken close to the time that the Armstrongs arrived; Granny Armstrong dressed just like that. Woolpack felt more like a small pub: redolent of beer, but a new owner had plans to restore it to its 'former glory'.

As to the farm buildings there were drastic changes. The former farm end of the longhouse comprised of the old byre, the hulls and stable with the hayloft above, has been converted into homes. The doors and windows tend to keep to the original openings and have the approved trim, sky lights have appeared in the slate roof. That bit of farmyard and the old orchard, suitable for pigs to root about, was now a lawn with a child's swing set in the middle of it. The lawn and the swing set are imported ideas like the umbrellas. It feels a little like seeing a costume drama where inadvertently a more modern item, from a much later era, intrudes. Around the corner of the farmyard one sees that the old barn with its attached pigsty is also a conversion. I read online that you can rent it; that it has underfloor heating. The pigs would have liked that, but the renters will not know of them. The new byre, recessed into the bank, is now converted into a large house with an acre or so.

At the back of the inn, the dipping yard is now the start to the path up the Rake, the public access to the fell. There are no sheep dipped or sorted here, there was no sign of them. But then, by about 1989 I am told, that dipping was no longer mandatory and can largely be replaced by injections and sprays. Is there still a Woolpack flock? The short answer is no: there are no Woolpack sheep on the Eskdale Common, presumably for the first time in centuries. When the flock came off the fell it was split up and sold, but the National Trust is said to have some sheep in their Woolpack fields.

I did not see the old sandstone trough with the water running through it, but there was a trough at the front of the Woolpack, displayed as a decorative item. Presumably, no passing animal has to be watered in the yard trough, no sheepdog, no ducklings as might have been in the past. In fact I saw no animal at all around any of Woolpack's buildings. There were no hens in the hen fields. New in the backyard was a granite wall separating the steps at the back of the inn from the new homes in the outbuildings. This symbolic wall was a fearful shock but entirely rational since there is now no need of a connection between the inn and the farm because the farm does not supply the inn any longer. Does it bother any new resident that the productivity of the land has been so drastically reduced?

The fields are the same; they are the least changed. I can see that the theory of fields keeping a lot of a farm's history must be correct. Cow Field, Holm Bottom, Tarn Ling – iconic names, they could not sound better. The fields still had their own individual character but for the most part appeared empty of farming activity. Granda's garden, once a most admired and productive place, full of vegetables, fruit and flowers for the inn, was now a wasteland of self-sown sycamores – doing well in the carefully tended garden earth. (Or it could have been a pocket of conscious 're-wilding', an experiment of the latest in environmental thinking that is starting to be talked about. Granda's garden was starting to look like the 're-wilding' experiment at the Old Shop of a century before.) I walked over the Front Field, past the spot where Alastair and I were when his voice broke. It had been warm, late in the afternoon and late in the summer, and we were raking hay. For us, valley sounds were stilled as we agonized over the sudden croak – whatever now?

I looked down the wooded banks by the river to the long expanse of the Holm Bottom – mercifully, there was a hay crop growing, the grass interspersed with its wild flowers. And that turned out to be the best feature of my stay. When I got back to Penny Hill in the evening, Margaret asked me if the hay there was ready to cut. I had been gone 50 odd years but for a moment they slipped away; I was still known in Eskdale, and worth asking about such a matter. I grew a little. It was a change, however,

Catherine at the Woolpack trough.

that it was a subject for a female decision. I found too that I had all the locals outrage when I subsequently registered that a large patch of the hay in the Holm Bottom had been flattened, presumably by a mindless picnic. The smallest child in our day would not have flattened hay – how could you cut that, what cow would you deprive of winter feed?

Doctor's Bridge looked just the same, the rushing water sounded the same, still amplified under the span, but it is no longer a hidden place. Bathers and walkers tarry. The bathers scream at the fast moving cold water that rushes fresh off the fells; they thrash about, chasing away the shoals of little fish. Unfortunately, one cannot now speak of Doctor's Bridge without remembering the internationally reported horror story that ended there, in this idyllic place. Walkers at the bridge that day, in 2010, were witness to Derrick Bird, the taxi driver from a town on the coast, ending his shooting spree ahead of the pursuing police. He left his car near the bridge, at a place previously remarkable for its wealth of spring flowers: anemones and bluebells, primroses and celandines, tiny violets under the hazels. Then he walked over Doctor's Bridge and up Low Birker Wood to turn the gun on himself. Doctor's Bridge – Bird must have known about it too.

The hikers are guided by a new sign on the footpath to the church, an new announcement that it is an ancient 'right of way', a bridle path in this case. These signs are a shock, but logical since we are now on public property, it is not just a path by the river and Woolpack fields as it once was. Otherwise, the walk down to the church was as always: the same fields, hills, trees on the river banks, the same views. It was obvious that there was more bracken about; at an old swimming place it was right down to the river, a place it had not previously reached, and I saw no stock anywhere that day to trample it down. It was difficult to decide if there was more gorse, another problem on rough grazing. Then just before the church, below the deep pool of Birker Dub, some adults watched as their young threw large rocks from the banks into the middle of the beck. Again the dismay. Even as children we knew that the river channel had to be clear to cope with the not infrequent heavy rainfall. The beck could roar into a flood, very suddenly become a spectacle, show another side of its nature.

Wordsworth was memorable about the heavy rain and its effects. 'The rain comes down heartily, and is frequently succeeded by clear, bright weather, when every brook is vocal every torrent sonorous.' We had limited ourselves to the little flat stones suitable for skimming over the Dub. Curiously, and we have only recently discovered this, Paddockwray owned a little bit of land here. It is quite a distance from the farmstead and fields, near where the iron girders go over the Esk; it must have been a bit of necessary river access in medieval times, for fish and possibly for washing sheep.

St. Catherine's Church was the same, still open, the same ambience, the same colours through the stained glass, but the old lectern was missed – stolen. Hard to get around that one. The church yard had been expanded into a neighbouring field but the headstones of the family and others, the memories of christenings, weddings, and funerals were all still there. The headstone of Tommy Dobson, the Eskdale huntsman, was still prominent by the porch; distinguished by his likeness and those of his hounds looming out of the stone. The path from the church to Trofuss Bridge was as always, but there was a new car park at the bridge. The dub at Trofuss had many bathers and a rope for swinging out over it and dropping in; a left over, possibly, from a film made there. The slow moving water here looked different, there were bubbles, presumably persisting from the jumps. I don't know if there are still salmon or how they cope.

Family christening party.

Going up the fell from Woolpack towards Eel Tarn was as ever, except that there was a snaking bright blue plastic tube going up the Rake to the stream up top, it was a new way of getting water. Out on top there was the same vegetation, the same bog asphodel where one crosses the stream, the same scents of moss, bracken, and bog myrtle. I didn't notice any frogs – they had been a big feature in our day when we had to step over them. There was an increased amount of bracken again; it quite choked the path to Eel Tarn. Apart from not being trampled by so many hooves, bracken will not now be harvested, certainly not for Woolpack. There is not the same call for animal bedding or for cover for the winter vegetable heap. A long time ago, bracken was taken for thatch, and at one time, it was commercially harvested for potash. As one looked back from the fell there were the same fantastic views of the valley, and the same clouds of midges above one's head. There were probably fewer sheep ticks waving around on the grass in anticipation of a passing warm body.

The old peat storage house just before the tarn had been converted into a little cabin, using the old door and window. A lovely idea. It could only have come about with public ownership of the land; in feudal times farms

DeeDee and Catherine at Eel Tarn.

had turbary claims on peat houses. Although we ourselves did not cut and dry peat, some were said to be still doing so until the end of the Second World War. Perhaps the Stony Tarn peat house has been converted in the same way; that one would be most satisfactorily hidden and reclusive. In this light, one would imagine that the old gamekeeper's lodge at Burn-moor Tarn to have become very valuable as a possible conversion; an actual house on the fells overlooking Eel Tarn with fabulous views of the high fells, dominated by the frontal aspect of Scafell and Black Apron. I admit that they would be wonderful places to live. There are supposed to be pike still in Burnmoor along with minnows; apparently acid rain has killed off the insect life that used to sustain trout.

So far Paddockwray has been a survivor. The farm is still locally owned and still has its flock and we are all grateful for that. Some day, however, those now valuable outbuildings may be developed.

At a glance the village of Boot appears a lot busier than it used to be, there were a lot of people about and to a large degree it too is now owned by incomers. Looking over the wall into Bridge End yard by the pack horse bridge to the mill, it was a shock to see that the long barn had been converted into a row of little townhouses, each with a tiny garden out front. The farmhouse and the farm must have been reassigned as well. The huntsman, Art Irving, used to live there. The last time I visited he showed me his beehives in the garden. I was just looking at the mill itself and at the Esk flowing by, when I was rudely yelled at by an officious in-comer from the cottage opposite. He demanded that I '…keep to visiting hours' – the mill has become a 'theme park' then, for sure, and it had been a real working place in my life time. To quote Eric Wood, 'the coloniza-tion of villages has changed rural life beyond recall.' In Eskdale's case, that must apply to Boot village and to much of the upper valley.

A visit to the Roman Camp on Hardknott showed it to have been more completely excavated, the perimeter walls and the central building walls reassembled and now higher. Similarly, the separate rounded Roman Baths have been excavated. The camp is easier to get to than it used to be; one can park at the base of the pass and climb up, and there is even space for a few cars at the site itself. There was a constant stream of traffic negotiating the steep narrow road on the pass and a few parties walking around the site. The anomalous flat space of the parade ground was not sign posted, so there was no-one there. Quite gone are the days of a one-to-one visit with the mostly forgotten stones peaking through the waving grass. I wondered if the Roman sandstone block from in front of the old byre had been recovered and put back in place.

Looking back down the valley from the camp, the view was as impres-sive as ever, the tracery of the field walls on the green grass, the rounded trees, the snaking beck. We ate our lunch gazing down towards the sea – tomatoes were fine now. To the north there was the always surprising sideways sight of Slight Side and the Scafell range, the central peaks, their bare rock contrasting with the green of the valley below. One sees just how close we are to the central massif of Scafell and Scafell Pike; it is possibly the best and easiest to get to view in all of upper Eskdale. Co-leridge said it well. In his notebook he wrote of '…the contrast between the beauty of the lower dales and the bare sublimity of the great high fells, strong colours everywhere'.

Then looking down and north east is Upper Eskdale itself – the bit at the head of the valley that has the proper name. There are no farms beyond Butterilket and Taw House, and one can follow the beck on either side up to the rise of Esk Hause. There, routes from Eskdale, Wasdale and Lang-dale meet. Esk Hause is one place from which to climb Scafell and Scafell Pike, somewhere too, there is a route to Borrowdale. Upper Eskdale and Esk Hause are not much visited: one may meet no one there, but it's just possible to be suddenly terrified by a screaming jet coming over the top, flying frighteningly low – it is a training area for the RAF.

My complaints must sound trivial, even laughable, in the face of all the preservation efforts by individuals and institutions: worries about bracken or gorse, fish being frightened, hay grass flattened, rocks being hurled about, the stream of cars, previous private or working spaces now being entirely public and developed outbuildings. Nevertheless, the change is dramatic and ongoing. It feels as if we, the central fells and the old families there have been swallowed whole.

Consider the agricultural output of our day, although the land was designated as 'marginal', the hill farms produced food not only for the resident population but also an excess for others. They exported sheep, cattle, and wool. Milk and butter, poultry and eggs were produced, vegetables and animal feed, and even some cereal crops – all organic, free range and sustainable. Locals and visitors were largely fed off the land until quite recently. Now I imagine the reverse to be true; for the bulk of the residents and visitors, a lot of food must be imported from elsewhere into the fridges and deep freezes that we did not have in the early days. Since the nation as a whole is said to produce only a sixth of what it consumes, this could be considered a problem. It is true that there are farms that are still working and so agriculturally productive, but the total output must be much less than it once was.

To be fair, the numbers of incomers are not solely responsible for the decline of productivity, there have been other factors, general to the area. The epidemics of BSE (bovine spongiform encephalitis) in cattle, and the Foot and Mouth disease affecting many animals in the 1990s have played their part, encouraging farmers to sell up in the Lake District; although I do not think either directly affected the farms in Upper Eskdale. Farm incomes have also declined due to rising costs, the decline of subsidies, and the effect of global prices making what can be produced there less valuable.

Before BSE, and Foot and Mouth, there were the man made disasters at Windscale and Chernobyl that affected farming in our part of Cumbria. Windscale was the former name of the nuclear plant on the coast near Seascale, now known as Sellafield. It started out making plutonium and later made electricity. In October of 1959 the rods caught fire resulting in clouds of radioactivity. Since the prevailing wind is from the west, Eskdale and its fells were affected. Subsequently there were a cluster of childhood cancers around Seascale. I was not at home at the time of the fire but Alastair said he had to dump milk for a month. On previous visits back, I had seen vans going around testing samples by the side of the road in the valley; it was not clear how much testing was done on the fells.

The Chernobyl disaster was much worse than Windscale in terms of total discharge of radioactivity. On the 2 May 1986, the cloud from that disaster was over central Cumbria when it rained heavily, so that the high fells with their common grazing areas were contaminated. Subsequently there were restrictions on selling sheep or eating mutton, as they were radioactive. Eskdale was included in the exclusion zone. There was a great deal of testing of meat for radioactivity for more than two decades. All of this led to market losses. I was not living there in the 1980s of course, and Alastair was no longer there to provide first hand information. For awhile the beaches were out of bounds for swimming but I think that was due to a leak from Sellafield, one beach was said to be safe if one wore Wellington boots.

The relative decline in agricultural productivity means that, to some extent, both locals and visitors to Eskdale now have the same modern concerns about food as people in the city: a lack of certain knowledge about its origin, how it is produced, whether it is safe to eat, its nutritional value, its comparative lack of flavour, what the environmental cost of its production is, ignorance about how domestic animals and agricultural workers are treated, suspicion of the corporations' possible short-changing business practice. Even at the time I grew up we had the answer to all of those questions. Similarly, we knew where the water came from and where it went; what could be composted and what could not. The old inhabitants had to know about all of those things. While they made the land work for them, they still managed to leave attractive countryside with a clean river, although some insecticides were a blot.

In feudal times, the peasantry had to cope with the dictates of the aristocracy and their hunting preserves. Hunting and farming make different demands on the land. But the landed aristocracy were none the less committed to country life; in our corner they had accommodated the farmers and the professions that supported farming. The aristocrats of our time, those that we knew, appeared to be acting in the interest of the locals, were involved in the decisions about country life affecting its continuity.

These days farmers have had to deal with the conservation groups, their wishes and rules, and the groups demanding access, looking for the ancient rights of way. The 'the right to roam' restricting what the farmer can put where. Walkers may forget to close gates, may object to farm practice or to farm odours. More recently there has been something of a different order, farmers may be paid to remove their sheep from the fell in line with changing public policy.

The middle classes from the cities have lost the memory of subsistence farming and mostly lost the skills necessary for it. It is quite normal for them to buy everything, to be dependent on food from far away places, and to focus narrowly on price and recipes (very often of foreign cuisines developed in distant landscapes). And then there was still in our day a certain urban stereotype of the farming community as slow witted. I think it meant the lack of street wise people. Jokes about the general backwardness and innocence of country boys and girls were legion, but the sobering fact is that the boot was quite on the other foot. I can see how the urban got that way; farm work is physically demanding and complicated, it takes time. I think of our old peoples' thick and calloused hands after decades of physical work. City work is a holiday by comparison, with all kinds of leisure and freedom. Then there was a later time when farmers were pampered with government subsidies.

Farming is not a job like any other: it feeds people, it has implications in land use, is likely to be in conflict with industry and recreation, it has importance when thinking about population. In feudal times there was the idea that the number of stock and general management of Eskdale should be that to sustain the population without unmanageable stress to the environment, as described in the Eskdale 24 Book. That looks like a long time ago, now it seems recreation and urban demands are more obvious.

Who are the large landowners in the Lake District today? The National Trust is a private society funded by the public. Along with the National Park it is committed to conservation and preservation and to coping with the demands of the public. The National Park and the planning board were established in 1951 to restrict unwelcome change. The National Trust and National Park now own most of the land in the Lake District, and a large part of the rest is owned by the government's Water and Forestry Commissions. Water is being taken from the lakes for Sellafield, and for cities in Lancashire. Forestry has planted some areas with conifers, notably the valley of Ennerdale. The acreage in private hands is getting smaller; and government imposed death duties play a part there.

In 1983, Hunter Davies gives an interesting list of the land owners in his book *A Walk around the Lakes*. Here are his figures of 30 years ago –

they tell their own story, a decline of private ownership and the increase of public ownership.

The National Trust	90,000 acres
The National Park	22,000 acres
The North West Water Commission	40,000 acres
The Forestry Commission	30,000 acres
Private estates	49,000 acres

These figures are, of course, now out of date; the National Trust, for one, has continued to buy. And there have been changes since the 1990s, for instance the EU Common Agricultural Policy on uplands. English Nature has paid farmers to remove sheep from common areas (via the Rural Payments Agency). The idea was to help the plants that sheep cropped. This organization was succeeded by Natural England who, I read, aim for 1.5 sheep per acre in summer and 1.125 in winter on Eskdale Common. I understand that the two conservation areas of Scafell and the Screes, both classed as Sites of Special Scientific Interest, were judged to have been overgrazed and sheep there reduced by 40 per cent. The over-wintering of sheep on the common is now reduced. There is also a move to return more cattle to the upland to reduce bracken and encourage heather as cattle eat the longer grass. So removal and fragmentation of the Woolpack flock is in accord with the official agricultural and environmental policies coming to bear on Eskdale and the common.

How was it for the local people before the onslaught, what was the quality of life? Pre-war we were living in a largely pre-industrial way, with more than a whiff of feudal times, fairly insulated from economic problems of the 1930s and from the world wars that were catastrophic for the rest of the country. Possibly we were one of the last enclaves in England to be opened up to a completely modern existence. By extension back into the Middle Ages, one can get an idea of how it was for people: they lived close to nature, everything had to make sense to them, their lives would have been full of the personal, and of course the work was unrelenting.

In the Middle Ages, however, there had been considerable violence close by on the Scottish Border, and we were just south of the Border Marches. Although I doubt that the reivers would choose to rob the upper valleys since they needed to have a clear getaway: the sheep would have to be gathered off the fell first, and they walk slowly. Reivers preferred to go to more easy country, in an easterly direction. Nevertheless, we are told, the reivers did on occasion get as far as the Lancashire border.

By the 1930s there had been law and order for three centuries. Possibly, for a while, we had the best of both worlds. Auntie Gladys maintained the best time in the Lake District was before 1914, before the wars, and she could be right. Although we lacked urban amenities in Eskdale, there were a lot of advantages: there was physical and mental space, and no evident homelessness or hunger in our time. There had been deprived people in the past it is true. At the time of Coleridge's nine day hike of 1802, he encountered homeless groups and begging – presumably some of the landless. I have to think very hard about any crime committed in my time in Eskdale. I really can't come up with anything at all: our doors were unlocked and we felt we knew everybody. One sees that we were closer to how humans are programmed to live, even though the pastoral lifestyle is itself a world away from that of the hunter-gatherer. How we live now in the cities is confining: small apartments or houses, with a small garden (if one is lucky), small parks, largely separated from nature, little exercise, the desperation about going somewhere for holidays.

It is true that Eskdale was always changing, but only very slowly. Over the centuries we suppose that upper Eskdale had been very much altered by agriculture. It was a long way from the wild, a lot of wild life and the large game had gone. Originally, the valley floor would have been wooded supporting a great deal of game. To the Romans, it would have looked a very different place: more fish, more deer, wild pig, bears and lynx perhaps. Hutchinson's *History of Cumberland* of 1793 is interesting in this regard. He comments on the quality and girth of the old oak beams uncovered in Dalegarth Hall, constructed about 1599 (the date was in the ceiling). Hutchinson speaks of 'distant ages' when 'the country abounded in timber trees', and again 'when we are informed that a squirrel could travel from Dalegarth to Hardknot mountain, by the tops of trees, the forest was so closely wooded.' In Hutchinson's time 'the rivers have salmon trout and eel, the lakes trout, perch, pike and eel.' In our day, big fish did not often get up as far as Woolpack, and the tarns have changed due to acid rain. Hutchinson writes that 'common birds of the district are eagles, grouse, crane' – those are now gone. He mentions martens and wild cats – I did once hear someone say they had seen a pine marten – but I suspect they are gone too.

The desire to re-wild and to cut back grazing is the latest thinking with which upper Eskdale has to cope. Since the National Trust is now the main landowner, it has to work out how to keep the farms going, how to replace the original farmers who have left, to decide what and how to conserve. Geoff Brown thinks that the current practice of renting to the interested and hoping they can make a go of it may have to be replaced by salaried managers.

While writing this I came across a book titled *The Plot* by Madeleine Bunting. This book was fascinating to me as it is very much on my subject: she touches eloquently on most of the problems I have seen. I recognize many aspects of the situation of which she writes. It seems that the destruction of viable farming country in Northern England is not confined to the Lake District. She describes the process near Scotch Corner, Yorkshire, where a farming community, also with centuries of work in its creation, is losing ground to those looking for somewhere quaint and authentic. She points out that while one can sympathize with both farmers and incomers, one ultimately has to worry about the land itself: its viability and future, its productivity. It is just possible that the Lake District may survive better because of the strength of its protective organizations.

There is one paragraph of Madeleine's book that I would like to quote as it encapsulates a great deal. 'Within a few decades, the area has gone from a modest backwater where a living was hard earned to a place of whim and fantasy in which prices affordable to millionaires swamp older measures of value such as the capacity of the land to provide a fair living or the emotional commitments to place.' And again 'This is not just land for a leisured society to play in...'

Geoff Brown talks about the Lake District Park as a possible World Heritage Site under UNESCO, in the category of cultural landscape that considers the link between man and nature. He refers to the fact that it has the necessary depth of time: more than 900 years of continuity of cultural practices. Apparently, there are not many landscapes that have the necessary depth of time to qualify for this designation. He refers to Susan Denyer, the Secretary for the International Council on Monuments and Sites, who lists other places in this category: south east Turkey, northern Yunnan, the High Alps, and the northern Caucasus.

All of that relegates us to a time in history. We were just around at the transformation of an old landscape into a very different place. At the time I admit, we were not so conscious of its history as a farming community; we were just very absorbed and busy. Those who lived in upper Eskdale, for over 900 years, were intimate with their land.

Now, the mid and high level fells are largely empty of wildlife, restricted in species, with no trees, nothing taller than heather or bracken; and it is the centuries of grazing sheep that have been largely responsible for that. Other players have been those in the past who chopped down trees; even the government itself with its subsidies for stock on upland farms.

Eskdale and its common has been admired for itself, for the look of the countryside and the old farms, for its walks and climbs. The preservation societies have tried to keep all that. The policy today is to improve the ecosystem – now that sheep are not as valuable as they once were. I have not yet understood the ultimate aim of Natural England: to what point in history it is thought desirable or possible to return. I believe they talk of restoring trees and shrubs to the ghylls. I admit, the prospect is exciting, to think of more trees on the fell; how far up would they go, what wild life might come back?

In defence of the old residents, I would like to quote another bit of modern thinking by Dan Barber, the famous American chef in his book *The Third Plate*. He talks about '...the last vestiges of cultures that evolved in accordance with nature, of diets that listen to the seasons and the ecology and as a result are rewarded with the best possible flavour' and of whole farm cooking '...they developed a cuisine that adhered to what the landscape provided.' We were a vestige. Our cuisine was nutritious but restricted, dependent on what we produced. As children, Alastair and I were profoundly shocked when we were given our first shrimps. They looked like pink grubs to us; we looked at each other in horror. We were being treated to lunch by our sometime Woolpack guests, our good friends the Heywoods, and were taken to Manchester for a short visit.

It must have been a shock for any locals or visitors who read George Monbiot's article in *The Guardian* newspaper of September 2013. There, he described the fells as some kind of desert: a depressing sight and said there was more wildlife in Birmingham. He is right about the restriction of species but it was the word desert that was the shock. Locals had become accustomed to hearing the Lake District being rhapsodized by the poets; had become accustomed to it being a place of pilgrimage. They must have got used to the idea of the application for a special status at UNESCO. However, it cannot have been a surprise to farmers to read that farming changed a landscape – that was their job, working with nature.

The fells are not completely wild, they have been grazed by hundreds of years of sheep.

How did the native born regard the fells emotionally? They did not consciously feel at odds with the fells as alleged by Monbiot that they must be. Their whole lives attested to their regard and care of their farms and fells. Still it is quite true that vanished species did not get much attention, and they should have. Imagine that last deer being driven into the lake; presumably it was thought to be competing for forage. Quite a bit of farm conversation was about predators – and one only has to see a savaged lamb to get the point. How did the local people speak of the fells? They certainly did not talk about walking or climbing or hiking or peak-bagging or bird watching or particularly of botany, in an objective fashion as visitors do.

The local's vocabulary emphasized the fell itself and their involvement with it. The expressions we used were restricted to 'going to the fell', 'being on the fell' and 'coming off the fell'. Sheep, or the men, were said to be 'at the fell'. It came over as akin to a spiritual or religious activity, something like going to church, being in church or coming back from church or at church. The fells were our huge hinterland – a gift, a bounty, a mental release and hallowed by the feet of our previous generations. Farmers were not so conscious of their historic privilege, they had the same complete and overriding sense of belonging as those who had gone before them.

We did not really understand that the ground beneath out feet was so completely desirable to the nation. There were no fearful discussions about the future at home, and while I was there, no negative comments on change. Not even the hotelier Armstrongs seemed nervous. We enjoyed our visitors and were cooperative with the authorities. I was lucky to have been raised in upper Eskdale, and to have had that family connection with previous generations.

To go to the fell was easy for us: just a stone's throw away. From Woolpack kitchen one walked out on the flagged floor up the granite steps to the yard then steeply up the Rake. The Rake was the short transition zone: between one realm and the other – between valley and fell. At the Rake gate to the fell there used to be signs of sheep: a few droppings or strands of caught wool. For centuries the flock had funnelled through the gate; their dainty black hooves had polished the stones. A further short pull up and one is out on top. That was it. The everyday dropped away. Already one overlooked the valley; looked back on the green and the cultivated below. Looking up the rocks were jagged; stones set in moss. There was a quiet, maybe a faint echo of a waterfall or sense of a breeze. There was fell freshness and fell scent. Our other place. Like the fields, the fell is still there – what will come?

Father's sometime aphorism at the dinner table: Mar-gar-et,
Don't forget.

Time Line

About 2000BC	Stone circles
About 700BC	Bronze Age ended? Barnscar.
122AD	Hadrian's Wall – Carlisle to Newcastle.
400	Hardknott Roman Camp.
About 900	Norse invasion.
1066	Norman invasion.
1086	Domesday book.
1093	Carlisle Castle.
1148	Calder Abbey (Cistercian).
1242	Butterilket Farm run by religious order from Furness Abbey (Cistercian).
1300-1600	Peak Border reiving time.
1445	Eskdale Church.
1530	Johnnie Armstrong hanged.
1542	Battle of Solway Moss – a major official retaliatory Scottish incursion to the south of Carlisle, after a provocation by Henry VIII.
1562	11X Great-grandfather William Porter of Weary Hall, Bolton, near Cockermouth died (antecedent of Granny – Hannah Tyson). He had provided men to fight against the Scots. The family had land in Eskdale and Wasdale.
1587	Book of Eskdale – detailing rules and routes for stock to the Eskdale Common.
1596	Kinmont Willie freed from Carlisle Castle.
1603	Union of Crowns – James VI of Scotland and 1st of England.
1600s	Records of Tysons in Eskdale.
1663	10X Great-grandfather John Dickinson (antecedent of Granny – Hannah Tyson) noted as being the tenant at Arment House (opposite Paddockwray), and paying the General Fine at change of ownership.

1692	John Vicars of Peel Place died. (his daughter was an antecedent of Granny Hannah Tyson).
Early 1700s	Records of Tysons in Wasdale.
1723	Eskdale School endowed.
1734	Doctor's Bridge widened.
1754	Possible record of Armstrong antecedents in Kirklinton, north of Carlisle.
1778	West's guide book published.
Late 1700s	Records of Leeces on south Cumbrian coast and Munros on north Cumbrian coast.
1789	Definite record of our Armstrong branch in Kirklinton.
1793	Last deer on Scafell.
1802	Coleridge's walk down Eskdale.
1810	Wordsworth's guide book published
1835-65	Lumley Kennedy's ships built in Whitehaven.
Mid-1800s	Armstrongs in the hotel trade.
1868	Great-grandfather Thomas Leece killed in explosion at Blackbeck Powder Mills, Furness.
1871	Armstrong Great-grandparents first proprietors of the Borrowdale Hotel.
1896	National Trust formed.
1914	Armstrongs at Woolpack.
1951	National Park formed.
1955-66	Wainwright guide books.
1979	Eskdale Common went to the National Trust.

Bibliography

Barber, Dan, *The Third Plate*, The Penguin Press, 2014.

Brown, Geoff, *Herdwicks,* Hayloft Publishing, 2009.

Bunting, Madeleine, *The Plot*, Granta, 2009.

Davies, Hunter, *A Walk around the Lakes*, Hamlyn, 1983.

Durham, Keith, *The Border Reivers*, Osprey, 1995.

Eskdale and District Local history Society, Census 1901.

Eskdale 24 Book, Whitehaven Record Office, David Bradbury, James Peirson, 7 Oct , 1959.

Eskdale Project, www.PastPresented.co.uk, David Bradbury.

Percy Survey 1578.

Whitehaven Record Office, Churchwardens records, YPR 4/16.

Fancy, Harry, *Shipbuilding in Whitehaven* – a checklist, Whitehaven Museum, 1984.

Fraser, George McDonald, *The Steel Bonnets*, Barrie and Jenkins 1971, Skyhorse Publishing, 2008.

Hankinson, Alan, *Coleridge Walks the Fells*, Harper Collins, 1993.

Hansen, James, *First Man: The Life of Neil A. Armstrong*, Simon and Schuster, 2005.

Hay, Daniel, *Whitehaven – An Illustrated History*, Michael Moon, 1979.

Sawyers, William, *A List of Shipping corrected to 1840*, Michael Moon, 1975.

Scott, Sir Walter, ed. *Minstrelsy of the Scottish Border*, Thomas Henderson, London, 1931.

Tacitus on Britain and Germany, trans. H. Mattingly, Penguin Books, 1948.

Winchester, Angus J. L., *The Harvest of the Hills*, Edinburgh University, 2000.

Wood, Eric S., *Historical Britain*, Harvill, 1995.

Wordsworth, William, *Guide to the Lakes*, Hamlyn, 1983.

www.naturalengland.org.uk.